MEMOIRS OF A SABOTEUR

MEMOIRS OF A SABOTEUR

Reflections on My Political Activity in India and South Africa

by

NATOO BABENIA

as told to

IAIN EDWARDS

Mayibuye History and Literature Series No 58

**MAYIBUYE
BOOKS**

Published in 1995 in southern Africa by
Mayibuye Books, UWC, Private Bag X17,
Bellville, 7535 South Africa

Mayibuye Books is the book publishing division of the Mayibuye Centre at the
University of the Western Cape. The Mayibuye Centre is a pioneering project helping
to recover areas of South African history that have been neglected in the past. It also
provides space for cultural creativity and expression in a way that promotes the
process of change and reconstruction in a democratic South Africa. The Mayibuye
History and Literature Series is part of this project. The series editors are Barry
Feinberg and André Odendaal.

Printed and bound in the Republic of South Africa
by The Rustica Press (Pty) Ltd, Ndabeni, Cape Town.

D4133

Dedicated to Pravina
With Love

CONTENTS

Acknowledgements.   ix
Abbreviations.   x
Introduction   xi

Part One

A YOUTHFUL STRUGGLE FOR INDEPENDENCE
South Africa and India, 1924–1949

On the Horizons of Youth.   5
Unsettled.   12
A Volunteer for Action.   18
Frustrated Ambitions and Recklessness   35

Part Two

ORGANISED VIOLENCE WILL SMASH APARTHEID
South Africa, 1949–1964

The Bitterness of Seeing.   45
An Activist on the Streets   51
The Return of the Saboteur.   60
Turning Up the Heat   74
Just Before the End.   85
The End.   95
Another Past   98
Back to the End.   99
A Different Story. 109
Back to the Trial 110
Judgment Day 111

Part Three

CAST IN STONE IN A HELL HOLE
Robben Island, 1964–1980

Leeukop Prison 117
Prison by Prison to Robben Island 122
First Tastes of Hell 124
The Longest Day. 128
Going Alone. 131
The Quarry. 135

Trouble Shooters and Slim Mense 138
Saamwerke 140
Robben Island Prison 141
Coifimvaba 144
Strip Search 149
Spy 13 150
Influx Starts 152
Lieutenant Bosch 153
Hunger-strike 155
July 1966 161
Campaign Against Tyranny 165
Education and Culture Struggles Begin 167
Culture Takes Off 171
Our Own Comedian 174
Flea Invasion 176
Mary 176
Spare-diet 177
Air Manoeuvres 178
News 178
Hospital 182
Suicides 183
Our Second Hunger-strike 185
Record Club 185
Tit Bits 186
Hospital Cleaner 189
SWAPO 191
Bad Guys 193
TV Generation 194
Farewell! Comrades! Release! 194
Glossary 199

ACKNOWLEDGEMENTS

I acknowledge with great respect the assistance Iain Edwards gave me with his deep sense of understanding of the problems I faced. I had but an inkling of the mammoth task I had set myself. It is not easy to glance through the pages of my life: at times with ecstasy and at times with pain. I had to allow Iain to see me through his eyes and not mine alone. This was hard.

I have been, and still am a political activist, for the last fifty-six years. During this process one hurts oneself and others with whom one works. To put this down in writing is no easy task. Here Iain came to my aid! He listened and listened and found a way through this dilemma. A way forward!

If readers appreciate what I have written then I must say "Well done Iain!" Thank you for being patient with me!

I would also like to record my gratitude to others who have assisted Iain and I. Gareth Coleman for his stimulus in initiating the project. Deanne Collins, Ronnie Kasrils, Enver Motala, Ian Phillips, Harold Strachan and Linda Zama for advice and encouragement. The Centre for Socio-Legal Studies and the Centre for Social and Development Studies, University of Natal, Durban provided financial assistance and the staff of the registrar of the Supreme Court, Natal Provincial Division, Pietermaritzburg and the Local History Museum, Durban assisted with photographs.

All my personal papers, including sketches, writings and other personal items from my stretch on Robben Island are to be deposited with the *Mayibuye Centre*, University of the Western Cape, for eventual inclusion in the proposed Robben Island Museum.

Natoo Babenia
Durban
23 June 1993

Abbreviations

ANC	African National Congress
APDUSA	African People's Democratic Union of South Africa
ARM	African Resistance Movement
BCM	Black Consciousness Movement
COD	South African Congress of Democrats
COMPOL	Combined Police Headquarters
DC	(Robben Island) Disciplinary Committee
FRELIMO	Popular Front for the Liberation of Mozambique
ICRC	International Committee of the Red Cross
IDAF	International Defence and Aid Fund
MK	*Umkhonto we Sizwe*
NEUM	Non-European Unity Movement
NIC	Natal Indian Congress
NIO	Natal Indian Organisation
NLF	National Liberation Front
OAU	Organisation of African Unity
PAC	Pan-Africanist Congress
PLAN	People's Liberation Army of Namibia
SACP	South African Communist Party
SACTU	South African Congress of Trade Unions
SAIC	South African Indian Congress
SASO	South African Student's Organisation
SWAPO	South West African People's Organisation
TIC	Transvaal Indian Congress
UN	United Nations
UNISA	University of South Africa
USSR	Union of Soviet Socialist Republics
YMCA	Young Men's Christian Association

INTRODUCTION

Work on this book commenced in 1988 when I was approached with the request that Natvarlal 'Natoo' Babenia would like me to assist in writing his autobiography. Babenia had recently been released from nearly eighty days in a detention cell. Writing his autobiography became the central thrust of his life. For Babenia this was a defiant gesture against the state, a means to reflect on his own life and a way in which he could publicly integrate his life within the history of 'The Struggle'.

A mere introductory sketch of the story Babenia recounted easily revealed the enormous potential of such a project. Born in Durban but soon a youthful political activist and saboteur in India during the 1942 'Quit India' campaign, Babenia returned to Durban and during the political crises of the later 1950s was an organiser for the Natal Indian Congress. Soon an *Umkhonto we Sizwe* cadre active in the early internal campaigns, Babenia was convicted in the Pietermaritzburg 'Sabotage Trial' of 1963, sentenced to sixteen years imprisonment and sent to Robben Island. Babenia was released in 1980.

The broad sweep of Babenia's story was fascinating, and so were the recollections of cruel human ironies which seemed to provide pivotal turning points in his life. Here was an incredible journey through political activism and sabotage on two continents during crucial decades. At its most obvious, Babenia now publicly joins Arthur Goldreich as one of those very few early cadres of *Umkhonto we Sizwe* having previous experience as a saboteur. Goldreich served in *Palmach*, the military wing of *Haganah* in Palestine.[1]

The late 1950s and early 1960s is the crucible in which modern South African politics was forged. Babenia's life history is the first published autobiography by an *Umkhonto we Sizwe* cadre to join together four crucial aspects of that history: open political activism, clandestine sabotage, arrest, conviction and long term imprisonment.

Many have written autobiographic accounts of their experiences in left wing South African politics and detention without trial during

---

[1] Of course others within *Umkhonto we Sizwe* had previous military experiences to draw on, but as soldiers enjoying the protection of the state. During the Second World War for example, many white members of the Communist Party of South Africa joined the South African Union Defence Force. Other *Umkhonto we Sizwe* cadres had previously participated in some of the various revolts and rebellions which rocked South Africa between 1946 and 1964.

the late 1950s and early 1960s.[2] Few of those who would later become saboteurs have written of this period. Many have written of their experiences of the detainee cell and court room clashes between a vengeful state and political activists which marked the end of this period of political struggle. None are by the politicos of Robben Island.

For most of *Umkhonto we Sizwe's* cadres active in the first South African campaign, the terrifying world of the detention cell was but a prelude to conviction and sentencing. But cadres who have written of their lives on Robben Island never deal in any substantial fashion with their earlier experiences of politics or sabotage activity and court room climax. Babenia is the first to do so.

Possibilities and potential are a good start but a long way away from a final text. Some of the problems were apparent from the start. Babenia wanted to write about himself, to remember himself and to understand his history and identity. However, individual memories of the self cannot be separated out from social or collective memories.[3] Indeed Babenia, through writing wanted to be very much a part of the public history of modern South Africa. However, the politics of that history insisted on casting shadows over him.

The South African state was to cast a shadow over Babenia long after his release from Robben Island. However, this was not only because of his continuing political activity and his detention during the States of Emergency of the later 1980s.

All saboteurs take aim at existing state structures and social systems. While Babenia's Indian interlude may well have given him experience of underground work and sabotage, it prepared him little for the shadow which the South African state would throw over him. The Indian and South African states were widely different. The hegemonic powers and ideology of the South African state were unknown in the India of the 1940s. In this sense, armed struggle in India was thus relatively less mentally complicated. For the saboteur in India, legitimacy was possibly also more easily gained within a diffuse social structure where there was often no large distance between anti-colonial political movements within

---

[2] From 1962 onwards, the South African Police were given ever increasing powers, amongst which were statutory legal provisions allowing the police to detain and interrogate suspects without charge in solitary confinement for single or successive periods of twelve days. In 1963 this was changed to ninety days and in 1964 to one hundred and eighty days. For further details see the South African Institute of Race Relations, *A Survey of South African Race Relations. 1964*, (Johannesburg, 1965), pp 59–74.

[3] See J. Fentress and C. Wickham, *Social Memory*, (Oxford, 1992), p 49.

civil society and sympathetic elements within regional or local state structures.

This was not the case in South Africa where the lines between the state and the masses were crudely but effectively demarcated and constantly policed by the state. As every modern state does, the South African state acquired unto itself huge powers to structure ideological discourses. Part of this required the state to cover some of its historical tracks well. This it did, not only by celebrating and creating history, largely Afrikanerdom's, but also by suppressing other histories.

During the very period when Babenia was a political activist and saboteur, the South African state was assiduously engaged in dragging South African society through a process of massive restructuring. This was the age of what Rodney Davenport calls the 'Social Engineers': the leading ideologues and proponents of Apartheid.[4] The term, if properly understood, will conjure up the full image of a resurgent Afrikanerdom's determination to see their often highly brutal visions of reality fully and completely shackled into the physical and social landscape of South African life. Their aim was a controlled mass society in which the black masses were a politically tamed and obedient workforce.

Presiding over this were Afrikaner Nationalism's leading politicians. They were the political patriarchs of the South African version of the thrust into modernity and they demanded more than simple electoral tribute. They also desired the personal eulogy. They presumed, sought and accepted public acclaim. This was easily given by a loyal *volk* and the majority of the white electorate for to them the accomplishments of Apartheid's leaders were, after all, manifold. The state was triumphal, having imprisoned its leading political opponents and all but destroyed the African National Congress. An unheralded economic boom had created a mass white middle class consumer society. Afrikanerdom's leadership became heroes. In March 1960, just before the outlawing of the ANC and PAC, Prime Minister Verwoerd survived an assassination attempt at the Rand Show in Johannesburg. Verwoerd, the intellectual and political architect of classic Apartheid was soon raised unto a demi-god.[5] Afrikaner iconography and myths about individual

---

[4] T. R. H. Davenport, *South Africa. A Modern History*, (London, 4th edition, 1991).

[5] So much so that Dr H. F. Verwoerd's cottage in Betty's Bay, a Western Cape Province coastal holiday resort was proclaimed a National Monument. The politics of the National Monuments Council remains to be analysed. It is however significant that so many of the white triumphalist and so-called historic National Monuments were declared during the late 1970s and particularly in the 1980s. This was the very

leaders became a potent and essential force within white politics and whites' imagining of history. There were stories of success to be told and listened to. But the spoken eulogy did not suffice. Within white society this was a thriving era for autobiography, biography and arrant hagiography. This was a golden age to be remembered and written about.[6]

In terms of the Suppression of Communism Act of 1950 and various later statutory laws, the South Africa state gave itself the power to, amongst other draconian stipulations, prevent people it 'named' from any form of public speaking or writing. People so named were known as having been 'listed'. By 1962, 437 people were so listed.[7] This may now appear a small number, but within the anti-Apartheid activist ranks of the early 1960s, the toll was near crippling.

The South African state also made great use of the Suppression of Communism Act of 1950, the Customs Act of 1955 and the Publications and Entertainments Act of 1963, in terms of which a Publications Control Board was established, to prohibit possession of a host of material ranging from books, periodicals, posters, drawings to photographs and sound recordings emanating from 'listed' persons, banned organisations or other information discussing a wide range of topics in ways which were deemed 'prejudicial to the safety of the State'.[8]

Primary sources dealing with black and the more broadly conceived of resistance politics of the period do obviously exist.[9] All this material was banned in South Africa. People could also not legally

---

period during which the Apartheid State was under siege. See House of Assembly Debates, First Sitting, First Parliament, 13–16 September 1994, Mr B. A. D. Martins, columns 2724–2725.

[6] See for example F. Barnard, *13 Years in the Shadow of Dr H F Verwoerd*, (Cape Town, 1967), A. Boschoff, *Sekretaresse vir die Verwoerds*, (Cape Town, 1974), J. Botha, *Verwoerd is Dead*, (Cape Town, 1967), A. N. Pelzer (ed), *Verwoerd Speaks*, (Johannesburg, 1968), B. M. Schoeman, *Van Malan tot Verwoerd*, (Cape Town, 1973), Ben Schoeman, *My Lewe in die Politiek*, (Johannesburg, 1978), J. J. J. Scholtz, *Die Moord op Dr Verwoerd*, (Cape Town, 1967) or H. B. Thom, *D. F. Malan*, (Cape Town, 1980).

[7] See South African Institute of Race Relations, *A Survey of Race Relations in South Africa. 1963*, (Johannesburg, 1964), pp 37–40.

[8] See House of Assembly Debates, First Sitting, Second Parliament, 28 May–23 June 1962; Minister of Justice, columns 6989–7002 and South African Institute of Race Relations, *A Survey of Race Relations in South Africa. 1963*, (Johannesburg, 1964), pp 68–70.

[9] Such as the newspaper sequences of *New Age*, *Clarion Call* and *Spark*; *The African Communist*; *Sechaba*; the internal and exile editions of the journal *Africa South*; T. Karis and G. Carter's *From Protest To Challenge. A Documentary History of African Politics in South Africa, 1882–1964*, volume 3, *Challenge and Violence, 1953–1964*, (Stanford, 1973) and the larger microfilmed collections which lie behind the latter work and *South African Communists Speak*, (London, 1981). Michael Harmel's A Lerumo, (pseud.) *Fifty*

read or even possess copies of the numerous seminal scholarly works on South African politics written by political activists.[10]

Controlling historical pasts, the state only allowed the silence to be lifted in order that historical actors could be publicly demonised.[11] It was only the leadership of the ANC and its political allies, including *Umkhonto we Sizwe*, who were publicly and personally denounced as murderers, terrorists and evil traitors.[12] Ordinary cadres suffered a different but equally slurring collective naming. They were condemned not only as murderous traitors but also as misguided pawns lacking moral fibre and being led by white communists.[13] This appeared in speeches, writing and later, television.[14]

Although Babenia had never been 'listed' and thus could write and be quoted, he was living in South Africa and did not want to leave. A vast array of legislation ranging from the Publications Control Acts through the Prisons Act to the Internal Security Act thus bore down on him. These laws laid down near absolute restrictions on and severe penalties for the publication of matters dealing specifically with banned organisations, central themes in South African politics and experience of incarcerated life in South African jails. And yet without as lucid an account as memory and desire would allow of these very historical issues which statute deemed illegal and often seditious, there was clearly little point in conceiving of any form of published historical recollection of Babenia's life. Vast and thus critical swathes of Babenia's past life seemed to be controlled by a state determined to proclaim an ownership over his past. This was a possessive desire, not to instil

---

Fighting Years, (London, 1971) could also fit into this category. A more recent, extremely useful and never banned addition is S. Johns and R. H. Davis, (eds) *Mandela, Tambo, and the African National Congress*, (New York, 1991).

[10] For example Brian Bunting, *Moses Kotane*, (London, 1975), Govan Mbeki, *South Africa. The Peasants' Revolt*, (London, 1964), Edward Roux, *Time Longer Than Rope*, (London, 1948) and Jack and Ray Simons' *Class and Colour in South Africa, 1850–1950*, (London, 1968).

[11] It was during the State of Emergency declared in March 1960 that the South African Broadcasting Corporation, a public utility, dramatically changed its policy towards political matters to direct unambiguous support for the Nationalist government. See G. Hayman, and R. Tomaselli, 'Ideology and technology in the growth of South African Broadcasting, 1924–1971', in R. Tomaselli, *et al, Currents of Power*, (Bellville, 1989).

[12] See for example House of Assembly Debates, Second Session, Second Parliament, 13 May–28 June 1963; speech by the Minister of Justice, columns 7765–7772.

[13] *Ibid*, columns 4644 and 4670.

[14] See R. Tomaselli, 'The face of the ANC' in M. Graaf, (ed) *Hawks and Doves: The pro- and anti-Conscription Press in South Africa*, (Durban, 1988).

loyalty from Babenia, but to ensure others of a security derived from the state's boastful stranglehold over historical terrains.

With the Apartheid state in power, readers intent upon seeing the pasts which Natoo was so much a part of had to rely on a number of polemical and often highly distorted, hysterical books, some by South African government agents, which unashamedly present anti-communist and anti-ANC views.[15] Significantly, for a long time these books remained the only texts on the subject legally available in South Africa. A more recent addition to this *genre* is Pike's detailed but unreliable, splenetic and paranoid ravings attacking left wing ideas and various political organisations with fervent anti-communist missionary zeal.[16]

Primary source material on *Umkhonto we Sizwe's* early operations is obviously virtually non-existent.[17] If the state's archives do hold collections on *Umkhonto we Sizwe* these have not yet been publicly disclosed.

Never has a history of so central a theme in modern South African history had to rely so heavily on the remembered pasts of historical actors recalling, interpreting and imagining their own life histories. The world they made was the dangerously subterranean world of clandestinity and anonymity which is the preordained home of the saboteur. Within this world the cadre speaks and acts. Oral communication was both such a vitally necessary and highly dangerous means of ordering an armed struggle. This, within an ANC-led political movement where the very formation of *Umkhonto we Sizwe* created huge controversies with cadres being heavily criticised as 'adventurists' and 'terrorists' and with the 'armed

---

[15] See for example B. Mtolo, *Umkhonto we Sizwe. The Road to the Left*, (Durban, 1966), H. H. W. de Villiers, *Rivonia. Operation Mayibuye*, (Johannesburg, 1964), G. Ludi, *Operation Q–018*, (Cape Town, 1969), G. Ludi and B. Grobbelaar, *The Amazing Mr Fischer*, (Cape Town, 1966) and L. Strydom, *Rivonia Unmasked*, (Johannesburg, 1965).

[16] H. Pike, *A History of Communism in South Africa*, (Germiston, 1985). Interestingly, this book's distribution in South Africa has been prohibited by court order after a Supreme Court judge detected inaccuracies about his own past activites as mentioned in the work. Some would say that these were hardly amongst the most glaring errors which the book reveals. For an important critique of this work see I. Phillips, 'Carping on Communism: Comments on Pike's *A History of Communism in South Africa*', *Journal of Natal and Zulu History*, vol X, 1987.

[17] The ANC's operational files from the early years in exile in London contain only limited information dealing with the earlier campaigns. This collection is now held in the Mayibuye Centre, University of the Western Cape, which also holds the private collections of a number of leading activists and a substantial collection of interviews with *Umkhonto we Sizwe* cadres.

struggle' facing almost impossible logistical, political and tactical obstacles.[18]

In 1986, a souvenir issue of the *Umkhonto we Sizwe* magazine *Dawn*, commemorating the twenty fifth anniversary of the founding of the organisation, was devoted to cadres from the early campaigns writing short accounts of their various activities. Clearly writing under close editorial supervision, articles range from giving lessons on the early campaigns to *vignettes* on specific incidents to disclosures on the events leading up to the formation of *Umkhonto we Sizwe*.[19] Distributed clandestinely within South Africa, this publication was for a long time the only really significant source providing an insider view of the operations of the early campaigns. Even the publication of this material went against the wishes of some senior *Umkhonto we Sizwe* leadership who felt that security concerns mitigated against disclosure and the political needs of public and written commemoration.[20]

A number of sophisticated and analytically intelligent works on the politics of the later 1950s and early 1960s are available.[21] Key political activists have also written political analyses of the early campaigns.[22] However, within much of this the actual operations of *Umkhonto we Sizwe* receive little attention.

There are still few historical analyses of *Umkhonto we Sizwe* operations. We have the stimulating but brief analyses by Howard Barrell,[23] Stephen Ellis and Tsepo Sechaba[24] and the impressionistic

[18] See H. Barrell, 'Conscripts to Their Age: African National Congress Operational Strategy, 1976–1986', (D.Phil., University of Oxford, 1994), Chapter 1.
[19] *Dawn* Souvenir Issue, (Lusaka, n.d. circa 1986). For official histories produced after the ANC was unbanned see the video *MK. The People's Army*, (Johannesburg, n.d.) and *Submit or Fight. 30 Years of Umkhonto we Sizwe*, (ANC in association with Learn and Teach Publications, Johannesburg, 1991).
[20] See interview by Howard Barrell with 'Mac' Maharaj, 19 November 1990, Rhodes House, Mss/Afr s.5121. I am grateful to Howard Barrell and Claire Brain, Archivist, Rhodes House, Oxford for access to this material.
[21] See for example C. Bundy, 'Around which corner? Revolutionary theory and contemporary South Africa', *Transformation*, 8 (1989), R. Fine with D. Davis, *Beyond Apartheid*, (Johannesburg, 1990), P. Hudson, 'The Freedom Charter and the theory of national democratic revolution', *Transformation*, no 1 (1986), S. Johns, 'Obstacles to guerrilla warfare: a South African case study', *Journal of Modern African Studies*, vol 2, no 2 (1973), T. Lodge, *Black Politics in South Africa after 1945*, (Johannesburg, 1985) and F. Meli, *South Africa Belongs to Us*, (London, 1989).
[22] See for example J. Slovo, 'South Africa—no middle road' in B. Davidson *et al*, *Southern Africa: the New Politics of Revolution*, (London, 1976) and B. Turok, 'The search for a strategy', in R. Milliband and J. Saville, (eds) *The Socialist Register*. 1973, (London, 1974).
[23] H. Barrell, *MK. The ANC's Armed Struggle*, (London, 1990).
[24] S. Ellis and T. Sechaba, (pseud. for Oyama Mabandla), *Comrades Against Apartheid*, (London, 1992).

and again brief comments by Heidi Holland.[25] Works of this sort often give useful but very brief, tantalising snippets of information, often gained from interviews with *Umkhonto we Sizwe* activists from the Natal Regional Command on early operations in Durban.[26]

There are an increasing number of readily available and published documents written by key actors in the political struggles of the period. Indeed a main thrust of much publishing endeavour over the last couple of years has been focused in this direction. These works, often reprints of earlier banned material, have their own strengths and weaknesses and cover the early years of *Umkhonto we Sizwe*, trial and imprisonment in particular ways.

The first edition of Nelson Mandela's *No Easy Walk To Freedom*,[27] contains a selection of Mandela's speeches, papers and trial statements from 1953 and ends with his address to the Rivonia Trial in April 1964. In a similar vein, the first two editions of Nelson Mandela's *The Struggle Is My Life*,[28] give a sometimes identical selection of Mandela's speeches, writings and documents. With the publication in 1990 of the third edition, the story is taken further, with the inclusion of statements made by Mandela on contemporary political issues and negotiations with the state over the release of political prisoners. In this edition there are also comments on life on Robben Island by 'Mac' Maharaj, a member of *Umkhonto we Sizwe* Johannesburg Regional Command and imprisoned for twelve years on the Island and Michael Dingake. Both Maharaj and Dingake deal mainly, humanely and circumspectly with Mandela's living conditions and his role within the prison.

In a volume compiled by Adelaide Tambo, *Preparing For Power. Oliver Tambo Speaks*,[29] we have Tambo's brief comments on both the early stages of the armed struggle and the Rivonia Trial, with his latter comments being made on the eve of the opening of that trial. As with Mandela's writings, these are in the form of formal speeches.

---

[25] H. Holland, *The Struggle. A History of the African National Congress*, (London, 1989).

[26] For other analyses of *Umkhonto we Sizwe* see E. Feit, *Urban Revolt in South Africa*, (Chicago, 1971), H. Strauss, 'South Africa 1960–1966: Underground African politics', *Institute for Commonwealth Studies*, Seminar Papers on the Societies of Southern Africa in the 19th and 20th Centuries, (London, ICS, vol 3, no 16) and D. J. Tilton, 'The road to sabotage: The ANC and the formation of *Umkonto we Sizwe*', 'South Africa in the 1950s' conference, *Queen Elizabeth House*, University of Oxford, September 1987.

[27] N. Mandela, *No Easy Walk to Freedom*, (London, 1965).

[28] N. Mandela, *The Struggle is My Life*, (London, 1978 and 1986).

[29] A. Tambo, (comp.), *Preparing for Power. Oliver Tambo Speaks*, (Oxford, 1987).

Much of this recently published or reprinted work contains primary material of a formalised nature. This is important material, but there is much more.

From within lives suffused with political activism, bannings, detention, harassment and jail sentences we can also read a vibrant, and for those living in South Africa, a long banned literature of personal testimony on what was in essence a tragic period. From this we can feel the whole range of emotions which go towards creating and justifying the personal political and the mental and physical endurances which were the almost inevitable price for deeply held convictions. These are writings which lie at the centre of modern South African history.[30]

Internationally there is a rich literature expressing the human anguish and suffering experienced in the cells, torture rooms and law courts of the state. Here is a powerful literary genre of the modern age, where the individual truly comprehends the power of the state and its ability to instill fear, torture and cast aside those whom it decides are political dissenters.[31] Metaphorically the cell and court room trial are inextricably interlinked key images within modern South African literature.[32]

The South African sabotage and treason trials of the early 1960s were dramatic events. These trials, which when involving suspected *Umkhonto we Sizwe* members were often referred to as 'Spear' trials, are in themselves worthy of immediate analytic study. It was here that the state proclaimed success, holding the underground up unto

[30] See for example F. Baard as told to B. Schreiner, *My Spirit is Not Banned*, (Harare, 1986), M. Benson, *A Far Cry*, (London, 1990), M. Blumberg, *White Madam*, (London, 1962), B. Bunting, *Moses Kotane. South African Revolutionary*, (London, 1975), C. J. Driver, *Elegy for a Revolutionary*, (London, 1969), R. First, *117 Days*, (London, 1965), Q. Jacobsen, *Solitary in Johannesburg*, (London, 1973), H. Joseph, *Side by Side*, (London, 1986), N. Kitson, *Where Sixpence Lives*, (London, 1987), H. Lewin, *Bandiet. Seven Years in a South African Prison*, (London, 1974), A. J. L. Luthuli, *Let My People Go*, (London, 1962), P. Ntantala, *A Life's Mosaic*, (Cape Town, 1992), W. Mandela, *Part of My Soul*, (London, 1985), N. Mitchison, *Bram Fischer*, (London, 1973), M. Resha, *My Life in the Struggle*, (Johannesburg, 1991), R. Segal, *Into Exile*, (London, 1963) and A. Wolpe, *The Long Way Home*, (London, 1994).
[31] See for example H. Bernstein, *No. 46—Steve Biko*, (London, 1978), B Breytenbach, *The True Confessions of an Albino Terrorist*, (London, 1984), Primo Levi, *Survival in Auschwitz*, (New York, 1985), Ngugi wa Thiong'o, *Detained: A Writer's Prison Diary*, (London, 1981), Molefe Pheto, *And Night Fell. Memoirs of Political Imprisonment in South Africa*, (London, 1983), Aleksandr Solzhenitsyn, *The First Circle*, (New York, 1976) and Robert Storr, *Solitude, a Return to the Self*, (New York, 1988). For an analysis of some of these and other writings see K. Millet, *The Politics of Cruelty*, (London, 1994).
[32] See for example Dugmore Boetie, *Familiarity is the Kingdom of the Lost*, (London, 1969), Mark Mathabane, *Kaffir Boy*, (New York, 1986), Sipho Sepamala, *A Ride on the Whirlwind*, (London, 1981) and Miriam Tlali, *Amandla*, (Johannesburg, 1980).

the harsh, supposedly dispassionate and prosaic light of jurispru-
dential procedure.

In the face of this some accused adopted a linear line of logical
defiance as defence. Mandela bravely rejected the legitimacy of the
state and therefore also the court. Some, including Mandela, while
pleading 'not guilty', consistently refused to apologise for breaking
'the law' and used the court room dock as a platform from which to
make speeches, which because of the public nature of this trial,
could be legally disseminated.

Other accused treated the entire court proceedings with rude
contempt. Billy Nair, joint commander of the Natal Regional Command is an excellent example of such bravery, political astuteness
and steadfast cheek.[33] Despite pressing questioning by a state
attorney eager to acquire the information, Nair continually refused
to reveal the details of secret encoded messages between himself
and an undisclosed source.

Others falter, stumble and collapse. They were alone; in themselves, in body and mind, the guinea pigs of the state's new
methods of interrogation. They were also the innocents of an
underground which had barely anticipated the severity of police
tactics[34] and which had taken pitifully few real measures to protect
either the organisation or its often casually recruited cadres from the
consequences of prolonged detention and interrogation.[35]

Lacking the ability to play with power, detainees play by the old
rules and accept guilt.[36] In the mad world of the solitary cell, guilt
becomes a form of self-acknowledgement and a crucial form of
humanity which you dress in when facing your unknown but
seemingly all knowing interrogator.[37]

The trials were often absurdist events packed full of rituals,
drama and power struggles. Babenia's trial was even held *in camera*.
Some can understand the absurd and respond, whilst others cannot.
In the Pietermaritzburg 'Sabotage Trial' of 1964, Nair and Ebrahim
Ismail acquitted themselves supremely. How, only they know. That
is part of their stories.

---

[33] See A 30, NPA–NPD, 224/63, *The State versus Ebrahim Ismail and Others*, Evidence
of B. Nair.

[34] See the interview with Joe Slovo in *Apartheid*, Part 3, (Granada Television, 1987).

[35] Interview by I. Edwards with R. Kasrils, 3 December 1992.

[36] See D. Foster and D. Skinner, 'Detention and Violence; beyond Victimology' in
N. Chabani Manganyi and A. du Toit, (eds) *Political Violence and the Struggle in South
Africa*, (London, 1990).

[37] See also J. Jacobs, 'Confession, Interrogation and Self-interrogation in the New
South African Prison Writing', *Kunapipi: New Art and Literature from South Africa*, 13,
(1991).

However even the strong struggle amidst the shifting sands of judicial power. There were multiple accused and multiple charges, all requiring devious legal arrangements and strategies. There were discordant layers of remembered and created spoken evidence from both accused and the state. These could clash with submitted documents which often, despite their obvious falsity could acquire a primary legal status. In their spoken cross examination of accused, state lawyers could use documents to deadly effect. Although guilt can be privately accepted, court room scenes where lies and truths intermingle and where lies can convict and true human agency go unrecognised lead to considerable mental confusion. Fact, fantasy, oral examination and the seemingly clear writing of a legal code intermingled constantly in almost uncontrollable and perverse fashions. The court room was a warped place.[38]

The classic work on the subject is that of the Rivonia trial by Hilda Bernstein.[39] It deserves to be read by all those interested in the legal history of political trials in South Africa and by those whose wider interests concern the relationship between power and truth. The wife of 'Rusty' Bernstein, the only accused found not guilty at the trial, Bernstein presents an eloquent and humane insider view of the accused, the proceedings and the legal wranglings, farces and ironies which characterised South Africa's major political trial.

The Rivonia trial was the state's much publicised showpiece. In this and many, many other lesser known trials throughout the country, *Umkhonto we Sizwe's* underground cadres were convicted and sentenced. Police tactics and court room drama was a prologue to almost inevitable incarceration.

Up until now, biographical and autobiographical accounts of life within the ANC or aligned political movements during the later 1950s and early 1960s have rarely been joined with accounts of underground sabotage activity and accounts of incarcerated life on Robben Island. Men and, most especially, women have told of their lives into exile or to other South African jails, as either detainees or prisoners, but not to Robben Island.

This is an important point. *Umkhonto we Sizwe's* first cadres were mostly men and the vast majority of those jailed for political offences during those long repressive years were black men. After

---

[38] The best publicly accessible evidence of this are the lengthy quotations from the court record contained in Fatima Meer's *The Trial of Andrew Zondo*, (Braamfontein, 1987).

[39] H. Bernstein, *The World That Was Ours*, (London, 1989). See also the much earlier work by T. Karis, *The Treason Trial in South Africa*, (London, 1958) and B. Sachs, *The Road From Sharpeville*, (New York, 1961).

sentence their destination was Robben Island. This prison's politicos
have long understood what Neville Alexander terms the '*unspoken
injunction*' to talk about conditions on the Island, but it is only now
that their stories are beginning to be told in writing.[40]

There are still only two published autobiographies dealing with
life as an early *Umkhonto we Sizwe* activist. There are only two
autobiographies by *Umkhonto we Sizwe* activists of life on the Island
during the early years, a collection of political education lessons
written by an *Umkhonto we Sizwe* comrade for use on Robben Island
and a single volume of prison letters, some from Robben Island.[41] In
a recently released work, including many dramatic photographs,
leading prisoners, their relatives and jailers give short accounts of
their lives on the Island.[42] There is only one biography of a founding
Umkhonto we Sizwe cadre. This is the only book which covers the
spectrum: the activities of the ANC and *Umkhonto we Sizwe*, arrest
and conviction and life on Robben Island.[43]

The first autobiography dealing with *Umkhonto we Sizwe* activities
is, of course, the already cited work by Bruno Mtolo.[44] Durban
industrial worker and SACTU union member, Mtolo became a
member of the SACP and a founding member of *Umkhonto we Sizwe*
in Natal. Babenia and Mtolo worked together on the Technical
Committee of the Regional Command. As such the book is useful
but, whilst containing much interesting and verifiable information,
Mtolo's work must be treated with a particularly special caution.
Mtolo was captured and broken by the police. He then turned state
witness and was used by the state in the Pietermaritzburg and other
treason or sabotage trials. His name and parts of his history were
also appropriated by the state and used in their propaganda war
against the ANC. It is possible that this work was not even written
by Mtolo. The book is an anti-communist manifesto where the

---

[40] N. Alexander, *Robben Island Dossier, 1964–1974*, (Rondebosch, 1994), p vii.
Originally written twenty years ago after Neville Alexander's release from ten years
imprisonment on Robben Island, the dossier's original purpose was to hold the 'vile
deeds' (p vii) perpetrated on Robben Island up to a wider audience. The authorship
of the original manuscript was carefully concealed. (Emphasis added.)

[41] For fictionalised accounts see for example F. Anthony, *Robbeneiland My Kruis My
Huis*, (Genadendal, Kampen, 1983), D. Brutus, *A Simple Lust. Selected Poems including
Letters to Martha*, (London, 1968), A. Fugard, *The Island*, (Johannesburg, 1975) and
D. M. Zwelonke, *Robben Island*, (London, 1973).

[42] See J. Schadeberg, (ed) *Voices From Robben Island*, (Johannesburg, 1994).

[43] With regard to PAC history, there is Moses Dlamini's interesting account of his
two year stretch on Robben Island in the early 1960s. See M. Dlamini, *Robben Island
Hell-Hole*, (New Jersey, n.d.) For the trajectory of SWAPO history onto the Island see
H. Shityuwete, *Never Follow the Wolf. The Autobiography of a Namibian Freedom Fighter*,
(London, 1990).

[44] Mtolo, *Umkhonto we Sizwe*.

central theme of renunciation is personalised very much along the lines of 'Where I went wrong.'

Babenia has an interesting and spontaneous response to being demonised by Mtolo's cruel context and shadow. Listen:

> "Hey, Iain, that damn fellow! He lied about me. He said I was making bombs in my May Street place."
>
> "Yes, but Natoo, you were."
>
> "Yes, I know I was! It was *he* who could not make them. *He* got all the mixtures wrong. That is why his bombs never bloody worked! Hey that fucking shit, *he* coughed badly on us. He sold us out."

The second autobiography is Ronnie Kasrils' *Armed and Dangerous*.[45] Initially a youthful *Umkhonto we Sizwe* platoon commander in Durban, Kasrils quickly becomes a key conspirator in the Natal Region Command of the organisation. Kasrils and Babenia often worked closely together. Kasrils pays tribute to Babenia, but never actually mentions Babenia or deals with any of their escapades or encounters. Kasrils escapes capture by fleeing into exile as the underground structures collapsed. This gives Kasrils a different future and name: as Babenia and others from the Natal underground become politicos, Kasrils becomes part of the 'Odessa generation', sent for military training at Odessa in the USSR. *Armed and Dangerous* recalls the early sabotage campaigns in a rollicking style packed with daredevil adventure and masculine bravado cleansed of any sense of remembered trauma. This is possibly because the shadow of what happened to his much loved first comrades-in-arms hangs over Kasrils and restricts the ways in which he writes about the early campaigns.[46]

Then there is Fatima Meer's biography of Mandela.[47] This is an intriguing work. It combines, often in collage fashion, a mix of accepted wisdom and narrative explanation on the history of the period with often not widely known personal anecdotal details of Mandela, the person. Published during the initially secretive but later more public negotiations over a political settlement, in the book Mandela is a politician, not also the leader and the Commander-in-Chief of *Umkhonto we Sizwe*. Meer's treatment of the

---

[45] R. Kasrils, *'Armed and Dangerous.' My undercover struggle against Apartheid*, (London, 1993).

[46] See my 'Tales from the Underground: "Red Ronnie's exploits and *Umkhonto we Sizwe's* early campaigns"'. Paper delivered at the Institute for Commonwealth Studies, University of London and Queen Elizabeth House, University of Oxford, January and February 1994 respectively.

[47] F. Meer, *Higher Than Hope. Mandela*, (Durban, 1988, revised edition 1990). There are important differences between the two editions, but these are irrelevant in the present survey.

early years of *Umkhonto we Sizwe* is brief and ultimately unsatisfactory. Little evident attempt is made to address the very many important issues raised by the various shifts in strategy made during the early 1960s and the concrete implications for activists necessitated by these shifts. A biography of a leader of Mandela's stature should surely require this? Further, the section on Robben Island consists of comments, on a number of issues, woven around extracts from Mandela's letters from prison. These are often interesting, but a very particular form of biography.

In addition to the Mandela prison letters as contained in Meer's work, there is also Govan Mbeki's prison writings, *Learning From Robben Island*.[48] Willingly, to 'Oom Gov' went the task of writing wide ranging sets of essays for use in political education classes on the Island. Often based on articles he wrote prior to jail, the selection is extremely interesting and gives a clear idea of how comrades viewed the importance of the role of history within political education.

Those who read them now and find these lectures either blase or crude and rigid must remember when and where they were written and so gain a fuller appreciation of their path breaking tenor. In preparing these lessons, Mbeki had no access to his earlier notes and writings and had to rely on memory alone. Then one must also consider the audience. They were often poorly educated comrades who had only become literate on the Island through the endeavours of their fellow comrades.

Bundy's short biographical sketch, whilst thin on the early years of *Umkhonto we Sizwe*, does give a good analysis of the lessons prepared by Mbeki. What is missing is an insight into the nature of the teaching process and that crucial term, 'The University of Robben Island': words which have a seeming clarity of meaning which is beguiling. Further, we need to know who was being taught; for these were not lectures and lessons for everyone.

Patrick Lekota served six years on the Island and then was later detained for what seemed an interminable amount of time. During this time he penned lovingly composed letters to his daughter.[49] They range intelligently and freely over the whole panoply of history with care, but also a didactic insistence. His stories are all about 'struggle' history.

The first substantial autobiographical look into Robben Island comes in 1983 with the publication of Indres Naidoo's *Robben*

---

[48] G. Mbeki, *Learning From Robben Island*, (Cape Town, 1991).
[49] M. P. Lekota, *Prison Letters to a Daughter*, (Johannesburg, 1991).

Island.[50] Coming from a politically committed family knowing
Gandhi, Naidoo was one of the first cadres in *Umkhonto we Sizwe*.
Active in the Johannesburg area, Naidoo served ten years on
Robben Island, being released in 1973. For many reasons, he gives
few details of his underground activity. He hints at the ramshackle
nature of MK during the early campaigns and the possibility that
they had been penetrated by a spy, but then later embraces the
heroic. Similarly, during the brief page or two on his trial and
sentence he writes despairingly about how remote appeared the
time of liberation. He later views time and politics more optimisti-
cally. Here are different meanings in different contexts, all serving
their own often discreet purposes.

The book is essentially all about Robben Island. Its narrative
episodic style is similar to Babenia's sense of how Robben Island can
be understood. Likewise Naidoo's images of how the creativites and
evils of time have to be endured, understood and are modified by
the self or others are similar to Babenia's. Within these, feelings and
emotions, those most vulnerable of human qualities, shine in flitting
and often faltering momentary states. The episodic structure is there
ultimately, for protection.

The second autobiography to look in detail at experiences on
Robben Island is Michael Dingake's *My Fight Against Apartheid*.[51]
This is a vastly different book. An ANC activist who left to live in
Botswana, Dingake is kidnapped, brought back to South Africa and
convicted in 1965 of helping people leave South Africa to undergo
military training. This is a bizarre beginning to the fifteen years
Dingake spends on the Island. Dealing with many incidents also
recounted by Naidoo and Babenia but viewing them differently,
Dingake's style lacks the episodic tightness of the other two; instead
he writes in an eloquently articulate and freer style. It is a fine text,
but it seems to lack the intrinsic menace conveyed by Naidoo and
Babenia.

With an episodic style similar to Naidoo and Babenia, Moses
Dlamini stresses the need to understand the linkages between
Robben Island and his previous life, not only as a Pan Africanist
Congress activist, but as a human being with entirely mundane and
legitimate concerns.[52] His flashbacks to these lives are contextually
terrifyingly effective in their starkness and again their intrinsic
cruelty. His writings bear the same hallmarks of ordinariness and

---

[50] I. Naidoo, as told to A. Sachs, *Robben Island*, (New York, 1983). First published
under identical authorship as *Island In Chains*, (Harmondsworth, 1982).

[51] M. Dingake, *My Fight Against Apartheid*, (London, 1987).

[52] Dlamini, *Hell Hole*.

starkness that one finds in Naidoo and Babenia and that transferred
fascination with the people in power: not 'people's power', but that
of their jailers. Through them are reflected Dlamini's senses of
himself. In this, for him as with Naidoo and Babenia, there is an
understandable but tragic cruelty towards the self and perceived
places in time and history.[53]

During the last years of the Apartheid state, other autobiographies and biographies dealt with various other aspects of *Umkhonto
we Sizwe's* history. Tim Jenkin's account of Stephen Lee, Alex
Moumbaris and his escape from Pretoria Central prison, is arguably
the most daredevilish autobiographic account of all.[54] Albie Sachs'
life experiences are of a totally different kind and he writes in a more
reflective, personalised way, embracing not only 'The Struggle' but
a far wider and complementary set of human principles which
allow him to understand human trauma.[55]

The mid to late 1980s was a time of township insurrection,
expanding *Umkhonto we Sizwe* operations inside South Africa and
furious public debate over conditions in ANC/MK camps and
military attacks on civilian targets. Two biographies dealt with MK
cadres, both of whom were often publicly castigated as terrorists
and murderers. Both were sentenced to death for murder. Both
cadres were Natal operatives. Fatima Meer's study of Andrew
Zondo, who was executed for the Amanzimtoti bombing of late
1985, placed Zondo's politicisation within the context of a rather
two dimensional history of an emotionally disturbed youth growing
up in Apartheid's townships. The thrust of Meer's work was not
only to explain Zondo's actions. Through quoting massively from
the court record, the book served as a published indictment of legal
procedure and the death penalty.[56] Brian Rostron's journalistic,
detailed but sometimes factually inaccurate study of Robert
McBride is an important work providing a complex picture of
political motivation and action. However, all too often Rostron
seems to embrace and celebrate a brash adventurist style.[57]

---

[53] For interesting analysis of these writings see J. Jacobs, 'A proper name in Prison:
self-identification in the South African Prison memoir', *Nomina Africana*, vol 5, (1)
(1991) and 'Narrating the Island: Robben Island in South African literature', *Current
Writing*, vol 4, (1) (1992). See also C. Terreblanche, 'Robben Eiland: Nuwe drome oor
'n ou nagmerrie', *Vrye Weekblad*, 10–16 April 1992.
[54] T. Jenkin, *Escape From Pretoria*, (London, 1987).
[55] A. Sachs, *The Jail Diary of Albie Sachs*, (Cape Town, 1990) and *Running To Maputo*,
(London 1990).
[56] Meer, *The Trial of Andrew Zondo*.
[57] B. Rostron, *Till Babylon Falls*, (London, 1991).

Then there is Mwezi Twala's *Mbokodo*.[58] Joining *Umkhonto we Sizwe* in 1975, Twala receives military training in the USSR and becomes a military instructor at various *Umkhonto we Sizwe* camps in southern Africa. Twala is then incarcerated at Quatro rehabilitation camp and eventually escapes back to South Africa. Now an organiser for the Inkatha Freedom Party, Twala's account is explicitly aimed at publicly exposing the human sufferings endured in *Umkhonto we Sizwe's* various military bases. Twala has nothing to say on the early campaigns and his memoirs are really part of the current political conflict over the nature of the more recent history of *Umkhonto we Sizwe*.[59] Inevitably, this conflict has drawn in critique of the whole history of *Umkhonto we Sizwe*, and this organisation's own visions of itself.

When Babenia decided to write his political history, he had to confront not only the legal and emotional shadows cast over him by the South African state. There were two other shadows.

As Michael Mann has written, all societies are 'constituted of multiple overlapping and intersecting sociospatial networks of power'.[60] Within society, political movements and organisations develop their own discourses and principles and give themselves both histories and futures. Here lie the defining dreams and aspirations of a membership, the slogans; crucial for a largely illiterate audience, and the security. Here is a mental world, layered and often contradictory, that can explain so much. This obviously defines, thereby creating heroes and senses of loyalty. Inevitably and understandably this very creation defines heresy and disloyalty. This is another form of treason. By the 1980s, the ANC's view of itself and of South African history and politics had become extremely powerful and near dominant within South Africa.

---

[58] M. Twala and E. Benard, *Mbokodo. Inside MK: Mwezi Twala—A Soldier's Story*, (Johannesburg, 1994).

[59] Within this struggle to interpret history, various political organisations ranging from within the South African Parliament to the long standing left wing Trotskyite opponents of *Umkhonto we Sizwe* are seeking and using various oral and documentary testimonies to bolster their interpretations. The ANC has also commissioned four official investigations, all of which have conducted interviews and have presented written reports. Another three reports, one by Amnesty International have also investigated and commented on this history. See Amnesty International, 'South Africa: Torture, ill-treatment and executions in African National Congress camps', (London, 1992), Ellis and Sechaba, *Comrades Against Apartheid*, S. Ellis, 'Mbokodo: Security in ANC camps, 1961–1990', *African Affairs*, (1994), 93, B. Ketelo, 'A miscarriage of democracy: the ANC Security Department and in the 1984 Mutiny in *Umkhonto we Sizwe*', *Searchlight South Africa*, 5, (July 1990) and P. Trewhela, 'The ANC Prison Camps: an audit of three years, 1990–1993', '*Searchlight South Africa*, 10, (April 1993).

[60] M. Mann, *The Sources of Social Power*, (Cambridge, 1986), pp 518–21.

Under the almost insufferable conditions of South African politics, the operations of the armed struggle and the quest for wide-
spread clandestinity created structures, written and verbal and an
alternate culture of political activism. Along with new terms, like
'The Movement' or 'The Struggle', the clenched fist replacing the old
ANC 'thumbs-up' sign and songs praising masculinity and weaponry came new codes of identity, behaviour and secrecy. Within this
it is only the senior leadership of the movement who acquired a
personal public identity. Leaders' faces would appear on posters,
their words in writing and their praises sung.

The only other people to be given a public face, *persona* and
history were the 'enemy'. The most effective recent example of this
is the 1991 'Wanted for Apartheid Crimes' poster featuring a
photograph of F W de Klerk's face.[61]

The ordinary *Umkhonto we Sizwe* was publicly nameless and
faceless, underground and known by a *nom-de-guerre*. The classic
depiction of this is in the poster of an *Umkhonto we Sizwe* male cadre
dressed in camouflage sitting, AK–47 resting on one shoulder,
reading a book entitled 'ANC Speaks'.[62] That was the identity of
loyalty. It was entirely mythical: operatives never wore uniforms
when engaged in South African campaigns.

To this Babenia bore fealty, sometimes adopting a very hard line,
uncompromising political perspective. This was so that he could
define his dreams about the type of society he wished to live in. This
was a vision whose existence lay in the future. Doing these things,
Babenia thereby, understandably, acquired a second shadow. This
was however something that could suppress parts of himself: gentle-
ness, his literary abilities, his whimsical nature and spontaneity.

Because of the tragedies of its past history, the exigencies of the
escalation of armed struggle and its essential brutalising costs, good
and evil became crudely defined. Underground cells, insurrectionist
groups, revolts and gunfire battles with the state in township streets
are hardly the time or places where one recognises and tries to
accommodate the traumatised self. Good becomes depersonalised
into the heroic obedient while evil acquires a face and individuality.
This in a movement which takes its history very, very seriously.[63]

---

[61] 'Wanted for Apartheid Crimes', *South African Communist Party*, n.d.
[62] 'African National Congress 1912–1982', ANC Youth Section (UK Mission) and
ANC Youth Secretariat, Lusaka, Zambia, n.d.
[63] For an insight into the political worlds in which this history was written and the
nuances of these interpretations, see T. Lodge, 'Charters from the Past: The African
National Congress and its historiographical traditions' in B. Bozzoli and P. Delius,
(eds) *Radical History Review. History From South Africa*, (New York, 1990). For

It was only on the 16th of December 1993 during rallies marking the last formal parades of *Umkhonto we Sizwe* and the commemoration of Heroes Day that the ordinary cadres were publicly named, honoured as heroes and some given medals. During one such ceremony in Durban the 'veterans', all kitted in full military camouflage, Babenia included, were each individually introduced to a cheering crowd.[64]

This is Babenia's second shadow. Empowering, but layered with histories which embody many ironies and ambiguities. In writing he accepts parts of this shadow but shouts out aloud that other parts will simply not do. Babenia asks for a more humane view of the personal. Accepting the apartheid state's depersonalised cruelty is one thing, but within the struggle as well? If you understand yourself through displacement into powerful aggregations called the state and the movement, then you loose yourself. And surely it was afterall through immediate personal experiences, of suffering and hurt, that one developed an outlook on life which gave so much to a maturing political commitment?

And yet in making this memoir Babenia also needed to confront that other shadow. This was his own: private, secretive and layered in the most confusing fashion. Here were histories and meanings reflecting various parts of his own life and struggles with himself. Many concerned betrayal, shame and a long suppressed notion of pride. Ambitiously he wanted not only to convert memorised pasts into writing but also those verbally constructed times when he threw himself again, now as an MK cadre, into the underground.

This part of Babenia's life lasted only a couple of years at the most, and yet within this lay so much elemental drama, courage and confusion that it seemed to have compacted decades of experience not yet learnt whilst he lived through it. Other *Umkhonto we Sizwe* comrades in arms say the very same.[65] And from there Babenia emerges, as he probably accepts will be his inevitable fate: his anonymity ends when the state recognises him, replaces his name with a number, calls him a *Poqo*, and locks him away.

Within the desire to write there are also personal hesitations which constitute as important a barrier as do those legal and broadly political. Current personal political activity and a generalised fear or reluctance, which can often be expressed in a politicised

---

interesting comments on the way in which the history of the later 1950s became used and integrated into the politics of the 1990s, see B. Freund, 'Some unasked questions on politics: South African slogans and debates', *Transformation*, 1 (1985).

[64] *Daily News*, 17 December 1993.

[65] See for example interview by I. Edwards with R. Kasrils, 3 December 1992.

manner, seem to feed on these concerns.[66]

Parts of the eventual text were to remain silences until very much later. Some only emerged in the final moments of preparation. The normal human response to trauma and the lived reality of repression and acts of brutality is to eliminate them from consciousness. They constitute a deafening silence. Babenia wanted to and struggled to remember his often orally constructed pasts, speak about these and write. When written drafts appeared the finality of the text produced an added exquisite form of torture.[67]

Any form of autobiography is a form of self evaluation which creates its own cruel pressures on those brave enough to embark on such a journey. The explorer becomes the torturer, probing the traumatised self. In a story full of courage, humiliation, human error and sacrifice, personal recollection appears as a final act of betrayal. This not only of the self, but because of the humanity which the very structure which the chosen life history creates, the writer gives a personalised and thus profiled insight into the lives of comrades. Honesty, power, the self and those often ambiguous histories which sustain one over the years come into sharp relief and bear up, all too successfully, those images of the person's traumatised past. This is exactly the purpose and the inevitable outcome of such a self-inflicted task. However this does not make it comfortable or easy to live with.[68]

A lot of this was in the future. In the beginning we approached two problems simultaneously: how to align Babenia's desire to write with South African law and starting the process of writing. As it then stood South African statutory law was unambiguous. Babenia could write but because of the nature of his life history, it could never be legally published.

Pseudonyms are an inappropriate device for trying to disguise the authorship of an autobiography. Advice from an exiled leadership over authorship was, as it could hardly otherwise be, unhelpful. We dwelt on the differences between autobiography and the novel. It is probably true that the stories of these years could best be told through a form of magic realist text. We also, hideously, thought of dismembering the text and discussed false authorship as opposed to pseudonymity. These were of course futile paths. And anyway,

---

[66] For important comparative work on this subject see L. Passerini, (ed) *Memory and Totalitarianism*, (Oxford, 1992).

[67] For an important analysis of the tyranny of the text see J. Guy, 'Literacy and literature' in E. Sienart, N. Bell and M. Lewis, (eds) *Oral Tradition and Innovation*, (Durban, 1991).

[68] See the excellent analysis of these issues in J. L. Herman, *Trauma and Recovery*, (New York, 1992).

Babenia wanted his name. The legal and political implications of the unbanning of the African National Congress, *Umkhonto we Sizwe* and the South African Communist Party brought increased licence and thus welcome relief. The laws preventing Babenia from publishing his autobiography, although not immediately repealed, fell into disuse.

Babenia will forgive me for a personal comment. During the long years he wrote this text he was obsessed by the secrecy of his text. What he was anticipating was afterall illegal. And he was writing about clandestinity. So neatly handwritten sheets would be handed to me carefully rolled up, as is the wont of a politico, wrapped in newspaper so to conceal. Right up until the end he still did this, with his last two conspiratorial coverings being the edition of *Mayibuye* with Angela Davis' photo on the cover[69] and then his final writings lay comfortably within the *ANC Draft Bill of Rights*.[70] Both of them have always been entirely legal documents. He has embraced this second shadow. I have these covers in my study and maybe I should give them back.

At the same time work commenced. Initially we worked through a series of open ended interviews, charting out the larger canvas of Babenia's life in order to set a context for both of us. These would soon bear the marks of our two, not always similar preoccupations. Later Babenia assumed the true role of writer. It was now that a serious overall texture and character emerged. Producing voluminously, as the long drafts appeared we would then, within his chosen structure, discuss, seek clarity, order and search for silences. Some of these meetings were recorded.

In broad methodological outline we appear to have adopted the same approach as did Indres Naidoo and Albie Sachs for their co-authored account of Naidoo's life on Robben Island. We have taken the same means for acknowledging authorship.

My roles as editor and curious reader, historian, friend, facilitator and writer became intermingled. Tensions also moved me, consciously and otherwise, in important ways into that terrain most assiduously held to by the interrogator. Then, roles and responsibilities become confused, power becomes abuse and that secure measure of mutual trust so needed when discussing traumatic experiences brought into considerable jeopardy. I am neither comfortable nor familiar in such a situation and have deliberately restricted this form of editorship.

---

[69] *Mayibuye*, vol 2, 9 (ANC, October 1991).
[70] *ANC Draft Bill of Rights*, Centre for Development Studies, (February, 1993).

This project was never an interrogation. Interrogators seek the annotated, corroborated and convicted fact. This I never did. Historians and editors can ask harsh questions, that is after all their function.[71] However, ironically, even if their questions are not informed by the demonizing texts of the past, but by an analytically incisive and sensitive historiography, this still makes their questions appear as threats.

However, in the present context the historian as editor has most of all to listen and to learn.[72] But it was never easy, as there was a tension which scared both of us. I would demand answers and he would attack, "You whites do not know what it was like!". Good. I would listen to the creation of a history and write it down. Then I would ask questions, seek the contexts and search for amplification, silence and inconsistency. Then came answers, "No, Iain, you are missing the point. I did do this!", "As it stands it is fine." And also, "No, I must think about that some more". This maybe appears brutal to the onlooker and certainly was indeed to both of us. At certain times power was clearly in my hands. I hope I used it positively and creatively.

As editor I have not felt it either necessary or possible to provide annotated historical comment. Glossary or textual annotations have been restricted to brief explanations of words or terms which may be foreign to the reader.

For those unfamiliar with the struggle for independence in India, important guides could be Arthur Lall's, *The Emergence of Modern India*, Sarkar's *Modern India, 1885–1947*, and Schwartzberg's *A Historical Atlas of South Asia*.[73] With regard to the South African sections, a number of substantial texts which are of critical importance are now easily available.

Similarly I have not felt it necessary to provide biographical details on the many people mentioned in the work. For the sections dealing with India, Chopra's *Who's Who of Indian Martyrs* contains some useful material.[74] With regard to the South African sections, biographies of many of Babenia's associates appear in Tom Karis and Gwendolin Carter's last volume of the *From Protest To Challenge*

---

[71] See E. Tonkin, *Narrating Our Pasts*, (London, 1992), chapter 7.

[72] For important analysis of these tensions see R. J. Grele, *Envelopes of Sound. The Art of Oral History*, (Chicago, 2nd edition, 1985).

[73] A. Lall, *The Emergence of Modern India*, (New York, 1981), S. Sakar, *Modern India, 1885–1947*, (London, 2nd edition, 1989) and J. Schwartzberg, *A Historical Atlas of South Asia*, (Chicago and London, 1978).

[74] P. N. Chopra, (ed) *Who's Who of Indian Martyrs*, (New Delhi, 1969).

series.[75] It is however important to note that very many of the people Babenia associated with in South Africa have not acquired publicly noted biographic status.[76]

Ultimately this is and has always been Babenia's voice, asking me, right from the beginning to help him into, not around, his own histories. Demanding to be listened to, he ranged through verbal and written pasts, sometimes proclaiming fact, sometimes expressing remembered feelings and always analysing and seeking contexts. He held ultimate power and, as the going got tough, could have yielded and surrendered the vision of a published life at anytime he so wished. He chose consistently not to do this.

Babenia's story is interesting in four interwoven ways. Firstly, and most obviously, for the very fact that he is wanting to reflect on himself and his times, the various interpretations of his past which he has made for himself and has had made for him, and that he wishes to tell this story.

Then there is the historical terrain of politics which his life covers. Babenia must surely be one of the very few South Africans to have been actively engaged in the calamitous events which shook the Indian sub-continent during the 1940s; and this as a saboteur. Here one must remember that Indian civilisation embraced not only the spinning wheel but also fireworks. From this vantage his views on politics, and in particular Gandhian struggle, is rather different to the way in which South Africans have created a particular image of Gandhi. And then from India into the vortex of South African apartheid society. Using his Indian experiences he looked critically at much of black oppositional politics, finally throwing himself again into underground politics and then, finally, into a jail for a longer period and requiring more emotional endurance than anything his life experience had prepared him for.

This trajectory bears down directly on a third importance. His recollections are the very first real personal study we have which deals directly with four crucial aspects of our South African history which have not previously been integrated in forms of autobiographic writing. These are the political campaigns of the later 1950s,

---

[75] T. Karis and G. M. Carter, (eds) *From Protest To Challenge*, volume 4 *Political Profiles, 1882–1964*, (Stanford, 1977).

[76] None of Babenia's first comrades-in-arms received mention in the first volume of Shelia Gastrow's *Who's Who in South African Politics*, (Johannesburg, 1985). In the fourth edition of her work (Johannesburg, 1990) Rowley Arenstein, Ebrahim Ismael Ebrahim and Billy Nair receive entries. The full list of political prisoners held in South African jails still needs to be completed. The IDAF and the UN Centre Against Apartheid biographical list *Prisoners of Apartheid*, (London, 1978) as an important but incomplete reference.

xxxiv MEMOIRS OF A SABOTEUR

the activities of *Umkhonto we Sizwe*, detention and court trials and memoirs of Robben Island.

And then finally, all of this is being done not by a leader, but by an ordinary loyal cadre. These are the thoughts not of a great leader, nor those of the gloriously heroic anti-hero of the outsider, but by a small guy. He is brave enough to expose his traumas and to ask that society no longer remain deaf to the visions, memories, dreams and spirit of people like Natoo.

In doing all this he is asking us to reflect on something hugely big. He is calling our attention to the human face of political activism. His writings reject any idealised notion of an easy and clean political transformation. He shows just how cruel and messy are the forces of change as ironic twists become both cruelties and also forces of a transformation which he believes in steadfastly.

Writing the history of the inside operations of guerrilla forces is difficult.[77] Sound analyses of guerrilla warfare in other parts of Africa do exist.[78] South Africa still lacks a comprehensive understanding of *Umkhonto we Sizwe's* armed struggle.[79]

The time for heroic autobiographies and biographies of Afrikanerdom's leaders has now gone.[80] We may now have reached a point where more victims of Apartheid's social engineers are willing and able to communicate publicly about their life stories. This will not be an easy task. There are layers of trauma that will need to be uncovered and confronted if the desires to reflect are properly sustained. Describing such accounts Kate Millet writes:

> The French . . . call it *temoignage*, the literature of the witness; the one who has been there, seen it, knows. It crosses genres, can be autobiographical, reportage, even narrative fiction. But its basis is factual, fact passionately lived and put into writing by a moral imperative rooted like a flower amid carnage with an imperishable optimism, a hope that those who will hear will care, will even take action.[81]

Babenia is one such witness.

This is a history which is characterised by a tension between oral and written forms of public expression. Indeed the divide between

---

[77] See for example M. Stuart-Fox 'The Murderous Revolution', (Bangkok, 1986) and M. L. Lanning and D. Cragg, *Inside the VC and the NVA*, (New York, 1994).

[78] See for example B. Davidson, *In the Eye of the Storm*, (London, 1972) and *The People's Cause*, (London, 1981) and T. Ranger, *Peasant Consciousness and Guerrilla War in Zimbabwe*, (Harare, 1985).

[79] See Military Research Group, *The Other Armies: Writing the History of MK* (Working Paper Series, paper vii, n.d.).

[80] Witness the rather sordid infighting between F. W. de Klerk and P. W. Botha over parts of the latter's intended autobiography, the eventual publication of which is also troubled by the possibility of a small purchasing market for the book.

[81] K Millet, *The Politics of Cruelty*, p 1.

orality and writing in the very memorising and telling of this history
has been indelibly imprinted in witnesses' minds by state legislation
and repression and the need for secrecy and loyal anonymity.
Furthermore, the very formation and history of *Umkhonto we Sizwe's*
has also always been highly controversial; conservative and racist
condemnation and trenchant left wing critique challenge *Umkhonto
we Sizwe's* created images of the heroic soldier.

In the rapidly changing South African political world, it will be
interesting to see which of *Umkhonto we Sizwe's* cadres choose to
publicly remember their stories, how they understand their own
pasts, who they perceive as their intended audience and through
what medium they choose to relate their stories.

But the comrades of and thankfully now from Robben Island are
very certainly not the only traumatised selves. South African history
has dragged all of us through levels of elemental pain that carve
deep scars.[82] If the thrust for all of us to confront these pasts comes
from the efforts of the *politicos* of Robben Island: depersonalised by
number, demonised by name and abused mentally and physically,
then this may well be the final, ironic and very triumphal legacy
which they could ever bestow on us all. But first we must be ready
to listen and to learn.

Now listen to Natoobhai.

Iain Edwards

30 July 1993
and 20 October 1994

Postscript. Soon after the final two bibliographic entries in this
Introduction were completed, Nelson Mandela's autobiography
was published.

I E 14 August 1995

---

[82] See S. Marks and N. Andersson, 'The Epidemiology and Culture of Violence' in
Manganyi and Du Toit, (eds) *Political Violence and Struggle.*

PART ONE

A YOUTHFUL STRUGGLE FOR INDEPENDENCE

South Africa and India, 1924–1949

Babenia family shortly before their departure to India, 1936
Back (left to right): Bachoo (brother), Motiben 'Big sister' (a cousin), Shanti (sister), Maniben (mother), Natoo
Front: Maganlal (uncle), Kanti (younger sister), Dayalji (father), Chiman ('big brother')
Toddler in front: Dhiroo (Motiben's son)

Lutchme and Stainbank child (Stainbank album, Local History Museum, Durban)

Natoo Babenia, India, 1945

Gujarati Literary Society, Garda College, Nasvari, 1945.
Babenia seated second right. *Centre:* Prof. A.R. Trivedi, Principal of College. *Seated second left:* General secretary of the SRC

On the Horizons of Youth

I was born on the 28th of March 1924 in a little wood and iron house under the shade of a huge fig tree in Coedmore Road in Bellair. The fig tree is still there, but it's a bit lonely now that things have changed so much. My tree now is just so dusty against wire fencing in the quarry yard.

Although it's really only a little way from the centre of Durban, in those days I think we felt quite far away from the city. The mainline railway link between Durban and Johannesburg came right through Bellair. We could hear and see the trains weaving along around the tops of the slopes, but I don't think we ever used the train very often. I cannot recall anything of the city just below us around the Bay. For the Indians and Africans of Bellair the centre of our life was the Coedmore Quarry. The quarry was our horizon in Durban.

We lived close to the quarry, not on the top of the hills and ridges, but down at the bottom in and around the quarry lands. People spoke of our place as lower Coedmore Road. The Indian people of lower Coedmore had small plots of land filled with carefully tended vegetables and fruit trees. There was plenty of food. As the seasons changed, there were always avocados, mangoes, guavas, figs and wild cherries. The air was sweet.

We did not know the owners of this quarry well. We were much closer to the carved up rocky hills. Whites had greater horizons. But after all, it was their stones that became ballast on railway tracks. The railway lines! What a triumph! The railway tracks were quickly shooting all over Natal. Everyone knew about the railway lines. With those railway lines came a lot of new opportunities. The whites were settling in comfortably. And so were traders. Where the railways went so did the traders. Whites called them Arabs. They were another colonising elite; competitors in a way. Here was the cradle of new views.

You could feel the pace and excitement, even in Bellair. But for us in lower Coedmore Road the dust had already settled. Once you adjusted your eyes you could see clearly.

Astride the railway line through Sea View and Bellair were large houses in big gardens filled with palms, frangipanis and hibiscus. Many of the houses were of stone or wood and iron. Just like our family house. But they were very smart and had lovely gardens. Also, along with our family's, these properties had vegetable gardens, avocado trees and mango groves. These houses were on the higher ground with often good views of the city and the sea. I suppose some were really estates. These were the homes for many of Durban's wealthy whites.

5

We knew a lot about many of these families. The Shave family had lands on either side of the railway line with a level crossing in the middle of their garden. That sums it up quite conveniently. Now the Shave's were important people in the community. Mrs Shave laid the foundation stone for the local Anglican church. Their house was called *Kinfauns*. People say this is a place in Cornwall, England where the Shave family came from. Anyway it doesn't really matter any longer. But I also think these people felt closer to the city than we did. Then there were the Bawdens who were very prominent Natal politicians and railway people. They lived in a huge house built out of Coedmore stone.

And the Stainbanks. The Indian community in the area knew the Stainbanks very well. They were an old, well established Natal family who owned large tracts of land in the area. I remember people saying that Mrs Stainbank was a very kind and gentle person. She often used to say that my father was like a son to her. But it would be rude to call her a paternalist. Maybe she was but that is not the way I remember my parents talking about her. The Stainbanks also had a lot of influence in wider circles. So these were our local gentry.

As I have heard it said, the Babenia clan history dates back to my great grandfather who was a member of the *Anavil Brahmin* caste. During the wars fought to repel first Muslims and then the British imperial columns, my great-grandfather had formed and led a successful military force. As a reward he was given the right to collect and keep the taxes paid by the peasantry of the village of Baben. It was from this village that the Babenia clan took their name as well. For many years the Babenias, which was a small clan, lived close together in a smallish area of land. Say within sixty miles of each other. Most of us were land owning peasants. Quite when my father and mother had come to South Africa I cannot really say. From what I hear it must have been in the late 1870s. Maybe he came as a result of straightened circumstances in India. But my family did come as travellers not as indentured labourers. Very few Babenias came to South Africa.

In Durban my dad had once worked in the Indian Immigration Office. There was a lot of corruption in the civil service and people could become rich trying to help people enter the country. It was during this work that he had met up with Gandhi, a person who was highly revered by the small community in lower Coedmore Road. I have heard it said that in 1930, when Gandhi was imprisoned in India, the Coedmore people felt that it would not be befitting for them to celebrate *Deepavali*. Gandhi's India was so close to those very near the quarry.

Gandhi advised my father to leave his work. Dad understood and came to Coedmore. Here my father secured the trading franchise from the quarry company. Being so closely connected to the quarry changed our lives. When the quarry owners brought in more machinery and expanded, the owners took over our house and allocated us a two acre plot where my father built a new brick house. Two acres was a lot of land to own. My father had tenants as well. Africans who worked in the quarry. They used to help us in our gardens and in the home. My dad also rented a larger piece of land across the *Mbilo* river from the Stainbanks. He also supervised the Stainbanks' land affairs, seeing to cultivation and tending to their horses. That was exactly how close we were to the Stainbanks.

There were seven of us in our house. My father and mother, Dayalji Akhoobhai and Maniben Babenia and the five of us children. The eldest was my brother Chiman who sadly died in 1990, followed by sister Shanti, my late brother Bachoo, myself and young sister Kanti. Our house had no electricity and no running tap water. We burnt candles and kept two big tanks for rain water. It was the same with all the people living lower down Coedmore Road.

The quarry owners had built rows of corrugated iron barracks; rambling rusty affairs with little windows for their African men. Most of them were Sothos. Many were migrants, journeying far in search of work. Forced to leave their farms, maybe many had their lands taken by whites, the futures of the sons and daughters of African pastoralists were embedded in digging up the land of their forebears for settlers. An underground was bound to come sooner or later. Why not? Making the best of things some had made the quarry their new home. These were the workers who stayed with their families outside the compound and amongst us.

We were a rather poor and isolated little community. Our womenfolk used to wake up at four in the morning and *knap* stones for three pennies a basket. The women had to stop working at around seven in the morning so as to allow the African workers under Jack the Indian supervisor to get loosened big stones from the rock wall. They would use heavy hammers and iron pegs to break them up. Then at around one o'clock a whistle was blown, warning of blasting time. You could hear it clearly. Blasting was done by whites. Big stones from the blast would sometimes roll on or even through our roof. Once Chiman got saved by inches. This used to make Mrs Stainbank very concerned and it was through her pressure that the quarry owners gave us the new piece of land. Indian women with small chisels and hammers early in the day. Then African men with big hammers and supervisors. Then white men, explosives and whistles. It went on and on like this. Later in my own life I was first a blaster and then a *knapper*. But this comes much later.

Later I was also told a lot about my father. My father had his own mind and would do what pleased him most. He was a proud man. He never made much money. He was a humble man and as a good trader he was always giving things away. In the poor community you couldn't become too isolated. If he heard that an African died in the barracks he would send white and black calico for the coffin along with twenty five pounds of mealie meal, bread and sugar. If an Indian died he would send white and yellow calico and some rice, pea *dhol* and sugar. These were tributes to be delivered by Khumalo, our shop assistant who lived on our property.

On Fridays the shop only closed at nine o'clock at night. Being a pay day the place was chock-a-block with workers buying for the weekend. It was always an exuberant time, a little drunken, rowdy and very boisterous. As money went its rounds, so joy could easily pass into sadness and even anger. There was not much money, maybe not even real compassion, but the living had a powerful instinct for survival. In their own silent ways the iron pots, the calico sheeting in just so many beautiful colours hanging from wire hooks on the rafters, the sacks of mealies, rice and flour and the rich smelling tobaccos were the magic potions of the new land. The meaty smoke and guitar music of the drinking parties, the fights and arguments over the counter and the wails of children were all in a way paying their homage to the new life.

My eldest brother had left school in standard six to help in the shop. Even his Bellair Football Club members would often come along on Friday evenings and help behind the counter. I was given a chair where the ready to wear goods were kept and told to see that nothing was stolen. If an African looked at something with interest, I used to ask, *'Wena tanda lo ento'.*[1] If he nodded his head, I would take the article and give it to him and say *'Nagoo thata'.*[2] I never bothered to collect the money. My father used to be near me and he would make the price. However, one day I gave a chap a cap and he was going out with it. My brother, from the opposite counter, saw it so he came out from behind the counter, took the cap away, gave me a smack and chased me outside. Father was angry with Chiman. He told him never to touch me.

But that was the end of my sitting in the shop. I was happy as I had more time to play. But from what my mother told me later, I was often quite a loner whom most of the Africans called *Tukela*. I was

---

[1] *Fanagalo* for 'Do you want to take this?'
[2] *Fanagalo*, meaning 'Take it there.'

never a pusher and often left out of the pack. I would often wander around by myself. I was a bit whimsical in my childhood. One day while eating, Shanti said something irritable and I hit her with the enamel plate from which I was eating. She still bears a small scar on her upper forehead. In my mother's eyes I could do little wrong and I never really lost my whimsical streak.

My sister was a unique person, diligent, kind-hearted and loving. From my childhood I had always been receiving things from her and her friends. I was very fair haired then and my sister's friends used to be very fond of me. They were very fond of showering me with tops and marbles. In the mornings, at school inspection time, I always found that I had forgotten my handkerchief. Quickly a senior girl by the name of Margaret Ramragh passed me one. I was often so saved by Shanti's friends.

Coedmore was a great place for children to grow up. It was rather secluded in a way. The County Football Ground was a stone's throw away. There you could watch the men playing over the weekends or run around happily yourself. All the kids of the African workers and our families playing ball, fooling around in the nearby pond or collecting guavas, mulberries and wild cherries in the bush. One of my brother Bachoo's best friend's was Themba, a chap who, with his sister Ntombi, lived with their parents close by. Their dad was a worker in the quarry. I think he lived in the quarry barracks while his wife stayed just outside. One day I remember Themba fell into the pond and very nearly drowned. After we pulled him out my mom took him to the male barracks.

Us kids were I think quite innocent of much that went on around us. We just played around together. But us Indian kids could go to the Sea View Government Aided Indian School just along the top of the hill. That was where my father sent Chiman to receive his education for the shop.

There were tensions in the area. As I hear, there was a lot of business rivalry. One day late in 1934 one of our tenants, a tailor, hatched a plot to kill my eldest brother. It is said that this tailor had the support of another local Indian shopkeeper who was competing with my father. The tailor had gone to the quarry during a lunch break and spoken to a very hefty African worker. The next day he had returned to speak again with the same person. Jack the foreman had noticed these comings and goings and got the African, who was a good customer of ours, to tell him the story. He was being hired to kill Chiman. Then Jack asked him if he was willing to do the job. No, he could not do a thing like that. He had seen Big *Nkosana's* son grow up in front of him. Jack advised him to tell all to the manager, a Mr Dickson. The worker was scared that if he did this the *Mulungu* would fire him. Fair enough, but Jack promised to protect him.

At the time none of us little ones knew anything about it. My father and mother were worried but they did not utter a word. There was an awful lot of skullduggery around and my old father had a tough time plotting with the police. Eventually it was the manager of the Coedmore quarry who helped us get the police on to the tailor and his cohorts. The tailor was caught and got five years. He was an old guy and as we heard later, died inside.

During these depressed times everyone was trying to trick each other. This was why, young as I was, I had become drawn into the shop. Travelling salesmen used to worry us with goods that they could not sell elsewhere. We had to keep fast selling stock lines in those days and my father had to be extra careful about what he purchased. Chiman had been educated sufficiently and was now well groomed to take over the family shop. But further, Shanti and I, the youngest of *kakaji's* children would sit on either side of him when a travelling seller came to offer goods. Shanti would help choose materials and I would peruse the sweet selections. Young as we were, Shanti and I began to really know the inside of an Indian owned store. The shop had to stay in the family. And father was getting old. Chiman and eventually Shanti and I would have to take over.

But the pressure soon became too great and in 1936 my family sailed to India. The family had been stung. Coedmore was no longer a happy place for us. Times were bad. It seemed as if the community was breaking up with the winds blowing people far away from each other. India called. Both my brother Chiman and sister Shanti were now of marriageable age. In those days the bonds of caste and clan were strong. It was clear that there was no one in the Coedmore community whom my parents saw as suitable marriage partners for their two children. Maybe this had angered people? Even the tailor: maybe he had a daughter or son of marrying age? Anyway, such was not to be. As there were few other Babenias in the country, for our family's future happiness and prosperity, India was closer than South Africa. This was not snobbishness. When you are getting messed around consistently, then personal things become important. In the South Africa of the mid-1930s it was not hard to harbour a sense of grievance. India beckoned. My father was however not to see India. He died on the boat journey and was cremated at Dar-es-Salaam.

I do not think my mother had really ever intended to stay permanently in India. But the family in India had lost much of their position during our stay in South Africa. First we had to settle into the strange village of Palsana. It was not easy. The family house had been boarded up for years and our relatives were quite poor. And we could not get my brother and sister married quickly. Prevailing Indian custom was that if one loses a close family member, a wedding could not take place for at least a year. Then began the quest to find eligible marriage partners. This involved a series of rituals. Finding a suitable girl usually takes time. Marriage first and then love. India had got used to it.

In the latter part of 1938 my brother got married and returned immediately to South Africa. The following year his wife joined him. But it was only in 1940 that my sister Shanti got married to a young man by name of Amritlal Nichabhai Desai. Shanti and Amritlal were a lovely, happy pair. By then it was too late to go back to South Africa, where the law says that Indian adults who had left the country for longer than three years were not allowed back in. Palsana was to be my home for the next ten years. India had grown accustomed to arranged marriages. South Africa had not got used to Indians.

Palsana was much the same as many other villages. It is in Baroda State which was a relatively small princely state just to the north of Surat. Baroda is quite a flat area with the land principally devoted to peasant farming. There is a little forestry on the north east border, but the main cash crops were cotton, some tobacco and then, of course, cereals. In some ways the British had left the place alone, but they could not quite do it. By the 1860s railways, Britain's gift to India, were coming through the area. Then they just sat around as an importing and exporting crowd collecting revenues: from salt, irrigation works, forests and the usual customs and poll taxes . . . and of course from tribute and opium. In the great Indian Revolt of 1857–59 Baroda's northern border was just touched, but as a whole the princely state was known to be neutral.

This was another of Britain's gifts to Baroda. In an attempt to divide up India and prevent the spread of nationalism, Britain allowed the feudal princes to rule great parts of the country. It was in these areas where people had virtually no political rights and were shackled into a system of feudal exploitation. In around 1901 a small secret revolutionary sect had formed in Baroda, but quite what happened to it no one knows. Maybe Baroda was a little sleepy. In the 1918 Gandhian 'no tax' campaign, Baroda was again neutral although the campaign raged on just south along the coastline. The British had a constant fascination with administrative structures, so in 1933 Baroda, together with numerous states and estates in the *Gujarat* area of Bombay Province, was made part of the Baroda and Gujarat States Agency.

Palsana was a rural village with about three and a half thousand people. There were no manufacturing industries. The people in the

village never starved and led a normal peasant life. There were no
lights or tap water. It was just an ordinary village. The village was
simply a peasant village with peasants cultivating their own land
and others sharecropping. There were three flour mills, owned by
quite wealthy men. Everyone sent their cereal crops to them. We had
a few tradesmen in the village, a couple of shoemakers, a blacksmith
and a couple of tailors. Along with six small trading shops were a
number of cafes and a pub selling Indian liquor made out of palm
tree juice.

But there was more to Palsana. The difference between Palsana
and other neighbouring villages was that our village was a *Taluka* of
Baroda State with fifty one villages under its jurisdiction. You could
see this. Our village had a post office, courthouse and tax collectors.
As the centre of a large densely populated area covered with little
paths and roads, the village had a small wealthy class. Along with
the five bus fleet owners were state officials and teachers who taught
in the English language school, the two boys' *Gujarati* schools and a
girls' *Gujarati* school. Not only did this make life a little easier, but
it made for a much livelier politics. But of course only when one
wakes up. It was here that I grew up and found my own horizons.

Unsettled

In India, we had the All India National Congress fighting along
with the Communist Party of India for the total liberation of India
from the yoke of British colonialism. In Baroda we had the *Praja
Mandal* forcing the Maharajah of Gaekwad to stop being subservient
to the British and to throw in his lot with the Indian National
Congress. The Gaekwad State *Praja Mandal* was affiliated to the
Indian National Congress. Each province had a *Praja Mandal* affiliated to the main body and the sub-districts or *Taluka Praja Mandals*
were affiliated to the Provincial *Praja Mandals*. The Palsana *Praja
Mandal* had a wing for the women called the Palsana *Mahila Mandal*.
The *Praja Mandal* in our village held public meetings, raising issues
like the plight of peasants, schooling, roads and welfare and
drawing up memorandums for submission to state officials.

I soon became part of this mass movement. I joined the youth
volunteers while I was in primary school and we prepared stages
for public meetings. Politics was a part of school life. We didn't have
any real structures, all youths were more or less volunteers. It was
just part of life. For the Congress we were the helpers and
messengers. We were always around the village announcing things.
We had a conch shell first and later we got a bugle. With my friend
Nanu, I would go around the streets blowing the bugle telling the

people to attend mass meetings at the *chatro*. People came in their hundreds.

There were important ceremonies in our struggle. The most important was the Gandhi *Jayanti* which lasted for about seven days. At four in the morning the bugle sounded, waking people up. At about half-past five we would start getting the people into marching order. With the two national flags in front we marched the streets singing freedom songs and shouting freedom slogans. The flag of the *Gaekwad* state was just plain ochre and the Indian national flag had the Wheel of Progress in the middle of three stripes: green, ochre and white. The flags were hoisted on a specially built platform and the leaders would deliver speeches about Gandhi's life. At the end we sang the *Bande Mataram* and dispersed. During these seven days we volunteers swept the streets and did odd chores.

Gandhiji was a revered figure throughout India. Subhas Chandra Bose once called him India's greatest man. That was the feeling for him. Gandhi's dreams were those of the Indian peasants. He looked for the simple life; the drawing closer of the peasant and the wage earner and viewed the distinction between menial and mental labour with sadness. For us schoolchildren Gandhi's idea of basic education called up the dreams of many: mass basic vernacular education with schools becoming self-sufficient through cultivation and the selling of goods produced by youths in school co-operatives. The children would not be separated from either the beloved peasant or the cottage industry.

The second really big annual ceremony was when the All India Congress Committee elected its leader. The first one which I recall was when Subhas Chandra Bose was elected President of the Congresses in 1938. As with all leaders he toured India after his election. For us he was to be welcomed at Vithalnager, near Haripura. This was a sacred city of bamboos built just for this one ceremony. This place was a grassland with a river flowing nearby. In about three months a city of bamboos was built. It housed all the executive members, provincial leaders and about 30 000 volunteers. All the roads were named after our leaders. The city had an airstrip, a telephone system, electricity and a museum showing Gandhi's life work and Indian handicraft. There I saw an amazing piece of silk material of twenty yards long and a yard and half wide being pulled through a finger ring. It was hand spun. It really looked like a boom city.

As requested by the Provincial *Praja Mandal*, our village sent ten volunteers. That evening Subhas Chandra Bose was brought from the station in a chariot driven by fifty three pairs of bullocks. He was waving at the crowd as he went past. I was struck by his personality. But I am not too sure about my politics during this early period. If the truth be told I was half nationalist and half Marxist; half pacifist and half revolutionary, all together with a good deal of youthful inexperience.

One of our volunteers who went to Vitharlnagar was a friend of mine, Makan. He was an untouchable. Gandhi called them *harijans*. In our high school we had many *harijan* youths. We used to share desks and even food.

The untouchables were of two types in our area. The *Dedhas* who used to work on the carcasses of dead animals. The carcasses were dragged and thrown down at a particular place outside the village. Stray dogs, eagles and other birds fed on them. The *Dedhas* used to skin these carcasses and treat the leather to make sandals, whips, harnesses and other things and sell them to the peasants. They stayed outside the village and the other castes never touched them. Then there were the *Bhangis* who carried lavatory buckets, throwing the mess at the dump site. They got paid by each household for clearing the bucket. They also lived outside the village in a separate section. The *harijans* were seen as outcasts.

Gandhi fought against this. He even came out with a paper called *Harijan*. But it was not an easy battle and even some *harijan* leaders criticized Gandhi for being too slow in pushing for equality for the untouchables. I myself could never really believe in this derogatory nonsense. The *harijans* were people just like anybody else.

But it was in the cities that I saw a clearer picture of oppression. For me, it was the Communist Party of India which had the guts to confront issues head on.

In 1940 I joined Navsari High School. Navsari was an industrial centre about thirteen miles from Palsana. It was a Congress School. But the Communist Party was strong and had organised the workers at the two textile mills. At that time the Party in India never went to the high schools. Membership was almost exclusively from the intellectuals and working class leaders. Many shop stewards, leaders in their own right, were brought into the Party. The May Day rallies in Navsari were big. I am now 71 years old, but I can still picture an untouchable girl: tall, fair and with a maxi red skirt marching in front of the procession with the Red Banner.

One Friday evening I went to the Town Hall to hear a Marxist present a paper. He was very good. In a style I came to know well, he started his speech with the burning question:

'Given the situation as it is in India, do you think we can move into socialism after independence? The peasantry is wholeheartedly with the Congress and the working class is divided. On top of this, the accepted method of struggle is *Satyagraha*. This suits the bourgeoisie. Given this situation, can we move into socialism after independence?'

In answer he upheld the notion of a two stage struggle. A sixteen year old boy was a little young for this. But the point of all this was not lost on me. These were exciting times. The youth were really infected by so many new ideas. We heard a lot of new things which we would discuss on the bus back to Palsana. The Party was giving us a better view of India. It was a time of raging political discussion.

I suppose it all really started in 1937, the year when as a young boy I had arrived in India. In that year the Congresses had just won massive election victories in many Indian provincial assemblies. It was a huge victory, but soon the splits started creeping in. Its not easy to turn from being someone whipped for singing the *Bande Mataram* to taking your place in state structures. People said the Congresses were becoming the Raj. The Congresses aroused great expectations which were difficult to achieve. It was a heady mixture for a high school student. There were Left forays from the trade unions, great peasant movements, socialists, rightists, communists, and of course radical student groups—all within Congress.

And of course there was the war. Leaders got caught in the terrible confusion of the war. So did we. People battled over what position to adopt on the war and how the war affected anti-colonial politics. Was the struggle simply against fascism and if so did this mean we had to make temporary peace with or even support Britain, our colonial master? As the war changed its course people saw different things in the war. Bose went his way. He founded the Indian National Resistance Army and sought support from Imperial Japan and Nazi Germany. The communists said that one must support the war. The British saw in the war the means to regain control over India. Many felt that the British wanted to use the war to provoke the Congresses into doing something stupid. By the end of the war the communists had lost ground because of their support for the war. In these trying times the Congresses needed to regain their credibility and take the initiative. What really started the ball rolling for the Congresses was the 1942 'Quit India' campaign.

Looking back I would say that by 1942 I felt part of a loyal but left tendency within Congress trying to steer our leaders away from conservatism and see that the ministries did the right things. Not only had the Party made a deep impression on me, but I was feeling uneasy about certain trends within the Congress. In this regard, my involvement in the ceremony marking Gandhi's birthday in 1941 and events soon afterwards were crucial.

Congress leaders in Palsana decided to have a chariot with Gandhi's photo drawn by seventy two bullock teams. I told them that I could get a bagpipe band from Navsari for ten rupees. They agreed and I hired the band. It was a spectacular scene. But I did not feel that great. It was a troubling time and here we were mobilizing people behind the cult of an individual. That was the way of the East.

After the Gandhi *jayanti*, our leaders took us volunteers to Surat for a treat. All our leaders were in their late twenties and early thirties. Their wives were members of the *Mahila Mandal* and traditionally were our sisters-in-law. Sometimes one or two leaders used to speak to us harshly. So we used to complain to our sisters-in-law, seeking the 'soft touch' approach to grievances. And it used to work out fine. We were too young to put our complaints personally to our leaders. They were too high. The sisters-in-law were our chief volunteers. They could put our case more vehemently and even close the bedroom door as a punishment. The day after we had put our complaint we used to find the leader concerned grim. We stayed away from him but met our sister-in-law and she would tell us everything would be fine. She would tell us that she had starved him last night. The talkative ones used to say, "You should have heard him knocking at my door" and then laugh. We used to tell them not to do that.

But despite my anxieties, a youthful enthusiasm was never far away. In 1941 the All India Congress Committee was going to meet in Bardoli. Our local daily newspapers, *Gujrat* and *Pratap* announced that the leaders would travel along the Tapti Valley Railway line from Surat to Bardoli and stop at various key stations along the way. The country was to be joined. We went off to Chalthan Station. I had my two hand-spun garlands with me. People were chanting Congressites' names on the platform. I got into the compartment and garlanded Bhoolabhai Desai. Bhoolabhai Desai woke Rajaji. He was sleeping! Can you imagine it! I also put a garland around Rajaji's neck. As many people were trying to come in, Bhoolabhai pulled me near his seat and asked where I came from.

"I am from Palsana!"

"If you are from Palsana, you should know Jaywantrai Desai."

"Yes, I know him!"

"If you see him, convey my regards to his family! How is that *Ashram* in your village?"

"There is no *Ashram* in our village."

"Isn't there a *harijan*, who spins and weaves cotton and makes *ghee*?"

"Yes, there is one. Poojabhai and his brother run it."

"You see, I remembered! I was there about twenty years ago to see Jaywantrai's mother!"

With the roar of slogans and clanking of the wheels the train moved on.

The next day Nehru was going past. Again people thronged around the train, presenting him with gifts, garlands and showing him homespun cloth. I was in the fore yet again! We managed to get onto the coach, put the garland around his neck and moved aside. Nehru spoke to me briefly about the garland, complimenting me and encouraging me to spin an even finer thread. As more people wanted to see him, I moved further back. He spoke to some activists. The guard blew his whistle and waved the green flag. After a while I could only hear the whistle of the train.

Soon Gandhi came to Bardoli. As usual he walked with Manu and Abha Gandhi. People got up and started chanting 'Mahatme Gandhiji ki Jai'.[3] When Gandhi got up to speak, there was a helluva din of chanting. He spoke of the war. He made his plea from the rostrum to the warring nations to stop killing poor men, women and children who have no interest in wars. He asked that warring nations should solve their problems by peaceful means. But he reminded us that we could not give our total support to Britain now that a war was on. Remember how 'Home Rule' had been promised after the First World War? Others, like Maulana Abdul Kalam Azad, Jawaharlal Nehru and Vallabhai Patel, reiterated what Gandhi had said.

Throughout all the excitement I had many unhappy thoughts. How could I have forgotten the Ashram? Was this because Poojabhai was a harijan? Had the cult of adulation gone too far? Why was I, who revered the Gandhian simplicity, so keen to get to the front of the crowds? Were we celebrating victory before victory? Why had Desai not been to Palsana, my beloved new home, for twenty years? And would Satyagraha really work? Filled with inner doubts, I listened eagerly to the debate around the complicated issue of non-violence.

In the Congress Committee the question which provided real fireworks was whether to adopt non-violence as a policy or a principle. Gandhi and a few wanted non-violence to be the principle and Nehru, Vallabhai Patel and the majority said that non-violence could only be a policy. There was a bitter controversy but non-violence as a policy triumphed. To me this made sense. I have always believed that the sabotaging of official buildings and targets which are symbolic of oppression, if accomplished with no loss of life, is the highest form of non-violence. It was very soon evident just how wise this decision was.

The year 1942 was the year of the Indian revolt. The 'Quit India' campaign, demanding that the British leave India, had captured the imagination of the youths, workers and peasants. On the 8th of

---

[3] Gujarati for 'Long Live Mahatma Gandhi!'

August 1942 dark clouds were looming over Bombay with a heavy downpour of rain. At a pre-dawn raid on that gloomy day, Gandhi, the Congress Executive and the Working Committee delegates were all picked up in Bombay and rushed to different prisons in special trains. Similar pre-dawn raids were made in other cities and towns and prominent leaders were picked up. By the time people woke up the entire leadership was behind bars. It was now that the leaders increased their credibility. From administrators in the Provincial Congresses they became our imprisoned leaders.

Popular anger was amazing. When people in Bombay heard about the raids they went berserk. British and Australian soldiers were raping our women in the name of the British Empire. A famous actress was raped by eighteen Australians and had to be hospitalised. In their hundreds Bombay citizens turned buses upside down, disrupted electrical and telephone lines and dug up railway lines. This was often done spontaneously but once the underground networks were established acts of sabotage became well organised.

When people heard they started something which the British never believed. Sabotage and guerrilla attacks were the order of the day. This was fine! When Gandhi launched the campaign he had said that there should be mass non-violent struggle on the widest possible scale but that if the leaders should be taken in, then every Indian who wanted freedom should be their own guide.

Soon the radical Congress leaders in each province gave their own interpretation to the broad concept of non-violence. Avoiding a massive police dragnet, many leaders formed underground networks everywhere. These groups went from district to district and from village to village forming more groups. Well known scientists came up with formulas to prepare bombs and these reached the underground units. Radio transmitters were established and the 'Voice of Freedom' was heard all over the country. In East Bengal and Provinces in the eastern sector, guerrilla bands formed. In Bengal and Assam, guerrillas took village after village and attacked the cities in small bands.

Sabotage became a primary task! It was realistic. Those who resisted, still clinging to a narrow view of non-violence were locked up or ended up the victims of police bullets. Of the costs to me personally, I had already made up my mind. At the hostel, I packed my books away. The dust had settled and my eyes were wide open.

A Volunteer for Action

I was young, cocky and dying to become involved. It was the same amongst all of us volunteers. We boasted amongst ourselves of our heroism and attempted to outdo each other in our radicalism and ability to undertake brave deeds. We eagerly sought the attentions of our leaders. They had wider concerns and more mature perspectives. I am sure that sometimes they felt us to be precocious, selfish and bothersome. Of political nuance we knew little: that was for 'our leaders', but we often saw through different eyes to those of our leaders.

And it was incredibly easy for us! Our leaders needed us as the shock troops of the *Praja Mandal* and for those host of tasks: courier, guide or activist that were so essential to the underground. But there was more to it. We were up against a simple state. Appointed officials lived amongst us, were known to us and were often Congressites. In their daily duties they would often have to work closely with the village headman whose accountability to the wishes of the community could confuse any unwanted change or intervention. But above all the peasant countryside is fiercely parochial and dismissive of strong government. This is what made the Congresses strategy during the 'Quit India' campaign so successful. We had so much freedom in which to act.

We, the young in Navsari, were known as Young Tigers. On the 8th of August 1942 Raghunath Naik and I led a procession through the streets, closing all shops and schools and calling for a general strike. Young boys and girls harassed shopkeepers hesitating to close. We raided, opened cool drink bottles, drank a little and smashed bottles in the street. Word spread that the Young Tigers were creating havoc. This made things easier for us. We found shops already closed. As we approached the Jamshedji Tata Primary School we got the Young Tigers into an orderly column and barged through into the premises. Children grabbed their satchels and fled. The principal refused to formally close the school. On his wall was a life sized photo of Jamshedji Tata, a multi-millionaire industrialist from Navsari. He had funded the building of the school. He and other Indian businessmen were making a fortune from the war. I threatened to smash the photo. The principal saw we were serious and relented. We took his signed note of closure and pinned it to the notice board.

It was the same at the girls' school. The principal colluded with the police in trying to trap us but we evaded her and all the girls marched out boycotting lessons for a week. At another of the schools built by Tata, some reactionary blokes started to get really aggressive, but our brothers from the Gandhi Physical Gymnasium came to our assistance and sorted them out properly. By this time many workers from the textile mills and youths had joined us.

According to instructions we converged on the Lunsiqui sports-ground where loudspeakers had been set up. Quite who planned this I never knew. Speakers explained the significance of the 'Quit India' campaign and told of what had transpired in Bombay and other cities. As we left Raghunath instructed me to attend a secret meeting that night. Police reinforcements were coming and our leaders, who had already gone underground, wanted to prepare further organisational activities quickly. At the meeting it was hard to make out faces because of the darkness. But I could distinguish some of the voices. To my surprise Thakorbhai and Lalbhai were there. Thakorbhai was married to my paternal aunt's daughter, Subhadraben. Thakorbhai and Lalbhai had been very active in Surat and had in fact been in Bombay on that fateful morning of the 8th of August. However they had evaded capture but there was a reward of three thousand rupees on each of their heads. As with so many people wanted in the British territories, they sought refuge in the princely states. As soon as they moved in they established an underground with their headquarters in a farmhouse near Gandevi. However the Nasvari police quickly tracked them down and raided the farmhouse. It was a piece of very bad luck. The cops were looking for stock thieves and instead bagged eight underground cadres. Now they were starting again. Through their own channels they were in contact with Ram Manohar Lohia, Achyut Patwardhan and other Socialist Bloc leaders. Those were the left-leaning but not Communist leaders within Congress.

Other voices were also familiar. The first voice I heard was that of our teachers, Raghunath Naik and Janak Dave. We were told to split into pairs and go around villages spreading the message that all government officials had to resign and that the war effort had to be crippled. Dinkar Desai and I had to cover the villages Supa, Gandevi and Kachiaviad.

We were also responsible for setting up accommodation in case any of the underground leadership needed it and for setting up contacts between various areas. The underground was going to establish a printing press and we should help with the distribution of leaflets. A method of making a homemade duplicator would be made known to all the underground cells. We were also to collect all reports of atrocities committed by the police. The code word for contacts should be 'Inquibab Zindabad'.[4]

We were in Supa when we heard that there had already been some shooting in Karadi Matwad. This frightened us so we scuttled back to

_____
[4] *Hindi* for 'Long live the Revolution!'

Navsari for orders. We were sent to Karadi Matwad where we made our first pamphlet, calling on the revolutionary youth to burn down the police station and courthouse and for government officials to resign. We went on distributing for the next couple of days until the cops started looking for us. It was then that my mother sent word that I was to return home. Sister Shanti was going to Baroda to join her husband and I, according to the message, was to accompany her.

By this time things were really hotting up in Bardoli and Surat. The British were clamping down heavily and using the India Detention Act, picking up as many of the leaders as possible. As a result, Chandramani Bhatt, one of the main leaders in the area, sought refuge with us in Palsana. For security reasons, he never took part in *Praja Mandal* activities but quickly set to work building up the underground. Palsana became one of the headquarters of the Bardoli District underground.

The underground structures became very active and we regularly received signed or thumb print attested statements of men, women and children who had been tortured and molested. Chandramani gave these documents to me and I filed them away. As the police were unable to arrest wanted men, their brutality increased and the statements poured in.

Soon I was being used as a courier between various underground groups. Once I had to go to Erthan to pass a message to Thakorbhai. It was quite an amazing journey. As Dahyu and I rode along in his bullock cart peasants would always look at us knowingly, ask where we were going and then, when we answered nod with relief. They knew! It was because of such incredible loyalty that one's tasks in the countryside were made a lot easier.

Thakorbhai and Lalbhai moved around a lot during this time. So I was kept busy. Once they even stayed with us in Palsana. They came early one night. Mother had prepared food and beds.

"Mamie, we do not eat any food prepared in *ghee* and we do not sleep on beds. Especially while we are still underground."

"There is nothing special that I have prepared, just puree and some curry! And about the beds! You sleep on beds because we have spare ones. If we did not have spare beds then that is something else."

"I give up! I give up! Mamie you are headstrong."

It was because Mother was like this that I nicknamed her 'Churchill'. But I never ever said it to her face. 'Churchill' could smack. Shanti knew I called mother this, but I steadfastly denied it. Shanti thought it horrible as Churchill was hardly popular at that time.

Then my mother raised the question of my activities. I knew something like this was coming. I had a suspicion when I received her orders to return from Nasvari.

"Mamie, Natoo is not doing anything wrong. He is doing what thousands of youth are doing. Do not be hard on him."

Now it was her turn to give up.

I was the go-between setting up a meeting between Thakorbhai and Mangoobhai, Hashmukbhai and Dhayabhai of our *Praja Mandal*. But I was always very aware of my youth and never ever stayed in on their meetings. I just did what I was told.

The following day I had to escort Thakorbhai to Tan. We would always travel very early in the morning to avoid the heat and any patrols. They were strangers; city folk, but I knew the countryside like the back of my hand, leading them through farmlands and going on quite a circuitous but clever route. This impressed them. I was 'Natoo the fox'.

As always I would not sit in on their meetings. I sat outside where the women would bring me tea. You can only sip peasant tea because they serve it in brass cups which become extremely hot. They were always very nice to me.

But from the slithers of talk which I was never averse to hearing there were problems in the underground. The cops managed to break groups up too easily, and some had ceased to exist. There were also too many underground networks. As escapees from the coast came in they started undergrounds and the whole thing had got out of hand. Further there was much discussion over the precise purpose of a successful underground. Was it merely to continue giving direction to the ongoing mass struggle on the streets and if so what were to be the relations between *Praja Mandals* and the underground? Or was the underground to concentrate more on sabotage? If so why had so little been done? And again was the underground to be separate from the Congresses or the local *Praja Mandal* leaders, who were often also underground? A lot of personal animosities and ambitions also bubbled up, obviously disguised as political differences!

Much to my amazement the question of guns also came up. During their travels, Thakorbhai and many others had been impressed by how many people were asking the underground for guns.

"The trouble I and Lalbhai face is that wherever we go, activists are asking for guns! We don't have them, so how are we going to deliver them?"

Lalbhai added:

"Another thing is that some activists did manage to get guns, but lost them to the police in raids. That is very silly. And it gets a lot of other people into trouble."

The meeting, which had now swelled to over forty people, hammered out a policy on guns. If people wanted guns then they should accept that they were guerrillas not saboteurs and that if they wanted to be guerrillas then they should get it into their thick heads that when police raided them, they fought to the last bullet. If they had still not realised that only sergeants carry revolvers and so raids could easily be repelled then they were not worth the name guerrilla. This was quite a strong line against guerrilla activity.

Looming over the whole meeting was of course the question of political lines. In the Palsana *Praja Mandal* there were some leaders who were Forward Bloc supporters and some were pure Congressites. It was the same amongst those underground from the coast. It could get quite confusing. Within all this I often remember people talking in terms which sounded to me like straight socialist insurrectionism. Now these differences had for long been part of the Congresses make up, but the 8th of August 1942 had altered the game very much. Underground structures were being set up, new people appeared in the area, people wanted leadership and leaders could talk in different languages and want different structures and power bases. It was all quite confusing and the tempo was getting faster all the time. They had to learn how to work together. This they all knew. But I do not know whether the issues were ever really resolved. I noticed that when we led processions now and then the Forward Bloc supporters shouted aloud 'Subhas Chandra Bose Ki Ja'.[5] We volunteers would take it up and shout Bose's name loudly. The other leaders kept quiet.

Palsana was quite active by then. We had many meetings deliberately aimed at breaking the ban on processions. There were plenty of arrests. Sister Kanti once got taken in, but as there were no jails for women in the area, the women had to be released. I first got arrested the day after Kanti. We appeared in court after five days. We were very militant and gave the magistrate a hard time:

"Your name?"
"Natoo *Azad*."[6]
"Your age?"
"Still growing."
"Your occupation?"
"To fight for Independence."
"Have you got anything to say to this court?"
"Yes! Let me sit in your chair and judge you!"

---

[5] *Hindi* for 'Long Live Subhas Chandra Bose!'.
[6] *Gujarati* for 'Freedom'.

"Not today. When you get freedom, do that!"
"That won't be long! I hope you are still around."

We were an insolent and hot tempered bunch. Our leaders knew this and would often use this to great effect.

When confronted by our leaders, most of the tax collectors in the Palsana area resigned. However one was recalcitrant and became abusive. We could hear him insulting our leaders from the verandah where we were standing around. It angered us. Navin was enraged.

"Tell him we will burn his house! Don't plead with him! We will see him tonight with our burning torches!"

This shocked him and he came out to see who we were. Our leaders mildly explained that we were uncontrollable and if anything should happen to his house, he should not blame them. He agreed to resign, but as a warning we capsized the bench on the verandah as we left.

The practicalities of the policy was quite complex. While the general rule was to get officials to resign, there were sympathetic people in the civil service whom Congress wanted to remain in their posts. In Palsana, Dixit, the chief of the Special Branch was always very reasonable. He and his brother Laxman played cricket in the same team as many of the *Praja Mandal*. We had a number of teams. I was then in the Multani Cricket Club, which was comprised of both Hindus and Muslims. When Dhayu got into some trouble in Baroda, Dixit was told to interrogate him. Although he knew otherwise he accepted Dhayu's startlingly weak explanation that he had been in Palsana all the time. Now Dixit wanted to resign and we had to work hard getting him to stay on. Further he also agreed to tip us off in case of any emergency. However he would get very sore when we abused the information. Our leaders worried a lot about this. We felt a lot less.

One always had to be on your guard because the security police were also not above playing little games. The Poona police sent some municipal workers into Palsana. Well, they wore municipal uniforms and were busy sweeping streets. But in fact they were spies, just keeping a lookout and gathering pieces of information. Our cops knew nothing about it, but we found out. The *Praja Mandal* leaders informed the village headman who instructed people to have nothing to do with them. But it was a catch difficult to ignore. People could just not resist it. I remember an old village man making fun.

"Is your government going soft in the head or something? It is so nice that they are sending you to sweep up. It is the first time they have ever bothered. You must come more often. Oh, incidentally the path outside my place could do with some attention. You will be popping by. . .?"

Of course the sweepers soon left. In India it is very hard to send strangers into a village for information. Even hawkers are known to villagers. A stranger attracts attention and people zip their mouths. In cities it is different.

In Baroda we did know of two informers. One was a doctor's daughter and the other was an elite prostitute called 'Kum Kum'. Both were pretty wenches. Both were also ostracised. People were even reluctant to sell them food. Kum Kum, who was studying at the university, left and went to Bhavnager in Kathiawad. I saw her there in 1946.

Although I was still very active in *Praja Mandal*, Chandramani Bhatt had been impressed by my eagerness and so I was invited to one of the underground meetings. There the question of sabotage was discussed at length, targets were approved and new materials for sabotage were explained.

At that meeting one of the delegates, Dhirendra, sought advice on how to obtain a revolver. I was eager to help and said it was easy. The village police superintendent used to hang his holster on a wall peg in his office. It soon vanished into our hands. Through success I became a courier carrying bombs from our underground to Bhiku Patel who was operating from a village near Bardoli. For security reasons I was only used to ferry things to Patel and only Patel.

After I had proved myself doing four such calls, Dhirendra showed me how to prepare a bomb. He knew his job and could even make booby traps. He was very secretive about it. I found myself fitting into all of this easily. I wanted to try my hand, suggesting bombing the post office. Dhirendra consented and gave me a square castiron block with explosive powder inside and a long homemade fuse attached to a hole in the block. It was quite a crude device and one had to move fast because the fuse only took a minute to burn. I was also given three bombs, which I wrapped in brown paper; for Bhiku, who had been instructed to come by in his horse and carriage to collect.

According to instructions, that night I hid the bomb near the court house, hung around with my friends for a while then left, saying I was going for a crap. Using Bachoo's bicycle I moved fast. I placed the bomb and lit the fuse, which I had already slightly modified by scrapping powder off at three inch spaces to make it burn slower.

It was a good blast. There was lots of smoke and soon a crowd formed. The blast had cracked the outer wall of the post office. This was the third bomb blast in our village. I do not know who did the others.

Things had not gone so well in Bardoli. An activist who worked in the court house had placed a pressure bomb under the chair of an official, a Mr Whitfield. He had found the thing and became excited. Suspecting student involvement, he had a few rounded up and beaten. They were treated by a doctor sympathetic to the cause who passed photographs of the wounded guys to the underground for safe keeping.

I was soon in the thick of it, attending a secret youth congress in Baroda. There I stayed with Shanti and her husband, Amritlal in Amritlal's father's very large two storeyed house in Koti Pole.[7] A mill owner had built four huge blocks of flats for his workers, but as a declared Congressite, there was always room for anyone seeking refuge. Amritlal's uncle, Morarji Desai,[8] was a trustee of the mills of Ahmedabad, Baroda and Bombay.

Desai's nephew was a member of the Communist Party of India. He earned his living selling booklets and books. He was studying in Ahmedabad. His beliefs made him an outcast in the family and only his sister stood by him through thick and thin. It was from him that I learnt of the deceit and tension within our movement.

He took me around one of the mills. The wages in these mills were low and Morarji Desai did nothing to raise them. They also used the time honoured tactic of supplying food as part of the daily wage. Strikes could not be called because the foreman and shop stewards were Congressites who were surreptitiously paid extra for their assistance and any gleanings of information. If there was a strike the police were called and the strike broken up. For those who wanted to live out the belief that the working class should take the lead in our movement, the obstacles were considerable.

Not only did the Indian capitalist class abhor strikes, but they were dead against any militant violent struggle. They had too much influence within the Congress. People like Birla, Dalmia, Tata and others gave moral and financial support to the Indian Congress and as Congress members almost demanded privileged status. They were constantly hobnobbing with the provincial leaders and found that the petty bourgeois and aspirant capitalist elements within the Congress would easily listen to them.

At the secret meeting, discussion centred around evident organisational problems. Things just did not seem to be lighting up in Baroda. We were given home-made duplicating instruments and told to raise the level of consciousness in our villages. The following day the Baroda leader, Jashwant Chauhan, who was underground and very much sought after, addressed us at the same venue. The police bashed in arresting many. Jashwant managed to escape but

[7] A street name, Pole is the Anglicized version of *Porr*, *Gujarati* for street.
[8] Morarji Desai later became Prime Minister of India.

amongst those taken in were two fiery women stalwarts of the Baroda resistance, Shakuntla Parlikar and Luxmiben Patel.

But the underground quickly reconvened and three sabotage targets were selected: two truck depots and Baroda State University library. Three groups were formed with each one moving into a separate room to discuss their own tactics. This was done for security reasons. No one would know all the plans. Our group's target was the library.

Things quickly went awry. I had managed to get a key for the library but no one else pitched up to commence the operation. I was fuming with anger. This was my first real experience of the power of the bourgeoisie over the congress movement. I have not forgotten it.

The following day I was instructed to attend a meeting with all the other three cell members. Jashwant Chauhan was also there. He had convened the meeting to discuss further strategy. I was not satisfied. I put up my hand.

"Is there something on your mind?"

"I want to know what happened. Why they did not turn up at the appointed place."

My cell leader muttered something about being busy with something else and how they had been unable to contact me. This was all rubbish. I had been contacted very easily just that very morning. Jashwant Chauhan tried to smooth things over. He was anxious to forget the whole thing but eventually the truth came out. Jashwant had cancelled all of the targets. The truck depots and trucks belonged to Congress supporters! I was livid.

"A sympathizer helping in the war effort! Isn't it ironical?"

"No, it is not ironical! It is a fact!"

I was told that I was being too emotional. Jashwant later became a cabinet minister in Free India. Dhayu and I left. If the people in Baroda wanted to conduct acts of sabotage then they should do it themselves and sort their own problems out.

But not everybody in Baroda was as gutless. While Dhayu and I were fast asleep at Shanti's in walks Luxmiben Patel and another girl. Luxmiben wriggles my toes and wakes me up. She was wearing a suit and had a felt hat on. She always had her hair cut like a boy's, and with the outfit she was wearing she easily passed as a youth.

"When you enter a house, you always leave your hat on?"

She laughed and slowly removed her hat, taking a grenade out.

"You Luxmiben! You are going to blow your head off one day! Why don't you put it somewhere else?"

"It is quite safe where I put it. Wake old lazybones! Here, up! I have a little job for you."

It was the 15th of November 1943. The anniversary of the shooting of Babubhai Patel.[9] They wanted to place a lamp and flowers on the spot where he had been slain. We were to take the daggers she handed us and protect the two of them from any policemen. She had it in mind that we should kill any patrolling policeman.

"Nice and neat eh!"

"Natoo! You are bitter about what happened last night! Look! I am also against the decision taken by Jashwant Chauhan. Come on get moving."

I had never really thought about killing someone before. I was quite terrified at the prospect of having to make up my mind. Thankfully no one came. We all stood around the lamp, sang the anthem and left. It made me feel a lot more easy and fulfilled. We two returned to Palsana.

There was such an anger and excitement in one's gut that some-times you could not resist doing things which our leaders felt to be rash. In 1943 the King, Pratapsinhrao Gaeckwad came to our village on his stately tour. The *Praja Mandal* leaders were refused permission to present a memorandum personally to the King. But the headman of Gangahara, a stooge who had refused to resign was going to attend an official reception. We felt very frustrated by this. There was little we could do to him. We could not burn his house because he lived in the same building as a staunch Congressite and the property was rented. There was a clear rule that one could only burn stooges' houses down if they lived in government houses and were not renting from owners who could often be Congressite supporters. So we wrote an anonymous letter to him saying that if he attended he would be killed. Or we would get him later. He got upset and went to see the *Praja Mandal* leaders. They stressed that the letter had not come from them. They were very concerned and wanted to know who had written it. Mangoobhai came to see me. I feigned ignorance, asked about what the letter had said and when he told me, said that it sounded just right. He was upset and quietly impressed upon me that the leaders did not believe in things like that.

It was thus hardly simply a coincidence that when this same stooge asked the *Praja Mandal* for an escort for when he returned home, our leaders gave me the task. But it did not cow me. In front of the leaders, I showed the stooge an eight inch dagger which I had

---

[9] Babubhai Patel had been shot in a riot at Koti Pole corner in Baroda during the early stages of the 'Quit India' campaign. See Chopra, *Who's Who of Indian Martyrs*, volume 1, p 267.

tucked into my coat. He was terrified. I cruelly told him that because he was a wanted man I aimed to protect myself in case assassins associated me with him. When I returned from the mission, I was told not to overdo things, that the headman had not in fact attended the court paraphernalia and that they had secured his resignation.

There was a lot of bravado around amongst young guys. One weekend I was sitting in a cafe in Surat talking to Bhikhu, a friend of mine from the Nasvari hostel. We had not seen each other for a long time so we were catching up on gossip. Bhikhu said that he had read about my exploits with the King. At which point Bhikhu's friend Jashu looks up at me. He peers at me in a sneering sort of way and asks me if I believed in sabotage. I did not answer straight, but kept my distance. There was a lot of tension in the air and soon Jashu gets Bhikhu to rope me into bombing a cinema in Surat. He said he would get the bomb for me. He said that he wanted to test me. Bhikhu was worried and asked me if I planned to do it.

"Yes, just to show this guy a point."

Of course nothing happened. Lots of excuses came my way. I remember giving Bhikhu and others serious lectures on how never to work with irresponsible kids. But actually we were fooling each other.

It was not long before I was really arrested. On the 20th of March 1943, Dhayu and I marched at the front of a huge procession. Behind me was Navin. He was the first guy I hit when I came to India. He had not spoken to me since then. While marching with the flag, I turned to him and said that if anything happens he must pick it up and look after it. After that it was okay between us.

Behind us were our leaders. The magistrate declared the procession illegal but the leaders refused to obey. Infuriated, the magistrate tried to get the police to open fire but they resisted. But the police superintendent did arrest the leaders and a couple of us youths.

The following day we appeared in court and pleaded not guilty. As always we all refused any lawyers to defend us. We were all found guilty. The leaders got four months imprisonment each and us four volunteers three months imprisonment. The whole village was there and some old people started crying. It was a turning point in the struggle in our village. The state was cracking down hard. The atmosphere was tense and our leaders had to pass a message that they should not do anything rash. We were taken to Nasvari Prison. Our families had bundled our bedding together and tagged these with our names. As political prisoners we were allowed to sleep on bedding. We made our bedding and started to sing freedom songs until we fell asleep. It was my first night in a real prison.

The following morning we met up with another group of activists who had already finished a month of their four month sentences. Amongst them was my Nasvari school physical training teacher Gandhi, his brother and some others I recognised. Under their guidance we learnt the ropes: going to collect one's rations, which one had to cook oneself and how to get extra rations by putting something heavy under the scales. As none of us could cook, our leaders cooked for us. On the third day after our arrival they were released. The jails were too full. This was the case in all Baroda State prisons. One batch is released as soon as a fresh batch arrives.

The prison authorities were fine. They allowed a visit from the second tier leadership who gave us a brief report on what was going on outside. Our jailer looked the other way when we smuggled some *bidi* in. And when we told him we could not cook he provided us with a common law prisoner who knew how to cook. In prison we never worked. During the day we were locked up for an hour after lunch. The only work we did was to wash our clothes. After fifteen days we were released. When they weighed us, I had gained three pounds. Pandya, our jailer said he did not want to see me there again.

While we were inside the second tier leadership had organised a total food boycott against the magistrate for his outrageous conduct. They had met with the community elders and all the shopkeepers had agreed not to supply him with anything. What really irritated people about him was that his uncle was a very prominent Congressite!

The magistrate was quickly humbled. His wife had recently given birth to twins and was unable to breast feed sufficiently. He was frantic, sending his peon all over the place looking for compliant traders but to no avail. Soon he was pleading with the village headman who refused to discuss the matter without our leaders being present. Eventually the magistrate had to make a total apology for his conduct and promise not to do anything in the village without first consulting a boycott committee which was simply comprised of our Congress leaders. We had practical control over Palsana. It was a total victory which gave us a surge of confidence.

We felt in the mood to confront bigger things. The Baroda State Parliament was then sitting to discuss the growing crisis. Most of the members of Parliament had resigned, with stooges filling their places. The Baroda *Praja Mandal* organised delegates from all over to demonstrate in front of the Parliament building. I was one of eight delegates from Palsana.

There was a great spirit amongst all the young volunteer delegates. We could get out of hand often. We decided to throw paint on Desai, a stooge from Vesma village. I was right there volunteering to do the deed. You do not get opportunities like that too often! It was not difficult to track the man's movements and as he left for Parliament I melted in with the crowd and as he approached his car I ran up and sloshed painter's ink all over him. Then I ran for my dear life back to Shanti's place at Koti Pole.

I was soon back in prison. That same afternoon there was a march to Parliament. The police stopped us, asked our names, we gave false ones and then they arrested us. They wanted as many marchers as possible in lockups to stop any trouble around Parliament. Soon batches after batches were brought in. By 4 pm there were some five hundred people there. Many were very young kids.

I was in a stroppy mood. I demanded to go to the toilet, but was refused.

"Well I am going to shit right here in the charge office."

I started taking my short trousers down. I just felt like being difficult. Five o'clock in the afternoon the whole lot of us were released.

In the short space of time inside, things had changed quite a lot outside. A march planned to surround the Parliament was blocked by a row of policemen. In front of them was a hastily drawn white lime painted line. Over the loudspeaker we heard that the police would open fire if anyone crossed the line. Our leaders saw that they meant it. One of the organisers made all us volunteers withdraw from the march.

But we quickly regrouped by ourselves in an alley close by. There were about twenty five of us. We decided to get flaming torches, march around and lure the cops into the side streets. We wanted them badly. And we knew that the cops on routine patrol in Baroda never carried guns. As we had thought, the cops fell for it dashing after us trying to bully us around. We fell on them, poking them to the ground with the torches and kicking the shit out of them.

Some of our leaders were probably a little worried by us but we were enraged by the cops. Very personal experiences produce a hatred. I myself remember once meeting a chap by the name of Raman Patel. He told me how his brother had been shot at Adas Railway Station. It seemed so vicious and unnecessary. About eighteen Baroda College students had organised themselves and went by train to Adas where they were to work among the peasants. On arrival at Adas Station they were told to line up against a railway coach. The police opened fire and my friend Raman's brother Ratilal, Ramu Patel, Mohantal Patel and Manilal Patel were shot dead. Another lost an eye and another had his leg shot to smithereens. It was later amputated. Raman told of how his dying brother had asked for water. Some women who wanted to assist were shooed away and a police officer came to Ratilal Patel, kicked him and said he should rather lick his boots.

Soon poems were composed about the massacre and meetings would often begin with speeches remembering the incident. At one meeting the student who lost his leg and the one who lost his eyesight were introduced to us. The horrific incident had brought the two of them very close together. After that I would often see the two of them bicycling around; the one eyed activist peddling with the other victim sitting on the frame. You do not forget these sights easily.

It was a brutal time. The harsh reality must come crashing down sooner or later. The more one succeeds the quicker the lightning must strike. But the banners remain proudly swirling above. Raman saw this.

"Natoo, haven't you seen a suckling baby stop suckling when it hears a procession song? Haven't you seen it kicking with joy? Is it really joyous? How will it remember? Should we celebrate if these sounds are etched deeply?"
"I see."

Actually I was not yet ready to see all so vividly. I had much to learn. I was still too caught up to see.

"Raman, I know what you mean. If a child stops sucking milk and kicks with joy, it is time for Independence!"

There were many like me. Workers, youths and peasants cut electric wires thinking those to be telephone wires and some were electrocuted by using wrong pliers. The struggle survived on it. Of course for any human there were always ways out. But these were paths so full of darkness and guilt. It was a piteous time.

If one was arrested for a non-violent act all one had to do to secure immediate release was to write a letter of apology. But amongst the eight and nine year-olds held by the police in the Reformatory none would write such a degrading letter. It was too much to do. Despite mothers' crying and pleading. But there were moments of shrewd humour. The kids knew in their hearts that the officials were embarrassed holding them.

"Ma, go home! I may be home before you!"

It was like this in Baroda so heaven knows what was happening in the fiery places like East Bengal, Assam, Bihar and some other districts. There the armed struggle was well advanced. Maybe it was easier because they were further ahead, but I do not think so. In East Bengal the armed struggle was at its highest peak. Free zones were established and a provisional government was set up with its own one Rupee coin. This new coin had on one side Gandhi's head and on the other side the national flag. To crush this uprising the British government spared no bullets; they even used planes. Men, women and children were shot at random.

In early 1943 I was called back to Baroda by another underground contact. A number of us were given weapons training. I was paired with Pushpa, a girl from Supa. Our instructor was a sympathetic army major, who taught us how to shoot the .303 rifle and use a bayonet. Thankfully we were never called upon to use our new found skills.

I never really knew what made her tick. She told me that she and a girl friend of her's were on the run after having killed a policeman who had tried to rape them. She was only sixteen years old but had that quiet determination and maturity of a person much older. I would accompany her often but she never spoke much. One day she just disappeared.

By the middle of 1943 I had to return to school. 'Churchill' insisted that as I was now in my matric year, the time to fool around had gone. I was a reluctant scholar and the school environment provided lots of scope for an irascible youth. There I met up with Raghunath who was part of a group who had set up a press in Nasvari. My activities were thus already known to others and they looked up to Raghunath and I with much respect and curiosity. However, although the school was a Congressite one, most of our good teachers were in lockups. The acting principal was not sympathetic to our political activities and insisted that both Raghunath and I sign forms stating that we would not engage in any form of political activism. We refused and sought the advice of Janak Dave who took the matter to the school board. The acting principal continued to harass us for some days until he was severely dressed down by the school board. He was embittered but there was little he could do.

But I was in no mood for this game playing. The son of our old physics teacher had just returned from Bombay; with two bombs. I wanted to make use of them. Raghunath agreed.

"Where are we going to place them?"

"One at the police station and one at the court house."

"All right. You speak to him and get the bombs, but do not tell him where we are going to use it!"

The poor chap wanted nothing to do with the operation but did hand them over to me. The bombs were two flat casings made of cast iron. Around the casing was a hollow wire with a thin string of fuse about eight feet long. At one end the fuse was connected to the explosive powder in the casing and the other end it was bent erect with the fuse string sticking out.

Raghunath was to take the police station and I, the court house. All you had to do was set the thing in place and burn the fuse string. You could also throw the bomb if you wanted to. We decided against this. Once the fuse lit you had three minutes to get clear.

Both bombs exploded as planned. Grinning with pride Raghunath and I separated immediately we heard the explosion. I had barely finished washing my hands at the outside tap in the hostel when the little chap is by my side.

"Was it ours?"

"Yes! Both were ours. The job is done and that's that."

Both bombs had done a lot of damage. Soon the school was buzzing with chatter.

By this time the acting principal was just an ordinary teacher and he blamed Raghunath and I for his demise. He was on to us, questioning our school mates and seeking any means to get us back. Now while Janak did get him off our backs, all the dust was in the air. When it settled it was clear that people disapproved of our activities.

It was a trying time for us. Most of our attentions were directed simply towards organising our lives in the hostels. The school hostel had been officially closed down but students and teachers could stay there free so long as they did their own cooking. Although we managed to scrape together enough to pay a cook, we had not yet received our ration tickets and basic foodstuffs were hard to get. We longed for rice! For a while we resorted to begging. It pained us a lot. We were in the middle of rationing because we were feeding British troops!

One day I met my mother's cousin Dhirubhai and while chatting I mentioned the problem to him. He directed us to his mother who was very kind. She got up and went to fetch the grain. She came with about a pound of rice and I opened my carrier bag. She poured it in.

"This is war time and grain is hard to get."

I told her that I appreciated this. I expected her to go and get some *dhal* or beans, but she sat down. We knew nothing more was coming so thanked her and left.

The strange thing was that beggars got their grain the same way. I had become a beggar! It was a very unhappy period for me and I failed that year.

In fact everything seemed to be moving away from me. As our political struggle moved forward it looked very much as if our leaders were ignoring me.

In 1944 I was back repeating the year, finally managing to pass.

In 1945 I entered Garda College and successfully completed my first university year with a second class pass. There I met up with Pushpa Kade again. However she was betrothed to another through an arranged marriage. I was deeply hurt. It is a love which I cherish up to this day.

During my college years I was active in the Youth Congress and in my second year became the secretary of the Gujerati Literary Society. But they were not stable years. I was getting too lost and did not apply myself. Exams came and I failed. I had to give up my studies and thus was parted from my closest friends. Dahyu obtained a good job in Baroda while Navin went to Bombay to further his university education. I applied and succeeded in getting a teaching post at a primary school at Palsana.

Frustrated Ambitions and Recklessness

1947 was a tough and long year. It seemed as if I was being pressed downwards.

The humdrum of school routine was simply made more testing through our shortage of staff. The headmaster had tuberculosis, was continually coughing blood and was quite unable to teach. Another left for East Africa. So two of us had to teach four standards. We would teach one class for half a period, give them work to do and then go and teach another class. Luckily I managed to convince Abdool, an out of work friend of mine from college, to join our staff.

With my encouragement, the students formed a student's council. I was their adviser. Their main tasks were to ensure that the classrooms and toilets were kept tidy and that all vulgar writings were rubbed off walls.

On 15th of August 1947 India and Pakistan became independent.

Fury became my companion and guide, filling my mind with thoughts of violence and aggression. It was not long before I found an outlet and a cause.

As communal slaughters erupted throughout India and Pakistan, the pace of events in Baroda became too quick. The situation had changed a lot since 1942. Many youths who were inactive had now joined in the struggle wanting some action. It was an unsettled time when instability came from various quarters. Many glorious strategies were quite irresponsible.

I became caught up in one such venture.

The new state was not yet fully in place. Indeed the big political battle in Baroda at that time was to force the King to join the Indian Union. The *Praja Mandal*, being particularly cautious in the potentially turbulent times, had given the King an ultimatum, threatening mass action if he failed to join the Union before the 15th of November. The *Praja Mandal* wanted the support of the volunteers. I decided to go underground.

Inside I was burning with fury, feeling humiliated and quite forgotten. A trapped small person given very little recognition.

I needed a small group of youths with the right temperament to do the type of work I was contemplating. My circle of friends became centred around disillusioned youths, many of whom had taken no part in the early political struggles. We became soul mates: Abdool Gafoormia, Bachu Desai, Nanu Naik, some others and I. To strike at the regime we needed guns. Soon, with the encouragement of Chandramani Bhatt who himself was feeling excluded and unrecognised by our leaders, I made up with Shamshuddin, a *dacoit* and a friend of Abdool's.

Over the years Shamshuddin had acquired notoriety as a bandit. As word had it he robbed money lenders and helped the poor around Ankleshavar. We were to obtain rifles, revolvers and other weaponry and rob the Baroda Treasury. In this way we believed we could cripple the King's authority and force him into union.

Shamshuddin was a tough guy. He arrived one day at *mamie's* house where I was still staying, disguised as a hawker. He had all the necessary weaponry. While we were checking the rifles and planning our operation he casually mentioned that he knew about Pushpa Kade.

"Do you still love Pushpa?"

"Of course! I do love her."

"Do you want her near you?"

"What do you mean?"

"If you want her, I can kidnap her and take her far away, and you can be with her."

"No thanks! Shamshuddin. That is not the way I want her!"

Pushpa Kade was not Pushpa the guerrilla, but my girlfriend from my days at school in Nasvari. I used to teach Pushpa English and *Gujarati* at her home while I was at 'varsity. I would visit her every day. I was the only guy allowed into that house! She was a cynosure of a hundred eyes! When she passes by some jealous guys used to shout *'Tidda wakra'*.[10] We remained good friends even after her marriage.

---

[10] *Mahrathi* for 'twisting her hips like a gazelle'.

Being a lumpen proletariat and to top it all a *dacoit*, nothing was impossible for Shamshuddin. He had eyes that looked like slits which may have been from his opium addiction. Abdool told me a lot about Shamshuddin's exploits but it bears no part of my life as a volunteer bound to a just cause.

But as we learnt from a morning edition of *Pratap*, our state did join the union. And so our plans fell apart. The leadership was jubilant but I somehow felt depressed. I had worked very hard to set up the underground cell. Today I can say that my depressive attitude was nothing less than immaturity.

I had to jerk myself out of this silliness quickly. We volunteers had work to do. We had to prepare for the ceremonial pulling down of the *Bhagwa Jando* and the hoisting of the new National Flag. I had an important role to play. I was even sent to Nasvari to learn the required protocol.

The whole village turned up for the ceremony. The entire police force was in uniform and the magistrate, as the chief representative of the defunct state, had to be present. As chief volunteer I gave the orders.

The policemen stood at attention. The Youth from Vesma got onto the platform, lowering the *Bhagwa Jando* and raised the National Flag. The Youth tugged a string and the National Flag unfurled and fluttered. The Youth, the crowd, the policemen and the Volunteers all saluted. The Youth folded the Bhagwa Flag. The Youth gave me the flag and saluted. I handed the flag to the magistrate and saluted. The Youth stepped back and came down from the platform. The *Mahila Mandal* sang the National Anthem and it was picked up by the people.

The National Flag, when unfurled showered flower petals all around. The people cheered. The National Flag for which we fought; for which thousands laid down their lives now fluttered against the azure blue sky.

Everything being over we dispersed.

After the Independence ceremony we had to concentrate on rural work. With Baroda State being a member of the Indian Union and with a whole lot of restructuring necessary, new provinces, districts and sub-districts had to be created as there was an overlapping of the two territories. But Palsana remained as a *Taluka* with some new villages falling under it and other villages falling into another *Taluka*.

To assist with the rural work and to maintain discipline, the village magistrate was given the task of forming a Volunteer Corps. We were to set an example of disciplined and loyal conduct to the youth of Palsana. I gathered together about twenty five other chaps

and I was elected Chief Volunteer. I chose Nanu Naik as my
Assistant. We were each handed a wooden staff, the symbol of our
importance and, dressed in our blue shorts, white shirt and Gandhi
cap, would drill each morning. We also had to keep the village
clean. We would have to dig pits and trenches for rubbish. The
magistrate was always appreciative of our work. When we met so
that I could report on our activities he would always offer me fruit
juice.

But I wanted out. I wanted to return to University and restart my
second year. On the journey to Nasvari we heard of Gandhi's
assassination. In Nasvari I went to the only place I felt home in: the
hostel. Everyones' eyes were red with tears. To compound things
the radio told us the funeral was the following day in Delhi. We
could not even get there. I returned to Palsana. All thoughts of
proceeding with studies had gone.

The following day Palsana honoured *Gandhiji* in a moving
ceremony. As we proceeded to the Mindola river, our *Praja Mandal*
leaders, the leader of the *Mahila Mandal* and I for the Volunteers all
carried poster photographs of Gandhi. People marching sang *Gandhiji's* favourite hymns. We reached the river, dipped ourselves in
the waters and let the posters float away. Our leaders then told us
about Gandhi and his sacrifices.

Soon the magistrate sent for me. He showed me ten new
wheelbarrows and fifteen spades in the courthouse yard. We had to
clear rubbish and dig latrine and refuse trenches throughout the
village, including the *harijan* areas. We worked from five in the
morning until easily six each night.

Around me my friends seemed to be succeeding. There were so
many opportunities opening up. But even my Congress ties seemed
of little importance. With a dedicated commitment I had kept a file
of underground activities and code names of people I worked with.
No one besides Chandramani and I knew of the file. One day after
independence Mangoobhai asked me if anyone had signed and
fingerprinted evidence of atrocities in Bardoli. He said it was very
important and that the Government wanted it badly. I told him
about the file, but that I had to take things out first. I took the file out
of the hole in the rafters and took out the coded contacts and handed
the rest over. Mangoobhai wanted to know how I had done it. I
could not tell him. That is the underground! This work had not been
part of the *Praja Mandal's* activities.

However this did not seem to matter any longer. Times had
changed. Mangoobhai said that no one's permission was needed to
take the files and left. Congress was planning on using the information during their deliberations on who should remain as local

state officials. My cherished files went without so much as a thank you.

I remember digging a trench the night before I left for Bombay on my way to South Africa.

I was born in South Africa but that did not deter me from getting involved in the struggle for total independence in India. I lived there for thirteen years and owed it to India. I was a dedicated cadre and gained a lot of experience and respect from the people I worked with. My village was proud of me. I have no regrets.

PART TWO

ORGANISED VIOLENCE WILL SMASH APARTHEID

South Africa, 1949–1964

™

Mayborne Cricket Club, 1957
Back (left to right): R. Moodley, Y. Osman, A. Khan
Second row: Y. Abrahams, T. Moodley, V. Moodley, D. Govender, M. Govender
Seated: M. A. Thajmoon, S. Moodley, H. Kajee, N. Babenia (captain), D. Pillay, N. Moodley
Front: L. Anand, I. Moodley

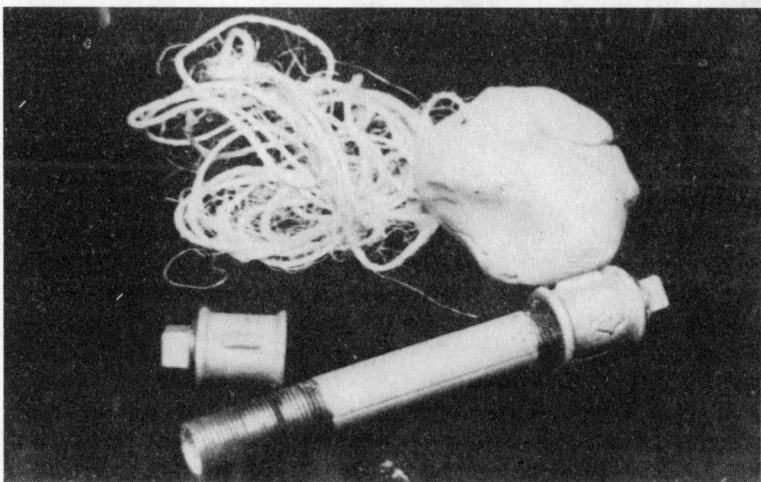

A pipe bomb (exhibit AE: State v Ebrahim Ismail and others, 1964)

Berea Road Station railway line after the bomb (exhibit AF: State v Ebrahim Ismail and others, 1964)

Dynamite cache (exhibit AE: State v Ebrahim Ismail and others, 1964)

The Bitterness of Seeing

On the 5th of October 1949 I left Palsana beginning a journey which was to bring me permanently back to South Africa. I was quite against leaving but my mother insisted. My uncle had recently died in Durban and I was to attend to his estate, see what was in it for me and if there was any immovable property left to our family, I should give power of attorney to our old lawyers Stocken & McClean. Then I was to return to India. So initially it was really only meant to be a short trip. But I wanted to stay put and as I argued, witness the moment of India in her transitional phase. My mother was implacable. It was not for nothing I nicknamed her 'Churchill'. In the end I told her with tears in my eyes that she was only interested in material gain and not my happiness. I was very bitter as I left with my younger sister Kanti and my brother-in-law Amritlal. They were to accompany me to Bombay.

Bombay hardly changed my demeanour. Much of the old India still seemed quite alive. My second class booking had already been confirmed but the travel agent said that there were no second class passages left. All the agent really wanted was to squeeze some money for himself. Seizing a slim chance I suggested that we should go home and pack the whole thing in. Amritlal, having none of this, telephoned someone in the Bombay Secretariat and gave the agent's name and number. A much chastened but still slimy agent found out that my brother-in-law was the cousin of Morarji Desai. I got my damn ticket. Influence can bear cruelly sometimes.

The 8th of October was a dirty smoggy day as I carted my trunk through the customs and boarded the *SS Karanja* which was going to take me some 6 000 miles away leaving my beloved ones and my beloved country to a land in chains. It was all too much for my sister Kanti. Even before the third hooter went my cousin took my sister away, wiping her eyes.

Fortunately I quickly met up with Doolabh Patel, who had been with me in the hostel in Navsari. We soon made friends with a couple of other deck class passengers who seemed honest, humble sorts. Things were feeling a little more normal.

But I was sailing away from a free India which cast a sad shadow. On board was a European, John Harding. He was being deported from Lahore in Pakistan for being a communist. He used to address the third class passengers and explain to them the cause of their misery. He pointed out that by not building cubicles with beds and toilets, the British India Steam Ship Company was saving space. People thus slept on floors with communal toilets and bathrooms. In this way the Company was making a fortune. He convinced them of

45

the wrong done. Bravely he then tried to explain to them the component parts of our society: the capitalist class and the working class. The struggle between them was called the class struggle and how in the end the conscious working class, the proletariat, will triumph.

I very much doubt if anyone understood the class struggle. Or if they understood him they did not want to align with him or his views. Because you see even the deck class passengers were nothing more than an aspirant bourgeois class. They had one leg in India and one in the African continent. They had a home in India and a business in Africa. Their allegiance was to money and nothing else.

John Harding was locked up as an instigator. His eloquence did not simmer down. He used to stand holding the bars of his lockup at the stern of the ship and address who ever was near. In the evenings Doolabh and I would take some oranges to him. We would chat a while, with Harding telling us about the communists he worked with and their shortcomings. It was a crucial time for me. As the ship plied on through the darkness, I could quietly reflect on my own activist past, Harding's and the ambitions of fellow passengers. I found very little wrong with Harding's views. I have never really forgotten him. I honed some anger in my gut. It felt good.

It probably made me a little sharp when I met my eldest brother Chiman in Durban. In his car on the way to Coedmore he asked me how the family was. I told him everyone was fine.

"Natoo, why did you give up your studies?"
"Where was I to get money for my studies?"
"Didn't you receive money from me?"
"*Motabhai*, when did you last send money to mother? Here, you ask me about money! If you had sent money regularly, I could have studied. Remember! I borrowed money to come to South Africa!"
"I don't know what you people did with the money!"
"Break it off! You sent money about two years ago, and that was a £100. What do you think we could have done with that money! And you want me to give you my power of attorney. I am not a fool."

The matter of my uncle's will was easily settled. My uncle had been a wealthy man, at one time owning all the properties in Argyle Street, East London. But by the time he died there was not much left. The money I got from the will I used as a deposit, purchasing my parents' old house in Seaview. I put tenants in and got £20 a month rental from it. But I could not keep up with the payments on the house so in 1958 it reverted back to the previous owner.

But what really did bug me was that Chiman constantly nagged me for money, asking me to lend him money from my share of the estate. He had his share anyway! I felt stifled.

So I went to East London to see my aunt Bella. However the Indian Immigration Act of 1913 restricted the movement of Indians from one province to another. Nevertheless, I decided to drive down without any travel document. It truly seemed insulting to have to ask for permission to move around in the land of one's birth. And I had been out of the country for far too long to be really worried about such things. I stayed with an old friend of my uncle's, Bhai, in No. 1 Mark Lane off St. Paul's Road. Here I met Peter Cassan and Iris. I got on really well with them. They were a lot more honest and open hearted.

One day David, a relative of my aunt Bella took me to Duncan Village and other slum areas. Africans in shacks, coloureds in shacks and even some poor whites in shacks. It was a shack town of one big community living in harmony though often empty in stomach. When we drove through, I saw kids playing, dogs scratching their backs, hens pecking the garbage dump and women with their hands on their hips talking loudly to the opposite neighbours. A thought flashed to mind. These people's forebears once owned land, healthy cattle and poultry, and today they have become victims with no land, no cattle and no poultry.

David turned around and we came back to St. Paul's Road and he dropped me near Mark Lane. I stood there and looked at Cardboard Mansions, owned by the rich Cassoojee. The building had no windows, in some rooms even no doors, but still people stayed. They had to. Once a month, mostly at the end, old Cassoojee used to come and park his car, get out and stand by the gate and shout.

"Gertie! Anna! . . . Maria! . . . Baby! Ava! . . . Rosy! . . . Floria! . . . I have come for the rent!"

The cardboard from the window would move and a head pops out. Then the next window and then the next.

"What you want? Rent! Its not month end yet!"
"Hey Cass, how about fixing the windows?"
"You old bastard, you come and worry us women, when our husbands are out! Heh! You got a cheek, Heh."
"Hey, darling! you want to visit me? Visit me!"

Old man Cassoojee would laugh, shake his hands in their direction and get into the car and drive away.

There was one thing of old man Cassoojee. He would never shout a husband's name, always the wife's. Sometimes these women would angrily throw stones not at Cassoojee but away from Cassoojee. The husbands lounging there on the pavement would burst out laughing. The anger of the women would turn against them!

"What the hell, you laughing for!"

"Aye Johnny, I had enough! Go find a job! You bastards! You laugh! But you can't bring a penny in!"

It would go on like this to and fro. Free cinema for the people by the people.

In East London there was an East London Indian Congress. Although it was largely defunct and ridden with infighting, some of the members tried to play a supporting role for the ANC. Severely weakened, the Congress soon became prey to those wishing to destroy Congress and start another body along the lines of the Natal Indian Organisation. It was a conservative political grouping formed by A I Kajee in 1947 to oppose the increasingly militant tone of the Natal Indian Congress. Leading the attack was the local Indian business community with Cassoojee at their head. He called a meeting of East London Indians in Keshavlal's Cinema. Hearing about the moves, Dr Appavoo, the Congress chairman, called up Peter Cassan, Iris and some others.

We went to the meeting thinking that we would be able to win enough support. It was a lesson. There were only about twenty five people present. And it became clear that the businessmen had caucused well. Cassooje made the point that the East London Indian Congress was clearly incapable of looking after the interests of the Indian community so another organisation had to be started. Appavoo then made it clear that the Indian community comprised more than just businessmen, and that the interests of Indian workers and poor had to be recognised. Rather, as Appavoo told the assembly, people had to make the Congress more active by taking up issues and attending meetings. All speakers insisted that the issue should not divide the Indian community. Then Patel from Bayswater Road stood up and moved that the East London Indian Congress be disbanded with its role being assumed by the East London Indian Organisation. A businessman seconded.

Iris moved a counter-motion that the East London Indian Congress be revived and perform its role in a democratic manner. I seconded. Twelve were for the original motion and six against with five abstentions. Up to this day I have not heard of the East London Indian Organisation. We knew we were beaten but also knew that some Indian businessmen would go on playing a supportive role to the ANC.

In January of 1951, the people of Duncan Village, under the ANC leadership of Alcott Skei Gwentshe, Douglas Sparks, Malcomess Kondati and William Mabona marched to see the mayor to protest against the Bantu Authorities Act. It was a very long procession with the tail-end of the procession still in Duncan Village while the leaders were at the intersection of Amalinda and St Paul's roads. I was taking photographs and helping the volunteers to keep marchers in fours. The marchers were chanting ANC slogans and singing songs like *"May-ibuye . . . Mayibuye . . . Mayibuye i-Afrika"* and so on. It was the first time I had heard the song, beautifully sung to the tune of *"Oh My Darling Clementine"*. The crowd was orderly and only wanted to meet and discuss matters. In fact a delegation met with the mayor a few days later. It was the first time that I became involved with the ANC.

Gwentshe was the chairman of the East London ANC and president of the ANC Cape Youth League. He participated in the Defiance Campaign and was arrested and given a suspended sentence. He was one of the first ANC leaders to suffer banishment when he was sent to an isolated area of the Transvaal in 1954 and then later confined to Frenchdale in the Northern Cape. He died in the 1960s in Transkei where he had been allowed to move to. In 1964 Sparks, Malcomess and Mabona were convicted on various sabotage charges. I met them on Robben Island along with two of Gwentshe's sons.

I had already started work as a vernacular teacher, teaching *Gujarati* students how to read and write *Gujarati*. But after about ten months the Immigration authorities started looking for me. Consequently I had to leave and come to Durban, where I found a room in Beatrice Street. In 1951 I married a girl from East London. From her I got two children, a girl Pravina and a boy Sharatchandra. In 1954 I moved to a two-roomed house in May Street. In 1956 my marriage came to end. We got separated. It just did not work. She was a substitute for Pushpa. I was still far too upset about Pushpa.

They were tough days. From when I arrived in Durban right through the decade I never had a job. I used to bum around and live off the twenty pounds a month rent which I got on the Seaview property. It was an okay life; very few pressures and there were a lot of guys like me around.

I have never been really sure why I stayed on in South Africa. Maybe things were a little better out here. Maybe I just could not face going back to India after all the bad memories. And it wasn't that I quickly got into politics here. Sure, things were beginning to move in Durban. Yes, I was always there at the marches and rallies at Red Square. But somehow I do not remember them as clearly as those first experiences down in East London. So I never joined the NIC. To me they were far too moderate. Compared to my activities in India and the pace of that final push towards freedom, the NIC's politics seemed very tame.

This was even true in 1959. Cassim Amrah was about to address a meeting at the Vedic Hall when some whites came and started kicking up dust. So the organisers switched off the microphone. I protested. But they were so scared of antagonising the rabble that I was pulled away from the stage. So I did not join. But still M D Naidoo persisted that I should join. I could not but I did become a volunteer as I really admired MD.

'MD' was really isolated within the NIC. MD was a Party member and consequently ran up against Monty Naicker and the very strong anti-SACP feeling in the NIC. He was also such a good speaker that people felt he had ambitions to take over from Monty.

MD also made a small political mistake. He represented the Greyville Ratepayers' Association in their struggle against attempts to proclaim their land white in terms of the Group Areas Act. At some point MD suggested that the land remain Indian. Now you could not say this. This contravened the NIC stance of total opposition to any form of racially exclusive land laws. For this he was forced to resign as one of the vice-presidents of the NIC.

The virulent antagonism within the NIC towards communists was so strong that even other comrades within the NIC were cautious about coming out too strongly. In 1960 our Greyville NIC branch elected three delegates to the NIC annual general meeting: Ahmed Motala, myself and Ebrahim Ismail, who was both a member of the NIC and the Party. We three wanted to rehabilitate MD. When the time for nominations for vice-president came we put MD up but N T Naicker, as the general secretary declared his candidacy invalid as the executive committee of the NIC had decided that MD was ineligible. There were no constitutional grounds for this behaviour and I objected. But Ebrahim somersaulted and failed to support me. It was like this in the NIC.

In 1960 Mrs Sushilaben Gandhi[1] approached me to work for *Indian Opinion*.[2] Ranjith Nowbath was in charge of the English section, while I was to write the *Gujarati* columns. Four days a week I would travel to the Phoenix Settlement[3] where the paper was produced with only one thing in my mind. To make readers conversant with the Congress Movement's policy. My views did not suit the liberal minded Sushilaben Gandhi. I soon realised that she would not do anything without asking Alan Paton.

---

[1] Sushilaben Gandhi was 'Mahatma' Gandhi's daughter, married to Mr Manilal Gandhi.

[2] The first newspaper in South Africa to cater specifically for Indian South Africans. The paper was started by M K Gandhi in 1903.

[3] Situated immediately to the north of Durban, a large tract of land purchased by Gandhi as part of his desire to establish a retreat, cooperative farm and experiment with the Tolstoi Farm ideas.

As the State of Emergency was now in full force, newspapers came under the scrutiny of the Government. On my day off the Special Branch created consternation at the Settlement. All political comment had to include the writer's name. Ranjith Nowbath had cleverly disappeared into the sugar cane when the SBs arrived. But he was also reluctant to take responsibility. So from then onwards all political reporting and opinion was 'written by Natvarlal Dayalji', my first two names. But the times were too hot for Sushilaben and despite pleas and offers to raise funding if this was her problem, she unceremoniously closed the paper down in August 1961. Much later she told my daughter Pravina that she closed the paper because of my political comments. *Gandhiji's* shadow grew smaller, even in the mango trees of Phoenix.

Yet as with India, in 1961 there still was a place for passive minded spiritual affirmations in a near burning South Africa. Sushilaben went on a seven day fast, pleading for the release of the emergency detainees. All through her fast we at the Settlement had a prayer meeting every evening. In the last day of her fast, Mrs Luthuli was to have come marching from Groutville to a meeting at Phoenix Settlement. Mrs Luthuli could not come but Johnny Makhatini, Fatima Meer and Sushilaben Gandhi made brave speeches. It was an important meeting. The quietness of her fast and our prayers were good for me.

Indeed it was with Ela Gandhi and her mother, Sushilaben, that I first visited the African shanties of Cato Manor. We had some food parcels and clothes to give to a social worker. The place looked deserted. Curious eyes were peering from behind windows and corners. I was a bit scared, but the woman social worker knew of our time of arrival and she came forward as we parked the car. In no time we saw people come out of their house and children running about. They had got the message that we were friends.

But things were hotting up all around me. And drawing me ever more clear to the centre of fire.

An Activist on the Streets

In 1961 the South African Indian Congress held its annual conference in Durban. Under R G Pillay, four of us volunteers took care of catering. Things went smooth. Thereafter the Durban District Committee of the NIC met in Merebank at Manual Isaacs' place and I was appointed a district organiser for our sixteen Durban branches. This was now a full time commitment. The money was not great, about £15 a month, but you could keep a roof over your head. And there were always comrades who would offer you tea and food. There was really no time for anything else.

By the time I was appointed it was clear that the NIC had finally become much more of a mass organisation where the interests and aspirations of ordinary folk had considerable influence. You just had to attend branch meetings to be struck by this. And the leadership was always aware of this. Of course in branches such as Durban Central, Greyville, Mayville and Cato Manor, a lot of professional people took an active interest in politics. But in other places such as Clairwood, where we were really strong and had three branches; Bayhead, Magazine Barracks and Happy Valley and in Quarry Road, the elected branch officials were most often workers.

As an organiser, I had to see that the branches met regularly and assisted in all campaigns. We also had classes for the branches. Every fortnight we met with the NIC General Secretary, N T Naicker. Leaders from all the Congresses briefed us of the Movement and sometimes leaders like George Ponen, Stephen Dlamini, Dr Randaree, George Mbele, Monty Naicker, Hassan Mall and M D Naidoo gave us news analysis.

I also had daily administrative work to fulfil at Lakhani Chambers.[4] Much of it involved filling out affidavits. The NIC was a political organisation, but much of its organising effort and thus its influence and power came from being really involved with social welfare issues. Say a branch found out about a poverty stricken person who needed help. They would investigate and if genuine, send the person along to us. We would type out a letter with the NIC letterhead and send the person to a grocer. Or to the Indian Child Welfare Society, who always responded as they knew the case had already been investigated. For this I had to help fill out the affidavits and go around to Kissonsingh's, the lawyers, to have the document attested. When we approached the Indian business community our letters were always signed by Kay Moonsamy, our provincial organiser who was also responsible for the business community. It was through such activities that the NIC was so popular. We would also do the same for people brought to us by the ANC, SACTU or community organisations.

When it comes to honesty, I think Comrade Kay comes out tops. He was a dairy worker, trade union organiser and ended up being NIC provincial organiser. He worked very hard and even banning did not stop him from doing organisational work. He often told me that working at grassroots level would improve the quality of our branches. We were proud of our branches because they had a working class nucleus.

---

[4] The building in Grey Street where the ANC, NIC and SACTU had their regional headquarters.

Since the ANC was banned all meetings were called jointly by the NIC, SACTU, the Congress of Democrats and the Women's Federation. The NIC, as a supportive organisation to ANC would get a hall, microphone and with the volunteers, arrange a meeting and bring out the required leaflets. I together with Kesval had to ensure that all our branches were at all times kept in touch with and active in everything that was going on in the Congress circle.

It was one thing to call meetings, quite another to organise them. For this you need co-ordinated planning. Now with the ANC being banned there could have been problems if it had not been for the Joint Secretariat structures. These had been set in place after the Congress of the People in order to facilitate an efficient working relationship between various political organisations. Policy issues and campaigns would be discussed by the Joint Secretariat and then sent to the organisations to discuss it. After the organisations had discussed it, it would come back to the Joint Secretariat to be finalised. Decisions of the organisations overruled all other factors. If a problem arose, a joint sitting of the organisations involved would sit and hear facts and solve the problem.

After 1960 these structures were a godsend to us. We knew how to work together, who to approach for specific tasks, who liked this or that type of work and how various groupings would feel about certain policies. Furthermore, and this was critical, it was through these long standing contacts that people developed a hard nosed loyalty towards the ANC as the primary organisation of the movement.

People often think that the banning of the ANC had a crippling effect. Sure one had to be careful. But those early years of the 1960s were heady days. Marches, the stay aways, workers flocking to the banner of SACTU. Sure we had to be careful but that was all part of the struggle. It was all a struggle of wits and for a while we were really moving.

When campaigning, you had to be careful. Say for example when distributing leaflets. Particularly when we targeted workers outside factory gates. It was always a little easier in residential areas and down Grey Street. So we always worked in groups. I would often team up with Barry Higgs or Mate Mfusi. Afterwards all groups had to report at the Congress offices. If a group did not report, we would go near the factory and make enquiries. If a group was picked up, we would notify Rowley Arenstein and he would go and sit on the cops. This way we kept a tab on every group.

But there could be tensions in our working relationships. The municipal Bantu Administration Board had begun to bulldoze an African shack settlement just near Umlazi. It was a relatively new place, made up of people who had been evicted from Cato Manor and had nowhere else to go. The municipality simply would not leave them alone. Elias Kunene came to the NIC office and reported the plight of the people. He asked what is the NIC good for if it could not help the people? I was hurt when he uttered that type of nonsense. Firstly, Comrade Kay never refused and secondly the NIC always helped the African people.

Kay and I sprung into action, writing letters and going around to the merchants. I took Elias Kunene and went around to wholesalers who gave kindly and then went to the Victoria Street Market and collected enough meat, fish and vegetables. Ratilal Kapitan of Kapitan Balcony Hotel gave twelve dozen loaves of bread. Soon we had delivered a truck load of stuff. We could have got two to three lorry loads but Elias Kunene was not willing to collect more.

I wanted to go to Umlazi to deliver the foodstuff but Elias said that the people's feelings are running high and it would be unwise for me to be there. Elias was an anti-Indian on the Africanist wing of the ANC. This type of attitude was expected from people like Elias Kunene and George Mbele. I have a good sense of perception and I make a man out for what he is.

It was always a pleasure to work with the whites from COD. But they were a different lot and you had to get used to it. They would always be there to put in the work but they were a rough lot. Some behaved like real outcasts. And the swearing! I remember once going along with Melville Fletcher and Barry Higgs to Howard College to hear a talk. There was Barry being really uncouth and gutsy. And his girlfriend was talking about cunts and all things. Real salt of the earth types. And clever as well.

Once Barry Higgs and I decided to paint slogans wherever we felt like. Fill the place up! He decided to do the Berea and Morningside area while David Perumal and I honed in on the Victoria Street Bridge and Grey Street. Hardly original but striking splashes of paint soon demanded the release of Mandela and Sisulu and the hanging of John Vorster. Strangely I recall that we only wanted a 'death to Verwoerd'. I wonder why we were so easy on him? Sadly our splashes could not stand the times. The following morning corporation workers were trying to scrub them out. Quick to respond some reactionary elements replied, using a municipal shed behind the Alhambra Theatre suggesting 'Hang Turok and Joe Slovo'.

Rowley was a pillar of strength during these years. He was always available to help us with some legal problem, or to help us get someone out of the cops' hands. He was a true communist. He never really charged anything for all his work. He had a disdain for matters of money.

"Have you got a couple of bob to lend me?"

"Sure Rowley, here you are."

"Ja, I want to get some milk and things for the people here."

Rowley was quite strange. In many ways he was so down to earth, always thinking of new ways to outwit the SBs and thriving on talking with ordinary people. Yet in other ways he seemed totally oblivious of much going on around him. He was somewhere else. But the cops used to hate him when they saw him stalking into their charge offices. Just like a cat after the rats. And he always looked like he already knew he was going to give them a clever time of it.

While the Emergency was being brutally enforced, Rowley received a threatening call. One night comrades went to Rowley's house and hid in the yard. Rowley was told not to open the door. It was the 28th of May 1961. The three day general strike was to begin the next day. It was imperative that everyone be protected.

At around midnight some white youths came armed and knocked at Rowley's door. No one answered it. They knocked again. Still no answer. Then Ronnie Kasrils, Melville, Leonard Mdingi; the contact from the Mpondo peasantry, and others made a dash with sticks in their hands. The assassins panicked and ran for their dear lives. Ronnie chased them along the street. One of the guys turned around and fired a shot from his revolver. The bullet hit the tarmac and a piece of tarmac glanced Ronnie on the cheek.

Ronnie came the following day to the *New Age* office, from where we were monitoring the three day stayaway. Ronnie found Ebrahim, M P Naicker and I there. He told us of the incident at Rowley's place and showed his cheek. Quite proud he was! Later that afternoon we popped around to Rowley's. The SBs had just been inquiring about the previous night. A big sick joke.

Of protests there were many during these times. Like when Dr Costa Gaziedes, who had been harassed from Baragwanath Hospital because of his political beliefs was driven out of King Edward VIII Hospital before he could finish his housemanship. There we were, Ronnie, Laura, Barry, Ebrahim, Kay Moonsamy, Sunny Singh, Riot Mkwanazi, nurses and others outside the gates protesting.

A guy by name of Neal Peetz was also with us. Because of his involvement he lost his job. Neal did not immediately get a job and thus the trio: Barry, Neal and I were always together. I first met Barry at MD's New Year's party and we became very good friends. He had literary abilities, was cool and very practical.

It was through this friendship that we decided to start a magazine called *Voice of the New Youth*. The logo on the front cover was done by Neal, leading articles by Ronnie, two poems titled 'Mother' and 'Colonialism—New Colonialism' by me and some articles by other people. Barry did the typing and also had a poem in the magazine. Ronnie and we clashed over the content. He wanted everything to be propaganda, but we wanted to propagate ideas. We went to Rowley who saw our point. The second issue also came out, but unforeseen circumstances did not allow us to come out with the third. Special Branch surveillance had increased. The NIC offices in Lakhani Chambers and the *New Age* rooms at Lodson House were under almost continual surveillance.

Yes, the ANC had been banned, but we had reformed with community organisations throughout the city. The spirit was incredible. And we had a real fight on our hands because the state was trying to convince people to participate in its own local government structures. We needed to show where real power lay and find the means to allow us to continue meeting despite the Emergency. So in July of that year a conference was called by the Durban Combined Ratepayers Association at the Vedic Hall in Carlisle Street. Ebrahim Ismail was amongst those who organised this memorable event. There were easily four hundred delegates representing well over a hundred community organisations from all over Natal.

The event attracted an even larger audience than we expected. Not only were there observers from the Institute of Race Relations and the Progressive and Liberal parties but also from the Durban Junior Chamber of Commerce and various Town Boards. Clearly these people were desperately worried about the state's failure to secure any substantial black support.

Ever the eloquent speaker, Jack Simons opened the conference, stressing how at this particular moment in our history the political battles of the Indians and indeed all progressive democrats had become fused with the struggle of the African majority. There was simply no other way forward. A resolution, proposed by Dr A H Sader of the NIC and supported by George Mbele for the African Residents' Association demanded universal adult suffrage on a non-racial basis. It was carried with acclaim! The meeting called for a boycott of the Advisory Boards. Delegate after delegate completely rejected Professor Hansi Pollack's view that the call for such a franchise would result in blacks loosing many of their white sympathisers. In the end it was only the two Non-European Unity Movement delegates who supported Pollack. We booed them down. I enjoyed that.

At about this time I met an American student from Harvard

University. He had been to the *New Age* office in Cape Town where Brian Bunting had referred him to M P Naicker. He was introduced to us as Peter de la Savoy. He stayed in Durban for some time and we became friendly. When time permitted I would take him around the city giving him a feel for what we were fighting against. I do not know whether he really liked it or not, but whenever we had a meal I would take him to my haunts and have bunny chow.

He knew my branch members and often Sonia, Peter and I went out together. Sonia arranged for us to go to a Jive Session competition at the Moon Hotel in Clairwood.

Well! I could not dance but Sonia was there to accommodate Peter. I was hopeless company and to top it all I was a teetotaller. We sat at a lovely spot in a lounge full of pots of flowers. My blessed luck returned.

They started calling rounds of drinks. Sonia knew that I did not drink but she said that I should make it an exception in honour of Peter. Drinks came but I held mine in my hand and when they took the floor, my drink went into the flower pot. With the second and third round I did the same thing. They were having doubles and it started showing. Sonia and Reggie started teasing me.

"Natoo, you say you don't drink, but you seem to be holding your own!"

I just kept quiet.

Sonia and Reggie took the floor. Sonia with her high heels started shaking her hips faster and faster and lo, she fell and twisted her ankle. We had to take her to the hospital to have the sprain bandaged.

After some time Sonia received a letter from Dar-es-Salaam. It was from Peter. He wrote to tell us that he had accompanied an African journalist, Joe Leeuw and Pam Beira through Botswana to Tanzania. Much later we heard that the same Pam had married Comrade Marcellino dos Santos of FRELIMO.

It was this kind of contact which excited us. Liberation movements seemed on the march all through the world. And we really felt very much part of this struggle.

When Maree, the Minister of Indian Affairs, came to Durban to set up the Indian Councils, the NIC held a placard demonstration in front of the building where Maree was going to meet Indian stooges. The branches were notified and quite a few people turned up, amongst whom were Kisten Moonsamy, Ebrahim and I. Only Nkosan Kajee was prepared to push through us and see the Minister. However during this campaign Ebrahim and I were taken to the Somtseu Road Station. The SBs let us go after taking our names.

But the state was taking a harder and harder line and during early 1962 tabled the Sabotage Bill. In protest against these moves we held a rally at Curries Fountain.[5] With the assistance of Sunny Singh, Ramie Beharie and some other branch members I organised the torches which were to be carried by the procession. We cut bamboo poles into metre lengths and on the day of the rally stuffed oil soaked rags on the tips and hid them behind a hedge at Shastri College.[6] It was a wonderful sight to see about a hundred and fifty men and women walking with the flaming torches in fours. In the ground they made a semi-circle with the torches while Alan Paton and others attacked the atrocious Bill before Parliament.

Following this was a demonstration on the steps of the City Hall. Amongst us were Ronnie, Riot Mkwananzi, Barry Higgs, Anne Nicholson, Eve Hall and Kay. The SBs came and Warrant Officer Wessels took down our names. I was standing between Eve Hall and Anne Nicholson with a banner saying 'Lift Ban on ANC'. Wessels came back to Eve Hall and asked her name again. As he left I looked at Eve. "He is just crazy!" she replied. Eve was a quiet and strong person. The police in Johannesburg were on the lookout for her and the cop wanted to make sure exactly who she was. As soon as the demonstration was over, Eve and Anne, who was a bit frisky, were whisked away by Barry Higgs. They were soon being hounded by the SBs in Johannesburg. Later they were convicted for being members of a banned organisation. Soon they were pulling a stretch.

In fact Wessels was a good guy. We would complain to him when the other SBs messed our places up when raiding. He would go back and take off with them. He was an old United Party supporter. One of the old school.

Sometimes the police did their proper jobs. During the biggest demonstration, organised by the newly formed Human Rights Committee, against the Sabotage Bill, a white racist hit a Natal 'Varsity student by the name of Bizzell. Johnny Makhatini and I caught him. Just then a traffic policeman saw us and brought the bloke to Bizzell, who identified him. The policeman then put the handcuffs on.

In Natal we had our own Human Rights Committee Branch, with Phyllis Naidoo in charge. As with all the organised marches, the NIC did most of the organising, even doing the catering. As organiser I was responsible for ensuring that all members of the Indian community did their bit for the cause. For this I had to circulate widely. As part of the Human Rights Committee campaign,

---

[5] The main Black sporting ground in the centre of Durban.
[6] An Indian school and the Indian teachers training college in Durban.

over Christmas 1962, NIC members had to go from shop to shop collecting money, clothing and groceries from Indian merchants to give to banished and detained leaders.

It was during this time we had one of the longest processions seen for many years in Durban. Protesting against the ban on processions was obviously not that easy, but our sharp lawyers had worked out that if four people walked together and another four walked twenty paces away behind and so on, then that does not constitute a procession. University students, NIC members, African workers and others, shepherded by our lawyers, joined in with the procession so long that the lead was near Smith Street Police Station and the tail near Natal Technikon. Nothing happened! The police were helpless! And we had beaten the ban!

During this time we were constantly in conflict with the police. One evening Ebrahim, Arvind Desai, Goolamnabi and I went along Grey Street pasting posters calling for a National Convention. Moving out from Lakhani Chambers, Ebrahim and I took the right hand side of the street and pasted our posters. But it was soon apparent that nothing was happening on the other side of the road. A night watchman said that the SBs had taken two young Indian boys away. We immediately got through to Phyllis Naidoo, who had just given birth to Sharad, and she contacted Rowley. The cops refused them bail, saying that it was an SB affair.

During all of this hectic campaigning I often had memories of my times in India. But none were ever so clear as the day when Chief Luthuli left to receive the Nobel Peace prize. He and his wife were brought from Groutville to the Himalaya Hotel by an Indian business-man friend from Stanger. They had lunch there with many well-wishers. The throngs around the hotel turned into thousands as the Chief left for the airport in an open coupe. Everyone was at the airport: banned and not yet banned. It was a veritable who's who. Many would have to settle accounts with the Special Branch a little later.

When the plane was about to leave our Chief walked to the plane amidst thunderous applause. He stood on the plane steps and waved. The doors closed and we slowly got into our car and drove back to the office. That day we closed the offices early.

This was the bite. Yes, our leader had given us international respect and recognition. And his own personal battles had finally been honoured. But it was a telling time for me. I could not but think of meeting Gandhi and Nehru, the garlands and the happy hopes and see the deep contrasts. India had soon gained her indepen-dence. In South Africa, it was a time when I felt we should move in other ways. We were not getting the 'Freedom in our Lifetime' of which Luthuli spoke. My own life seemed to be going nowhere. Our politics seemed to be standing still, caught in petty battles, making bravely defiant stands and shouting sacred principles into a dark hole.

The Return of the Saboteur

I commenced this journey in January 1962. I was messing around in the *New Age* offices when Ronnie Kasrils called me outside and asked if I would like to become a member of MK. I had of course known about plans for the formation of MK for a little while and only expressed my opposition to the loss of lives during this early phase.

> "Natoo, why are you afraid, if lives are lost?"
> "No Ronnie, we cannot let that happen. It is still early days and we need to let the people know we are here."
> "No! There won't be any loss of lives."

I felt it important to clear this up. Our success in establishing MK depended upon it. I was in.

After the June 1961 decision to form MK, Walter Sisulu had come to Durban. I met him briefly at MD's place. From there they went off to a meeting in Clermont.[7] Billy Nair and Curnick Ndlovu were appointed the Regional Commanders. Curnick was sent off to notify Chief Luthuli of the plans. At around this time Nelson Mandela also came down to Durban. He met with the NIC leadership. Many of them were not in favour of any form of armed struggle. These sort of chaps had their own line on Gandhian ideas and were unconvinced by Mandela's reasoning.

Bruno Mtolo was to head the Technical Committee. He was to be trained by Harold Strachan. Eric Mtshali was also there at the beginning. Under the Regional Command were the platoon leaders who were in charge of a number of cells. Each cell was comprised of four people. Ronnie was the platoon leader in the Durban area.

Ronnie and I had known each other for some time so it was quite easy to approach me about joining. We got along fine and somewhere along the line they had found out that I had previous sabotage experience. This was interesting as I had never mentioned it. Further, as I found out later, M P Naicker had mentioned to Billy that if Ronnie was looking for a sober minded chap I was the one. 'MP' was really the head of things, along with MD who was the adviser on legal aspects.

As MK cadres involved in acts of sabotage we were always highly conscious of the heavy responsibility which lay with us. It was early

---

[7] The African freehold township near Pinetown just outside of Durban.

days and our primary task was to announce to the people that a new phase in the struggle had begun. During this phase we had to establish an experienced and well disciplined network of activists and thereby show the people that MK had teeth.

In any case we only had small amounts of the powerful stuff. I think Bruno was the only one with a revolver. He was certainly the only one I ever saw with one. Ronnie had got a pellet gun from Graham Meidlinger, a COD chap who ran the T.B. Clinic in Lancers Road. Ronnie would put a cigarette up and make us shoot it. Afterwards you could often still smoke it.

What was our purpose? Well, it was quite complex and maybe even confusing. There was the idea that MK, through acts of largely small scale sabotage, would convince the state of the need to back down and start acting properly. But few of us really believed this fully. We recognised that from our small beginnings, MK would have to expand its operations.

Ronnie was clearly not yet finished.

"What about your wife?"

"To that end, you do not have to worry. I have been separated since 1956."

"Natoo, how old are you?"

"Thirty seven."

"Man! Don't talk shit! You look like you are in your late twenties! Gee weez man!"

Ebrahim was to get in touch with me.

That evening I duly reported to the *New Age* offices where I found Ebrahim, Absolom Duma and another African comrade whose name was not mentioned. Ebrahim informed us that Absolom was to be our cell leader. Duma, whom I knew very well, spoke about discipline, punctuality and integrity. We sat for about fifteen minutes and then left making arrangements for another meeting the following week.

All this soon changed. Ebrahim received word that he and I were not to be in Duma's cell. Because of pass laws and possible curfews it would be hard and dangerous for Duma and his friend to be seen with us late at night. No African could be on the streets after eleven at night. And Duma and his friend had neither work nor work seeker's permits. Thus if the police stopped them they would be put into lockups.

We met again in the Youth Congress office. I saw two new faces there. They were of David Perumal and Sunny Singh. I knew both of them as we often went out together distributing leaflets. The four of us were to operate as a cell with Ebrahim as our cell leader. We were all happy to have him as our cell leader.

Rightly so, Ebrahim was very heavy on discipline. Apart from the obvious need for discipline in a sabotage organisation, there was an extra imperative. Most of us were also activists within still legal organisations as well. So the cops knew us well. I had no problems with this. As Ebrahim was the cell leader, I had to listen to him and carry out his orders. It was here that I had differences with Ebrahim. These were more over questions of approach rather than strictly ideological or principled divides. I would always obey, but under protest. Most of the time I was right. As time went on we managed to iron these out.

When I was recruited into MK I was not a member of the Party. I only became a member once I was imprisoned. But even then I did not know this. I only found this out much later because 'Mac' Maharaj told my daughter. Apparently it became Party policy that jailed MK cadres became Party members after having served two years' probation whilst attending Party classes.

Now it was not that I did not want to join. I was game. I remember one day walking along with Ronnie and Ebrahim to the *New Age* offices when Ebbie says:

"Natoo we are walking in different directions."

They were going to Party classes. So I asked if I could come along as well. Ebbie just looked at me and said something like I was not sufficiently intellectually adept. And then of course things just moved too fast and by the time I was arrested, Ebbie had gone underground along with all the other Party structures.

Ebrahim had joined the NIC at the age of fourteen. Groomed by people like M D Naidoo, M P Naicker and Poomoney Moodley he soon developed into an activist of high calibre and integrity. He had an intuitive feel for politics with his analysis being on the whole excellent. But during the Sino-Soviet dispute, I thought we were going to lose Ebrahim. He became very close to Rowley, who was a committed Maoist. And Ebbie was active in the Youth Congress, where he had a lot of influence over chaps like Soobiah and Siva Pillay. Soobiah was a founder member of MK in Natal and Siva joined a little later. Ebbie was really difficult, being strongly anti-Soviet and always pushing *Peking Review*. "*Peking Review* this, *Peking Review* that. . . ."

But these differences over the Sino-Soviet split did not really affect MK operations because although their Chinese line was creeping into youth politics, there was only Ebbie and Rowley who believed. And anyway Ebbie began to drift away from Rowley. Finally, on Robben Island, Ebbie came back to us and from thenceforth on never lost his pragmatism.

But Rowley got the chop because he took matters too far. Both in terms of strategy and his own personal conduct. There were many divergent currents of political analysis within the Party and the ANC over the way forward. One group resisted the idea of any form of armed struggle and held out the hope of a maturing working class, led by SACTU, embracing a socialist politics. Others were exploring various forms of armed struggle.

As a Maoist, Rowley had very specific views on how to conduct an armed struggle. He opposed us not on matters of morality, but on grounds of political strategy. Rowley felt that we should first send people out of the country for proper training. They should come back inside and only then should we go bang. And because of Mao, Rowley looked up to the peasantry. I think his involvement in the Mpondo revolt simply confirmed his wider political perspective.

The whole way through this time Rowley had a group of young activists sitting at his feet. He was always very cool and persuasive in putting his point across. He never got angry, so he could win people over. But I know that he could never get Johnny Makhatini.

But he seemed to have a lot of influence over some of the NIC executive. That was the problem, because we never really knew whether our NIC executive supported us in MK or not. This was probably why, although NIC leaders were banned, the NIC itself was never banned.

Sometime before MK was formed, Rowley was called to a Party central committee meeting. Rowley argued and argued his line. Eventually I hear that Moses Kotane stood up and told Rowley that every time there is a decision to be made "You are standing alone. Why is this?" And then Kotane said something he should not have. He told Rowley to remember that "This is an Africans' struggle, not a white man's". Kotane lost his head. He did not mean it in a racist sense. He was just very cross and frustrated. He had no time to play.

It was because of this that Rowley was excluded from MK operations. But he persisted. And he probably felt angry at being left out. Ronnie made sure that those close to Rowley stayed out of MK. Like Barry Higgs and Neal Peetz.

But by the middle of 1963 Rowley really overstepped the mark when he issued a pamphlet under the name of the African Youth Society criticising us as adventurists. It was a two page typed thing. I know who typed it. It was on our NIC typewriter, not Rowley's. The man was banned at the time so he had plenty of time to sit around and type. This same comrade was always telling me to stay away from Ebrahim!

Rowley sent Kgalakhe Sello who, with George Sewpershad, was articled to Rowley at the time, around to the NIC office with a tied up parcel. He told me to distribute these things. I read them and

showed them to MD and Soobiah. The pamphlet was very hot. We
all agreed it was a crazy idea. I felt this was very irresponsible as it
put us cadres in jeopardy. I did not distribute it. Later, Rowley was
out of the Party.

Those were tough days. The repression was terrible and as
saboteurs, personal tensions and little niggling habits and mannerisms often came up in unfortunate ways. However one did get to
know one another well and try to overcome some of the irritations.
As an NIC organiser and MK activist I gained a sense of various
comrade's characters.

Moses Mabhida was one of Durban's leading trade unionists, the
secretary of SACTU in Natal, convener of the regional Congress
Alliance and, with Chief Luthuli's banning, the acting president of
the ANC in Natal. He was also clearly very close to the Chief.

I would always find him walking around in the SACTU offices,
like a tiger in a cage. He was a simple dresser, but having a very
forceful personality he would choose his words with considerable
deliberation. A long time resident of Cato Manor, it was Mabhida
who exposed police brutality in the area and really knew the mood
of the shack dwellers. When he gave us report backs on what was
happening there we really felt we were learning.

With Moses in the SACTU offices was Stephen Dlamini. Starting
off as an ordinary worker he then rose quickly, becoming an
organiser, ANC leader, chairman of the African Textile Workers'
Union and later secretary of the Municipal and Milling Workers'
Union. I got to know him very well.

During the 1960 Emergency, Stephen went into hiding, held
meetings and helped organise demonstrations against the detention
of Congress leaders. I remember one such meeting he set up at the
house of Jutabol, an NIC member in Cato Manor Road. I went to the
meeting with MD who, like Stephen, was also in hiding. MD was
holed up in Garnet Road. At the meeting were Rowley, Stephen and
two African activists. We were to discuss the question of demonstrations, the worsening situation in Cato Manor and activating the
residents' associations in all areas.

As we arrived Steve was about to have supper with his host who
had served a curry.

"Why aren't you eating the curry?"

Jutabol tells him that he is a vegetarian.

"Then you must just pick the peas and potatoes from the mutton and eat
it."

I knew Jutabol very well so I told Comrade Steve to leave him alone.

"Oh! Oh! Another vegetarian taking the part of this one?"

Everyone cracks up in nervous laughter.

There was a big joke about Comrade Steve. 'MP' tells us that, with the Emergency in force, the cops were scouring the townships looking for Steve. But they never found him. Steve knew so many women workers in the Domestic Workers Union who were living in *kaias* on the Berea, that he changed beds in white Durban every night while the cops combed the townships.

Steve's remarkable sense of craftiness was not just used only for politics. One day MP asked me to take Monty's daughter and Nad's niece to the hearing of Monty's Group Areas case, which Bram Fischer was fighting. The court was jampacked. There I am sitting and listening when Steve calls me outside.

"What are you doing here? People at the office are waiting for the affidavits to be filed and you are wasting your time here."

I said that I shall go at once. He squeezed past me and went and took my seat with a broad grin on his face. I knew Comrade Steve well so I left.

One day he really did catch me out. I had suggested to Kay, MP and Ebrahim that we play *faafi*. Ebrahim puts twenty five cents down with Kay and MP both putting their fifteen cents all on number nineteen. They won, each getting twenty four cents to the cent. There I am paying MP his winnings and Steve comes along. From that day onwards I was always a 'lumpen proletariat' to Steve.

Discipline was the utmost importance to Steve. Sometimes, just like Joe Slovo and Fred Carneson, when heated I used 'Fs' and 'Bs'. If Steve was there he would quietly say that there is something foul smelling here. I used to get angry.

"Comrade Steve, I am a bloody worker and I use workers' language. What is wrong with that?"

He would coolly reply.

"You are not a worker but a lumpen proletariat. You want to spoil Kay, MP and Ebrahim with your *Faafi*."

This used to get me.

And he could be quite trying to work with sometimes. One day he showed me the *London Observer* which had Nelson Mandela's "I am prepared to Die!" speech to the court. I should get a typewriter and type the whole thing on a stencil. I got hold of a typewriter and with my one hand typing I started to cut the stencil. It took an awfully long time. I took it to Comrade Steve. He asked me what it was? I told him that it was the 'speech'. He calmly told me to destroy it and took out of his pocket a printed booklet and said that he had the 'speech'. I could have it. I was very angry and was about to destroy it when Kay said,

"Natoo, keep it! We will run out copies for the branches."

This was Comrade Steve.

George Naicker and Comrade Steve were thick as thieves. They believed in the same ideology and almost always came to the same conclusion in matters of contradictions. But Steve used to blurt out his views while George used to nod his head sagely in consent. To have Comrade Steve around helped us sharpen our wits. People who knew him well understood him, just as I came to know him. His heart and soul was in the cause of the workers and he was committed to the principles of Marxism-Leninism.

George Naicker was our MK treasurer. I do not know where we got our funds from, but with George as treasurer we could hardly go wrong! Steven Mtshali, who was very particular when he gave evidence against us in court would meet George in Albert Park. Steven would recognise him as 'the man with the briefcase'. Later, on the Island, I was in the clinic talking to Curnick and there is George so I say to Curnick, "Look Curnick, here is the man with the briefcase." When I saw George again in Lusaka I see him with his briefcase. I say, "George, you still carrying your briefcase!" George did a tremendous amount of work and had no ambition. Up to this day George is still carrying his briefcase.

Curnick was as dedicated to the workers as Steve, but very different. *Nyanga*,[8] as we called him on the Island, he was secretary of the South African Railway and Stevedoring Workers' Union which shared our NIC offices. He was a hard worker and a stickler for discipline. But in contrast he usually needed free reins to show his own best. If one tried to manipulate him for one reason or another, he became lost and was unable to give his best. He has not really changed.

During the time when processions were banned, Curnick had addressed a meeting in the YMCA hall. He ended off by warning people not to march. As I was finishing up taking the collection tin around, one of the SBs, who had been taking notes came to Curnick saying that someone was organising a procession. He darkly warned that the cops were trigger happy and looking for excuses. Curnick and I dashed out and found an African youth organising a march. Curnick caught him by the cuff of his shirt and jolted him. He asked some of the Womens' League volunteers, Alzina Zondi, Quenneth Dladla and others to keep the people moving safely.

After another meeting, the cops had picked up a youth, flinging him into the van. The crowd was angry. Curnick went to the SBs

---

[8] Zulu, in this context meaning man amongst men as the solver of problems.

who got the cops to release the guy. An ugly situation was averted. The times were tight and one came to appreciate Curnick's decisive quick thinking and independence.

Although always very serious Curnick was able to use it in a way which gained him enormous popularity. He was also a powerful speaker and had that startling knack of being able to translate a moderate speaker's speech into a dynamic, stirring Zulu war cry. People clapped hands every second when he interpreted for an English-speaking comrade. M P Naicker had high hopes for him and the summary of his every speech was highlighted in *New Age*. 'MP' even encouraged him to play a very important role in the Kwa Mashu Residents' Association. It was through Curnick's leadership that the Kwa Mashu Residents' Association made great strides in the early '60s. It was through this Association that the ANC in Kwa Mashu was able to survive the banning. Indeed they were even able to call a public meeting in Kwa Mashu where they forced the stooges on the Kwa Mashu Residents' Committee to resign.

Now Ronnie really was very different. He would really lead from the front. He was a real *laaitie*. Even when he was banned he did not give a shit. He would go around to talk to Graham Meidlinger, who was also banned. They were not supposed to be talking to each other but Ronnie never cared. Graham used to get pissed off and tell Ronnie to go outside and talk from the stoep. Then Graham would phone the cops and say he could not get rid of Ronnie. Graham was very whimsical and did not join MK. But Ronnie was never phased.

During the protests about the American blockades off Cuba we were meant to stage a rally outside the American Consulate. Before I could get there Ronnie and others struck like lightning. The windows were smashed and the doors kicked, leaving marks all over the doors. Then they vanished.

Soon after joining MK, Ronnie came to me and said it be nice to see the ANC flag flying over Hoosen's Building in Queen Street, the tallest building in the Grey Street area. After a quick recce, which Ronnie in one of his excited moods said was unnecessary, we went to Lakhani Chambers and borrowed some money from M P Naicker. We needed to buy some material and a pole.

"What are you two guys up to?"

He just laughed when Ronnie briefed him.

"You chaps! You get funny ideas!"

But he was very pleased. We took the money.

Soon a large flag was flying nicely. Ronnie and I scarpered. I took the lift and Ronnie the stairs. He must have really moved. When I came out Ronnie was already far ahead of me. It was a sight to watch. Some smaller flags were also flying over Lakhani Chambers. Clearly it had all been planned.

At the office MP was on the fire-escape taking photos. As we left, Ronnie clutching his 'varsity books and a copy of *New Age*, Wessels and some other SBs asked Ronnie about the flags. I quickly slipped out.

"Jeez man! I've just come from 'varsity to get my 'paper. How should I know."

The guys down at the NIC offices were in fits. The cops were not having too much luck trying to get the flag down. Curnick pointed, "Look at those monkeys!" and everybody started laughing. In the end they just tore it away, leaving only the black strip flying. The next day that was also gone.

When a political campaign was in progress, we in MK would make our own contribution. The cops were often super sensitive so the jobs which were given to us could become quite dangerous. Sometimes the pressure showed.

During the Anti-Sabotage Bill protests, Ronnie was in charge of a slogan painting expedition. There were to be four groups. Each group had a car for a quick getaway. This was actually quite dangerous because often the only people with cars were COD people and not in MK. Such complication could compromise, but logistically we had few other options. Meville, Arvind Desai and I were to cover the highway from Westville to Berea Road. Meville was our driver.

When we came near Durban High School, Arvind went to keep watch while I painted. Hardly had I begun when I saw Arvind running. Arvind said nothing, he just kept on running. A couple of hundred yards away was a police van with some guy pointing at us from inside. We climbed in the car and Melville starts taking bends on two wheels. He turned into a street, found it was a cul-de-sac, climbed out and started running up a flight of stairs. I was right behind him.

"Open the door Melville!"

Then I froze.

"I don't bloody well live here!"

"Melville! Stop being cute! I am an Indian! I'll be locked up for house-breaking dammit."

The cops seemed to be long gone somewhere else. I was cool again. Using a torch we checked the car for any paint marks and left.

A cardinal rule was always to get back to your home as soon as possible. The cops were wise to who they thought was playing around and used to wait at suspects' places. This just to see who was in and who was out enjoying the night air. At the Ridge Road flat Ronnie was in a foul mood.

"We got into trouble with a night watchman at Weston's Bakery. How did you fare?"

He was in no mood to hear our explanation and insisted we return and finish the job like true cadres.

"Oh no! Not me. If you want it done, the paint, brush and bag[9] are there behind a tree trunk!"

But Melville, Dawn and I did take a stroll down that way and sure enough there were two police helmets protruding over the wall. Our suspicions were right. Dawn promised to tell Ronnie. The next day Ronnie did actually apologise, with a huge smile on his face. I came to know Ronnie very well and got used to his moody behaviour.

Nevertheless Ebrahim had in fact been picked up that night. Although MD succeeded in getting him acquitted on the slogan painting charge we did not need that kind of exposure.

In planning any MK operation emotions could never rule over pragmatism. Everything had to be plotted coldly, calculating the dangers inherent in sabotage. One always had to adhere to the rule 'if we could not do it today, then there is another day'. This was clear right from the start. We were meant to open our campaign on the 16th of December with a blast at the Bantu Administration offices in Ordnance Road. But the night before, our surveillance found that the night watchmen were drunk, so in we went. So one had to be reasoned and dispassionate.

One also needed serious discussion within the cells. During a planning meeting higher up the command, the petrol tanks at Addington Beach had been proposed as a target. Under protest I was sent to scout. My protest was that if we hit the target the prisoners in Point Prison would die and so would people living around there. The target was cancelled.

Much of our early work was in testing our explosives. Once, on instructions from Ebrahim, we met outside the Shah Jehan Cinema and with two plastic carrier bags took a late bus to the cemetery near Wiggins Road in Cato Manor. Ebrahim opened the carrier bag and took out a plastic bottle half full with petrol. He also had a piece of bicycle tube sealed on one side with explosive powder inside. He took out an empty capsule, opened it and put three or four drops of sulphuric acid into the capsule and closed it. Then he took the capsule and put it on the powder in the tube. The tube had a five inch long string attached to it. He opened the plastic bottle and then

---

[9] To cover your hand to prevent paint marks and finger prints.

inserted the tube through the mouth of the bottle, holding the string and screwing the bottle cap on. He said that the plastic petrol bomb was ready. He placed it about a hundred yards away on a patch of cleared ground. He told us that as he had used a small capsule so the bomb should go off in twenty to thirty minutes' time. While he was assembling all the things he explained to us what he was doing.

We waited for half an hour and nothing happened. Another fifteen minutes and still nothing. I went with Ebrahim to see what had gone wrong. Ebrahim picked up the bottle slowly, only to find that the tube with the explosive powder was submerged in the petrol. We threw everything away.

Then Ebrahim took a glass bottle full of petrol and made a hole in the cap with a nail. He inserted a wick through the hole and tilted the bottle so that the wick became wet. As soon as it was lit Ebrahim threw it against a rock. A flame shot up. He told us that it was called a Molotov Cocktail. One experiment had succeeded while the other had failed.

Soon after this, as I knew quite a lot about explosives, Ebrahim told me to take David and Sunny and show them a timed plastic petrol bomb. I made a mixture of seventy percent potassium chlorate, fifteen percent sulphur and fifteen percent fine charcoal. I cut a four inch bicycle tube and sealed one end with a solution. I made a hole at the unsealed end and ran twine through it and tied the twine. I got a gallon plastic bottle and bought half a litre of petrol and poured a little out and the rest I poured into the plastic bottle. I took a small and a big capsule and put them in a matchbox. I took half an eye drop bottle of sulphuric acid and closed it with a stopper. I put it, wrapped in tissue papers, into my jacket pocket. I took a piece of towelling cloth and soaked it in grease and pushed it also inside the plastic bottle. I put the cap on and put all the stuff in a carrier bag.

Off we went to a place quite near where we had undertaken our abortive test. From the carrier bag I took out the plastic bottle and told David to open the screw cap. I took the explosive powder and put it inside the tube. I told Sunny to hold the tube. I dusted my hands and opened the small capsule and dropped in three drops of sulphuric acid, closed the capsule and left the bottle of acid standing upright. I opened a bigger capsule and inserted the small capsule in it. I closed the big capsule and asked Sunny for the tube. I made a hole in the powder and put the capsule in. Thereafter I got the plastic bottle from David and slid the tube in, making sure it did not touch the petrol in the bottle.

I closed the bottle leaving the string attached to the tube sticking outside. I placed the bomb there and we walked up the hill. The acid bottle was back in my pocket. Whilst assembling the bomb I explained everything to David and Sunny.

We came up the hill and sat against the cemetery wall. I told them that it would go off in one and half hours. While assembling the whole thing I stressed that the acid drops must be dropped in the centre of the capsule and no drops must be on the outside as it could catch alight as soon as it touched the powder. Therefore I suggested that it was best to use two capsules, one big and one small.

We sat talking in whispers. One hour went past and it started drizzling slightly. Sunny became impatient but David told him to cool down. While we were sitting there we could hear echoes of voices on the opposite hill. They were voices of Cato Manor police station cops going off duty home to Chesterville.

An hour and a half later we heard a huge explosion and saw the whole area lit up by a bright pink light. We were able to see each other's faces clearly. The voices on the hill were subdued and we made our move. Sunny led the way as he knew the area and we scuttled through peoples' yards and lanes. Near Dormer Road we left Sunny and walked on. On the way I threw the acid bottle and the remaining powder away. We waited for about five minutes and a bus came. Police vans were going up and down. We jumped off at Shastri College and went home. Ebrahim was very pleased when we reported our successful experiment.

One day in September 1962 Ronnie came to see me. In the privacy of my bedroom he told me that he would be bringing some sabotage material for me to store. He then wanted to know if I knew anything about chemicals? I had taken chemistry at school and was curious about what was coming my way.

"Oh! Things like potassium chlorate, potassium permanganate, sulphuric acid, aluminium powder and iron oxide."

"Ja that's fine, I know how to store them."

"What do you think potassium chlorate is used for?"

"Ronnie, don't make me laugh! I know what it is used for by saboteurs!"

I was super casual. Anyway it was a bloody stupid question. Ronnie laughed.

"Bruno Mtolo will come and show you how to prepare explosive powder. Is that alright with you?"

"Why don't you show me how to prepare it? Why expose me to another person?"

"Natoo, I can show you, but I am not allowed to! You will be working in the Technical Committee sooner or later, so it is better you learn a few things from Bruno."

The following day I remember well. I woke up at five and bathed. After dressing up, I made a pot of tea. I was having my third cup of tea when Ronnie opened the door and came in. He told me that he had brought the stuff. Ronnie did not like tea so I did not offer him a cup.

"Where is it?"
"I parked the car near the lane entrance!"

Using the back entrance we carted a haversack and something else wrapped in a plastic bag up into my kitchen. Ronnie was quite careful with the plastic bag. He proudly announced that it contained a bottle of sulphuric acid. As I had no stove, I put a small two door cupboard in the kitchen fireplace. I took the bottle from Ronnie and placed it behind the cupboard where no one could see it.

"What's in the haversack?"
"Other stuff."

I carried the haversack to my room. Ronnie opened it and took out a bicycle tube, a bottle of potassium chlorate, a bottle of potassium permanganate, some fine charcoal powder, a box of empty capsules and three pairs of gardeners' gloves. I put all the stuff in a box, closed it and pushed it under my bed.

"Is it safe here Natoo?"
"Quite safe as long as you people don't frequent my place."
"No! No! No one will come to your place!"

Perish the very thought.

"Natoo, your branch should have meetings at some other house!"
"That is fixed! We are going to have all meetings in Minora Mansions, where we have a NIC branch member."
"Good! Remember, the stuff I brought is only for safekeeping."

Ronnie gave me a lift into town, dropping me off in Field Street because he did not want to be seen in the car near Lodson House or Lakhani Chambers.

On Sunday Bruno Mtolo came to my place with another carrier bag. He was to show me how to mix explosive powder. He took out some potassium chlorate and mixed it fine in a wooden plate using a wooden spoon. He took only one spoon of it. Then he took less than half a spoon of potassium permanganate and mixed it with the potassium chlorate. He mixed both powders finely. Then he took less than half a spoon of charcoal and started mixing all the three powders together. He advised me as he went along why a wooden plate and a wooden spoon should be used. A metal plate could cause friction and then powder will burn.

He then took a pinch of the mixed powder and placed it on a saucer. Taking a small bottle of sulphuric acid from his pocket he dropped two drops of the acid on the powder. As soon as the powder came into contact with the acid it shot up in a flame. I had to open the window to let the smoke out. In a few minutes it was all gone.

Then Bruno took out one small and one big capsule. He opened the small capsule and showed me how to drop a few drops of acid into it and how to close it. He told me that the acid will dissolve the capsule within twenty to thirty minutes. He said the big capsule took an one hour to dissolve. And if the small capsule with acid in it was inserted inside the big capsule it took about an hour and half for both to dissolve.

He told me the powder mixture was going to be our standard mixture. I told him that is good. There was however a problem. At that stage we only had about 750 grams of potassium chlorate. And chemical companies were refusing to sell the stuff any more.

I never at any stage told Bruno that Ebrahim had already shown me all that.

The next day Bruno returned with his carrier bag. In the kitchen he filled seven lengths of tube with some black powder. All the tubes had pieces of string tied to them. He left me with one of the filled tubes, two small and two big capsules, a half litre empty plastic bottle and a small bottle of sulphuric acid. I was to give Ebrahim the stuff. After he left I changed the charge, emptying the tube of its powder and making my own mixture using sulphur instead of potassium permanganate and filled the tube. I kept the stuff safe in the kitchen cupboard. The flat was filling up.

Ebrahim failed to arrive as planned that evening. But the next morning there he was knocking on my door. We were to use the incendiary bomb to fix A S Kajee, the only stooge to have attended the Republic Day ceremony in Pretoria.

Plans soon changed. After getting some petrol from the Royal Vulcanising Petrol Station we walked to Kajee's office in Alice Street. Ebrahim swore bitterly when he saw the night watchman sitting there smoking his pipe. To kill a bit of time we wandered around for a while with our bomb. The bloke was still there when we returned. It was getting late. We wanted to do something. Ebrahim said we should put the bomb on the train going to Kwa Mashu. Neither David or I were happy with the change of target. We planned to raise it with Ebrahim the next day.

Leaving the carrier bag under one of the flower seller's stalls just across from the station entrance, Ebrahim and Sunny went to buy the tickets. There were only two passengers in the compartment; an Indian and an old African. We chose a seat next to the door. As the train shoved off I went to the toilet to set the device. I used one small and one big capsule. Ebrahim pushed the bottle under the seat opposite us. It was so easy. It only took around three minutes. But you had to work fast! We had already attracted the attention of Indian waiters on their way back after work. And Sunny was becoming aggressive and sharp with them. He is always putting his neck out! I do not know what is wrong with him. We all got off at Churchill Road station and walked back to May Street.

Seven bombs had been planted that night of the 15th of October. Only four had exploded. Ebrahim said that ours had been the best. It had exploded near Duffs Road Station causing quite a bit of damage to the seats.

But Ebbie was mad with me. We were supposed to have alighted at Umgeni Station. I was undisciplined! He was quite wooden headed and couldn't see that with Sunny and the Indian blokes getting fiery we were jeopardising the operation. He raved about it to Ronnie who really sat on me.

"Natoo, if you do not obey orders we get rid of you."

He made his fingers into a gun and clicked his thumb down.

"Ronnie. You better be fast. If you are not fast I get you!"

Later Ronnie found out that Ebbie was in the wrong. And anyway it was not even the target. That was Ebbie's fault so I had one over him.

Whenever we went out to hit a target we always took snuff and chillie powder and sprayed it around the target so that the sniffer dogs could not smell our footprints. We also used Cutex when handling explosives so that we left none of our fingerprints on the explosives. This Ronnie had taught me.

To me the problem about the failing bombs was clear. People were putting too much petrol in the bottle. The tubes with the powder were about five inches long. If the tube touches the petrol then the petrol corrodes the tube opening and the powder gets wet. Once the powder is wet there is little or no chance of it burning. The bomb is a waste.

That day Ebrahim told me that I would be working in the Technical Committee in future. I was no longer in a cell.

Our Technical Committee comprised Bruno, Coetzee Naicker, who had been allowed into MK despite his brother MP's advice, and a fellow by name of Mkwanazi and myself. We only ever met once together: in MD's office. Of that I am very sure.

Turning Up the Heat

Soon the air was very tense. In August 1962 Mandela was picked up near Howick and regional leaders became very heavy. Lectures on how we should conduct ourselves in a more professional way came thick and fast. And we in Durban were supposedly not doing enough. Ronnie came down on us very strongly.

It was at around this time that Ronnie stopped me attending any placard demonstrations and meetings. The cops were always around taking names and photographs. Ronnie also told everyone not to call me 'Babenia', but 'Natoo'.

To make matters worse, by end of 1962 there were heavy tensions between us and elements within the ANC. Now there had always been tensions between hard line nationalists and more progressive elements within the movement. In the Durban area George Mbele, Dorothy Nyembe, Elias Kunene and others were the leading nationalists. They were often very racist in their attitude towards whites and Indians and took issue with SACTU people over the role of the working class. They certainly did not like the Party.

Now with the ANC being banned, there were no real structures whereby issues could be thrashed out. With the organisational mechanisms being absent, leadership battles could also not be controlled. It was very sad. If the 'M' plan structures had been set in place in the early 1950s as they were supposed to have been, things might have been a little different.

But it is funny how things worked out. It was really only in the Eastern Cape where the 'M' plan structures were really functioning. This was because of Govan Mbeki. And yet because they were so efficient and organised once the regime got onto them, they could just pull them all in just like that!

However it really was only from 1960 onwards that people started to organise new structures in Durban. Each township had its own *isolomuzi*. They were established, but not only were they obviously covert but often also functioned sporadically. And there was fighting within these structures. Many of the fellows did not want to do any work. They wanted to be leaders sometimes just to stop others from leading and sometimes to stop things from happening. Maybe they were scared. But they got angry with SACTU and Party people who put their all into it. This was why Curnick was having problems in Kwa Mashu. But MP was backing him in every way he could. We in MK had to keep close links with these civics.

It was a situation which was bound to produce renewed in fighting. Actually the very attempts to establish civic structures produced much tension. Curnick had already experienced this in Kwa Mashu. There Elias Kunene, Dorothy Nyembe and others resented his influence and success and were opposed to a SACTU organiser and Party member taking the lead.

So one day George Mbele, Selborne Maponya and Elias Kunene

tackled Curnick about MK. They wanted to know who were the MK members in Durban.

"How should I know. I am an ANC member and a SACTU official. I don't know."

"Alright Curnick if you will not tell us, we'll tell you. Billy, Stephen, Ebrahim, Ronnie, Bruno ...."

I hear it was a good list.

I suppose it really was not that difficult. We were always in and out of the NIC and SACTU offices which were right next door to each other. With a little guesswork they had put two and two together.

Mbele insisted that all MK operatives and functions fall directly under themselves. They were scared that power was slipping away from themselves and resented the fact that MK operated independently of the ANC. We always resisted this sort of demand. In fact Sisulu had clearly stated that the structures of MK would have to be separate from any civic structures. Mbele and his lot also did not like the Party and were opposed to non-African involvement.

It was the only course of action which MK could have taken. In principle MK functioned as the military wing of the ANC, with its task being to serve the political struggle. But organisationally this relationship had to function hierarchically: through MK channels to the High Command and then to political levels. And anyway there were many 'ANCs' in the shambles after March 1960. We pushed on.

The MK Natal Regional Command wanted dynamite. I went to Bellair with Ebrahim and checked out Coedmore Quarry and then the Clairwood Quarry. It was difficult to get the dynamite from Coedmore Quarry, but it wasn't difficult to get it out at Clairwood Quarry. We observed the place carefully and came back.

In the meantime there was some construction work going on in Pinetown. They had been using dynamite to clear rocks. Ronnie had heard about it so he took Eleanor, his girlfriend, there. Somehow they found the shack where the dynamite was stored. That night Eleanor got busy examining the lock and trying out keys from a whole bunch we kept. Nothing seemed to fit. When she was busy an African night watchman came wobbling by and peeped at them. Eleanor quickly grabbed Ronnie and started kissing him. The drunk African laughed and tottered off. Soon they found the right key, locked and unlocked the padlock a couple of times to make sure and left, leaving the place all locked up.

A day or two later Ronnie drove out there with a couple of cadres. After loading up as much dynamite as they could, they drove to Cavendish and buried half of the dynamite, putting the rest in George Naicker's garage. George was given instructions to put a fan in the place to keep the stuff cool. Later two tins of dynamite were taken out and buried at Treasure Cove Beach. That was a nice touch.

Ronnie could be very scurrilous sometimes. For this operation and others he would use Rowley's car. Of course Rowley knew what Ronnie was up to. Rowley could not use his own car at night because of the strict conditions of his banning order. And Ronnie was Jackie Arenstein's pet, so he could get whatever he wanted.

As bad luck would have it the dynamite that was buried at Cavendish was discovered by a herd-man who once worked in the mines. The original inhabitants of this land of ours often knew too much about land. This was a great loss to us, but we had enough to carry on with our activities. By the end of the week all the stuff was removed from the garage and put at different places.

I only got to hear about all this much later. This hardly surprises me as it was always a clear policy that while we would use the stuff we would never ask where it came from.

The pace was quickening. On the 1st of November Ronnie comes to the NIC office wanting me to prepare three bombs and bring them back to the offices. All this in less than an hour.

"Look Ronnie, I am going to prepare the explosive powder, but I am not bringing it to the office!"

"Aye Natoo! What are you scared of?"

"Ronnie, I am not scared! Get that straight!"

"Alright! Alright! Relax!"

I had not told anyone, but I had stored some of my stash at my friend Rasoolbibi's place. I was in a real rush so while she was helping me mix the stuff I think I pressed the spoon too hard into the mixture. A small spark flashed at the side of the chipped enamel plate. A huge flame shot up. The room was full of smoke.

"Natoobhai, my house is on fire!"

Of course it wasn't and in ten minutes or so the smoke was gone but you could smell cordite. I left to do the work back at my place. Half an hour later everything was done. After washing my hands and storing everything away carefully, I dashed off down to First Avenue to see if a taxi driver mate of mine could help me get to the rendezvous in time. My luck was in. Ronnie looked at me stiffly.

"Natoo, you are a few minutes late."

"Ronnie take the stuff and get the hell out of here!"

Ronnie left and I started thinking what a short time he had given me to prepare the powder. I made up my mind that if Ronnie wanted anything he should notify me six hours in advance. Having made up my mind I decided to go home. I had had quite enough for one day.

That night I was sitting at home with some friends when Ebrahim pops by. He was hungry so off we go to the Epsom Lounge in Umgeni Road. We had hardly started when all the lights went out. Ebrahim excitedly blurts out "Ah!" and claps his hands. He had obviously come straight from a job.

> "No Ebrahim!, this is stupid. Lets go back! I think my neighbours must be having something to eat!"

There Ebrahim and I sit down to some mutton curry and thick slices of bread. The candle light showed Ebrahim eating with a sly smile on his face. As soon as he finished, I told him to go home. I knew the SBs would raid his home. He was hardly an unknown. I ambled off home and lay on the bed reading *Spartacus* until I fell asleep. Sometimes you had to look after your mates because they clearly weren't up to it.

They had blown up some pylons just outside Durban. And sure as anything, Ebrahim had been visited. He had been at home the whole evening. So had Billy when they popped around to see if he was alright. This was the start of our first anniversary celebrations.

The next day Kay asks me where I was the previous night. I told Kay that I was at home with friends.

> "Why?"
> "Haven't you read your paper yet? Somebody blew up an electric pylon in Sarnia!"
> "Give me the paper, Kay!"

Barry was also full of smiles and funny. "No! Natoo, you were somewhere else!" Barry really did want to join.

There was a nice article in the *Rand Daily Mail* all about the sabotage. I thought that now we are really becoming professionals. Ebrahim said that now the racists would know that MK means business.

In India we learnt how to use the countryside to our advantage. Now, many debated the theoretical virtues of this position but it meant little when the weight of practicalities bore down. Our task was to advertise ourselves and make people aware of our growing strength. If we had conducted sabotage in the rural areas word would have spread very slowly, the state would definitely not have announced it and nor would the newspapers. In the cities it was impossible to ignore. People would see it and their newspapers would report it. Newspaper reportage had another benefit as well. There were really only two ways of ascertaining whether the operation had been successful or not. You must either go back and inspect and risk arrest from the waiting cops who knew our limitations well, or read about it at one's leisure. It had to be the cities. But it also meant that we had to be extra careful to avoid any loss of life.

In 1962 two days before Christmas and fourteen days after Nkosan Kajee's office was eventually blown up, Ronnie came to me at the office and said that I should prepare a pipe bomb which he would collect from my place at around seven that night. I said it would be ready. I mixed the explosive, poured it into the pipe, closed the pipe, put a little sulphuric acid in a small eye drop bottle and took one small and one big capsule and put them in an empty match box. This was the 'Babenia bomb'. A pipe bomb.

Everything was ready as Ronnie, who had brought Eleanor along, came spot on time. He chatted about this and that for a while and then left for the job. Before he left he told me where it was going to be used: Durban's main post office. The following day he told me that the target was a great success. He was very pleased with my technical skill and had come to rely on me a lot as Bruno Mtolo was failing him. It seemed as if, as we began to get more confidence, we could begin to behave a lot better.

On the 10th of January he wanted another pipe bomb. This time to place at the Bata Shoe Company offices in Queen Street. Led by SACTU, the workers at Bata in Pinetown were then on strike. Ronnie wanted me to accompany him on this mission. Ronnie came around 7 o'clock and I took the necessary stuff and left with him. We took the bus and jumped off in Field Street. We walked towards our target and found African boys sitting against the wall where we were to put the bomb. They were domestic servants working in the opposite flats. We could not put the bomb in the letter box as we had no intention of hurting anyone.

So we spent the rest of the night taking walks around the town. As we came near the post office a police van came with screeching tyres and stopped near us. My heart was in my throat. I quickly moved away from Ronnie. In a hurry, a policeman jumped out and posted a letter in the box and rushed back to the van. I let my breath go. So did Ronnie murmuring "A close shave". Ronnie had a way with words.

But the kids were still lolling around both times we returned. We agreed to leave the bomb in the gutter near our target. We sat in the gutter in Commercial Road. I took the bomb from my inside coat pocket and told Ronnie to feel it. He felt it and found it warm. I put the pipe bomb in the gutter and we took a walk to Albert Cinema where there was a bus stop. If the bomb went off in my coat pocket, I would have been a dead man.

It was around eleven and the bio crowd came out. Amongst them was Naidoo, an SB: "Hello Babenia!" I greeted him. He moved on.

"Are you scared of the SB?"

"Ronnie just do not start this again. I am not scared of the SBs but Naidoo knows you and me, and if anything happens tonight he will be able to fit the pieces."

"Alright! Alright! You can throw the capsules away."

"Why only the capsules? What about the acid?"

"Throw that away also."

I threw them in a scrap metal yard. On the way back we walked past our proposed target again. The boys were gone and I saw a smile on Ronnie's face. He said that we would now do the job. Ronnie insisted so I went home, got some acid and capsules and returned meeting Ronnie outside the Albert Street cinema. Ronnie said we had to call the whole thing off. I was mad.

"Ronnie, what the hell is wrong with you? First you ask me to throw the significant things of our operation away and then you send me all the way home to bring the very same things and now when I am here, you summersault like Carpio!"[10]

He cooled down. While I was away some cops had got an African and were harassing him for his pass. Ronnie had got angry and involved. They let the African go but had taken Ronnie's name.

"Did you give your correct name?"

"Of course not!"

We went to the scrap yard, recovered the pipe bomb and I took it to the *New Age* office and hid it. I made up my mind to discipline Ronnie the following day.

The following evening we met near the *New Age* office. Ronnie's conduct was, I said, uncalled for. I explained that in our type of work the target is the most important factor. His involvement with the policemen was a foolhardy thing. Emotions should be controlled and patience should be the keyword. He listened carefully and did not answer, only saying that we should do the job later that night.

At the *New Age* offices I prepared the timing device. I dropped some acid into a big capsule, opened one end of the pipe bomb, made a hole in the powder with my finger and inserted the capsule and sealed the pipe up. I came down and gave Ronnie the pipe bomb wrapped in paper. He took it and went to the target. Signalling all clear, I waved my hand and he dropped the bomb in the letter box.

---

[10] A United Nations official sent to Namibia with Marti Ahtisahari in the early sixties. He always pretended to be loyal to the UN mandate, but in actual fact he was bought off. So if anyone was selling out we would say "Hey man! Don't make a Carpio twist!"

As we were walking away we heard a big explosion and the whole area was full of smoke. It was Muslim people's big night and people started running towards Pine Street. Ronnie wanted to go and see the damage but I put my foot down and pulled him to West Street and put him on a bus.

The bomb had gone off but something was wrong. I had used a big capsule and it should have gone off after forty to fifty minutes, but instead it went off in five minutes. Clearly in the warmth the capsule had melted a lot quicker without one knowing it. The acid inside the capsule had to eat up an already weakened capsule. Therefore the damn thing went off so quickly. From then onwards I used a small and a big capsule all the time. Ronnie was convinced, ruffled my hair and left.

Ronnie had become the kingpin in our MK activities. Whenever we ran short of chemicals Ronnie travelled to Johannesburg and got it for us. We had lengthy discussions on explosives. We had a code name for dynamite. It was called the 'Big Fish'. Pipe bombs were called 'Little Fish'. I think we used 'cigarette' for petrol bombs.

The 21st of March was Sharpeville Day. The day before, on instructions from Ebrahim, we had gone to Treasure Cove. Ebrahim stopped me in front of a tree. We started removing the sand. Six inches under the sand I saw two five gallon tins wrapped in plastic paper. He took out fourteen sticks of dynamite for me to wrap in newspaper. I wrapped it up carefully. We broke a small branch with leaves on and used it to sweep away our footsteps as we walked away. On the bus back I kept the dynamite tight between my legs in case of any accidental knocks. An explosion would have finished our careers and innocent people would have died of our careless-ness. Ebrahim told me that David Perumal and Sunny Singh would be with us. He said that he was sorry to drag me from the Technical Committee, but since we once worked together, he was left with no choice. I was willing to assist because there was no other fourth person. I put the dynamite under my bed.

That evening Ebrahim came with David and Sunny. I took five sticks of dynamite and bound them together and put the fuse in with the detonator and tied it at the top. I ran a cordite line from the middle stick of one bundle through the middle stick of the second then into the third. The first bundle and the second bundle were to be attached to the two railway tracks and the third bundle to the signal box. I had to keep the cordite long enough so that it could reach quite easily to the two railway tracks and the signal box. The job was fixed. I had a matchbox full of explosive powder and the fuse attached to it.

Around ten we went to Victoria Street Bridge. We waited a while for a taxi to move away and then approached the target. Ebrahim told me to fix the timing device. I went to the municipal library toilet and filled a small capsule with sulphuric acid and closed it. I opened the big capsule and inserted the small capsule in it. I quickly left the toilet and went to Ebrahim who was standing on the bridge and handed him the capsules which I had put in a matchbox.

Ebrahim took it and went to David and Sunny who were already attaching the bundle of sticks. He put the capsule in the matchbox with the explosive powder. The railway line blew up that night after one hour and ten minutes. The SBs raided Ebrahim and Sunny and many other people that night. Workmen were up the early parts of the morning trying to fix the railway track. By morning trains were running fine.

I was told sometime later that on the night of the explosion Govan Mbeki was at M D Naidoo's flat in Victoria Street. When he heard the explosion, he dropped his hands and said, "MD some of the boys are active tonight!"

But things had not gone to plan. Our scouting had been bad. There was a late train on Saturday night. As it slowed down before the station it had in fact run over our blasted line. My ex-wife and my kids were on the train. Whether Ronnie kicked up dust with Ebbie about it I would not know.

The state was not backing down at all. Quite the opposite. They were going on the offensive. The repression was terrific. Up till then most of the guys in the police of the SBs were relatively good guys. Now they began drawing from Broederbonders in the Railway Police and these blokes were really mean.

Just about this time Billy Nair, M P Naicker and Kay Moonsamy were banned. They were also looking for Curnick. At that time you could only be banned if the cops actually served a banning order on you personally. There was a meeting at the YMCA one night and Curnick was due to speak. Curnick was then not staying in Kwa Mashu, but had taken up temporary lodgings in Room 316, A G Soobiah's Bakers Union Office in Lakhani Chambers.

While I was in the NIC offices three telephone calls came from women wanting to speak to Curnick. They said that they were his girlfriends. We knew this cheap trick of the Special Branch. I told all three callers that Curnick had not yet come from Kwa Mashu. I notified Curnick and he told me to switch them off.

At the YMCA, Curnick stayed behind the curtain and when his turn came to speak, he came out from behind the curtain and took the microphone in his hand. There was a helluva scramble by the SBs to reach Curnick. They shouted "Curnick stop it you are being banned!". It would have been quite funny if the circumstances had been different. This incited the women as their golden boy speaker was being banned. A huge war cry engulfed the whole place. Curnick took the banning order and with both hands made a sign to the people to cool it. He left the place.

Apart from giving them the usual stuff, Billy and Curnick were also banned from entering the offices of the NIC, SACTU and *New Age* offices. *New Age* was also banned and so out came *Spark*. With Kay being banned I took over his position in the NIC office. Though Kay was banned he continued with his activities. One weekend Kay and I attended five branch meetings and continued to do so for some time.

During this time Bruno came to my North Street home. He had left Steven Mtshali in the car outside. It seemed unnecessary.

"He knows the house because he has seen you enter. So what sense in letting him wait outside? Go, call him!"

Bruno was making a Beeton bomb. I just watched and drank my tea.

The Beeton bomb originated in Britain where it was used by burglars and safe breakers. To make it properly you use one part iron oxide and three parts aluminium powder. Plus a little explosive powder of course. You put it all in a mud container. It does not explode, but rather creates enormous heat. And a hell of a lot of smoke. It is very nice for railway lines and iron bridges.

Ronnie came by the next day. The Beeton bomb had not worked. We had a debate over how to make them. I told Ronnie that the quantities mixed were wrong. He said that they were right. I told Ronnie that I would show him the correct mixture. I took three parts of aluminium powder with a tiny spoon and one part of iron oxide and mixed it together thoroughly and put it on a saucer. I had some explosive powder on the ledge of my door post and on the top of the window frame.

"What is this?"
"Ronnie don't make a fuss. Its ready made but don't worry."

I put a little on top of the other powder and dropped out a drop of acid. The whole thing caught on fire.

"Hey! Natoo you bastard! The fellow, he's letting me down."

I had been interested in explosives for a long time. Some things stick in your mind because you like that kind of thing. Chemistry was one of my favourite subjects at school and also you could pick up some interesting things in detective books and there was some magazine from America called *Witches Magic* or something. There was also some Swedish chap who wrote about it. He never came out here though.

In June 1963 Kay was arrested in the Dayal Road Cigar Factory and charged with breaking his banning order. Rowley was informed, we told Kay's wife and took some food down to Kay at Wentworth police station. Rowley discussed the matter with Thumba Pillay. Bail was set. Rowley told me to collect half of it. Rowley managed to get him acquitted. When Kay came out he used to help George Singh in his office. But he was still very much banned. Things were drawing to a close.

As the cops moved in we found it very difficult to replace trained members. Right from the beginnings of MK we had deliberately kept the membership small. In the Durban area there were only about twenty of us active members. It was not that people did not want to join. I was often asked:

"Natoo, how do you join?"

I would give them small tasks.

"Well why do you not go and scout around this building, or that place and see what is happening. These are the types of targets that people in MK are interested in. And somebody will get back to you."

I left it at that.

Ebrahim was a lot keener. But he wanted to recruit youths. Sixteen and seventeen year olds. I was panicking. People like that are too irresponsible and you can't break people in at that age. By that time I knew this. I had been there already.

In MK you had to get a cadre discipline together to train and also we had to show what we were doing. But you could not have masses wanting to belong. Nor could you have things just happening in a chaotic fashion. But through both our MK and other activities we wanted to politicise. We knew we had to grow slowly, but we also often hoped that the people would just rise up. The times were like that. Billy always used to inspire us in this regard. Billy would speak of us lighting the grassfires.

In situations like this one finds it extremely difficult to set a proper pace. In fact we really had little control over these things. Ordinary folk were dying to become involved. MK had begun sending people out for training at the same time as trying to start up inside. This held problems. And the state was clamping down ever more fiercely. Under the Sabotage Act there were heavy penalties for acts of subversion and they could restrict people whom they thought were aiding us. Hence we lost a lot of eager helpers from COD and the NIC.

Melville Fletcher was a great guy who helped a lot. But somehow Ronnie did not want him in MK so he never joined us. The same for Barry Higgs. Barry was easy going, pragmatic and a ducktail. Even worse than Ronnie. He would sleep in parks and things like that. The chap was game. He would say things like "stop taking me to meetings, just give me the stuff and lets do the job". But Ronnie was against it. But Ronnie could talk to them easily. Not so for Ebbie who used to find it very difficult. You can't call people like that 'lumpen proletariat'. It was a pity that we had not got the COD guys really in. They were blokes who could handle guns and things. But because you make it your domain . . . .

The strains were beginning to show.

Just Before the End

Ebrahim was staying with me at my new place in North Street. But with Steve, Selborne Maponya, George Mbele, Curnick and Billy all arrested, Ebrahim went underground. So did Ronnie.

I have always felt that it was wrong to go underground. By disappearing you showed yourself. And that is going to cost you. Ronnie and Ebrahim should have stuck around. By that stage the cops were looking for Steven Mtshali, but not for them. I felt it was too premature. Up until the time I was arrested I remained as an organiser, messing around in the NIC offices. I was even still playing cricket for the Mayborne cricket team. It comprised guys from May and Osborne streets. There were quite a few politicians amongst us.

And the cops did not have much idea. When they picked Bruno up at McCords Hospital they released him because they did not have an inkling. Sure we were a bit loose. Ronnie would sometimes overstep the mark. And Billy would come round to my place. Billy had no business to do that. And then Bruno started not coming into the office. The cops knew immediately. They were always outside checking who was who. Three and three came together nicely. Ronnie, Ebbie and Bruno.

Ronnie, Ebrahim, Steven Mtshali and Bruno had gone underground. They got some little shack out in Kloof and, with Billy and Curnick inside, Ronnie, Ebbie and Steven became the new Regional Command. I never went there myself, but this was to be the new command centre. Four of them stayed there. Ronnie, Ebbie, Bruno and Steven Mtshali.

Bruno was still head of the Technical Committee. I was moved back to a cell. I was being pushed out. Ebbie could not work with me. Ronnie told me they were roping Siva into the new Technical Committee. Ebbie had pushed for Siva. They were together at Salisbury Island College where Siva was studying for a science degree. But this was bad news, for Siva could hardly remember how to mix various things together. I had to hand over all the powders and things I had to Siva. Siva had to take these to Kloof.

Things were getting hotter by the day, so in some senses it was
okay just moving to Kloof for hiding and planning. But they wanted
all the powders and stuff taken there as well. It was very stupid
because it made making and transporting bombs difficult. But
anyway, we hardly had any stuff left.

But this was more than just a strategic retreat. It was a regrouping.
We had expanded our operations. Curnick was very involved in
sending people outside for training. By that stage we must have sent
around thirty people out.

Now admittedly there was pressure on us from within the
movement to move in a more insurrectionist direction but in fact the
stated policy remained. But what was happening was that Ronnie
and Ebbie were becoming adventurist. They were growing more
daring and felt less strongly about the loss of lives. And with Billy
and Curnick detained there was no one to stop them. The only sober
minded of them was actually Bruno. Our next targets were set down
for the 13th of August. I have often said to Curnick that I am very
glad we were picked up because if we had done those jobs we could
have swung. Thankfully the 13th never came.

During those days we spent a lot of time taking parcels to Point
Prison and visiting relatives. Quenneth Dladla and Salina, Stephen
Dlamini's girlfriend, were real gems. It is in those circumstances that
you find true loyalty. Billy's wife Elsie was taking Billy's detention
calmly. For others it was not quite so easy.

On the night of Thursday the 1st of August I saw the lights
burning at G S Naidu's offices in Hoosen's Building. So I went along
but before I could enter R A Pillay told me that I should leave
because the SBs were already inside. This was dangerous because
George Naicker was using GS's offices. So I went home and got hold
of Dan Rajh and told him to open his tearoom. From there we tried
to telephone a butchery in Malvern to warn George about the raid.
But we never got through. We were now out of touch with George.
What we did not know at the time was that George was probably
still in Johannnesburg. As we found out later, his car had been found
and confiscated at Lilliesleaf during the Rivonia raid on the 11th of
July.

Later that Thursday night Ebbie comes around to my North Street
room. We take a walk to Poomoney's place in Carlisle Street. While
we walk I tell him about the raid on G S Naidu's place and that we
could not get to George. Then he tells me things are getting hot and
that is why they are moving things to Kloof. He gives me some
money to give to Siva for the taxi fare to Kloof. I felt pissed off, "He
is taking all the bloody stuff! What about the dynamite?" I felt that
if they really wanted to go their own way they should not leave the

dynamite where it was and incriminate me. I knew where it was buried. Ebbie tells me that he had already arranged things with Siva to rebury all of the dynamite. He went into Poomoney's place and I went home. I was feeling angry and hurt. In a way I felt they were dumping me after all that I had done for the Technical Committee.

Friday I am in the NIC office chatting to Freda, who was Curnick's girlfriend. In walks Steven Mtshali. His other name was Seshemane. Why he wants two names I don't know. About the very last person we should expect! In the NIC offices! The police were looking for him and this was not the place for him to come to. His wife had been picked up. Steven had just come from Rowley's office. Rowley had already assured him that everything would be fine because she was not politically active. We consoled Steven but he still seemed distraught. He said he did not like Rowley's attitude. I do not know what his case was because Rowley knew who was who. I told him that the SBs were using a ploy to get him. I advised him to go to his hiding place and never to go near his home. Freda promised to try and see his wife. He left, grim faced. Freda and I looked at each other. We knew we were in trouble.

Then Siva came asking when we should meet. I give him the money and tell him to meet me in North Street before ten o'clock the next day. While sitting there he asked me about ten times what time he should meet me. I was a little impatient with him.

Then I walked along to MD's flat in Victoria Walk to report about Steven Mtshali. I knew things were bad. MD just shook his head sadly and agreed. All of a sudden Siva popped in and wanted to know what time I could meet him. Now I was just fed up and wondered how the hell he became a MK member! MD told him off as well.

That night Phyllis Naidoo and I spent some time with Elsie Nair at Himalaya House. Phyllis then drove me back to North Street. Later I went to May Street, my old place, and got all the stuff that was in the kitchen and brought it to North Street and put it in a paper box. Back home I fell asleep reading a Western. I needed to relax. It was weird. They were leaving me behind. But I had just seen the cops raid, failed to get to George and then had spoken to Steven and Ebbie who were both on the run. I was scared and a bit confused. We were well into the dark hole.

By this time about half of our cadres were inside. But no key people yet. Ronnie, who probably also knew more about what was happening countrywide than we did, knew something would happen soon. So he was restructuring to avoid the possibility of everything falling apart if someone coughed to the police.

Maybe it was too much for me. Maybe I wanted out. Earlier I had spoken to Ronnie and told him that I had a passport and wanted to leave. He told me to stay. I know I was not the only frightened cadre.

On the Saturday Siva failed to arrive. I waited for an hour or so and then went to Dan's place. I had stored some aluminium powder there. When we needed some, Siva and I, separately, would go round and take some of the stuff. After Siva fails to pitch, I go to Dan's shop, buy a carrier bag and put the tin of powder into it and hide it back in Dan's shop, next to the empty milk bottles. From there I go to the racecourse where I meet Elsie and Poomoney. Elsie asks me to accompany her to Point Prison to see Billy.

Much later, David Perumal told me what Siva had in fact been doing that Saturday. Ebbie and some others had drawn up this pamphlet under the name of the Natal Indian Youth Congress. It proclaimed that the time for revolutionary action against the white colonial regime had arrived. The youth should support the Natal Indian Youth Congress's plan for revolutionary action in support of the Freedom Charter and *Umkhonto we Sizwe*. Siva had typed the pamphlet out on our NIC typewriter and then, on the Saturday, taken some girls out to distribute it. But when the girls saw what the thing was about they refused. One of them, Rookmoney, went and told 'MD' and said that they had thrown their pamphlets away.

On the Sunday Elsie, Salina, Quenneth and I take a bus and go to Point Prison. Afterwards I went to a cafe for lunch. There I see Siva. He started smiling when I ask him where he was. He says he got caught up but that he would see me Monday morning in the office.

That Monday on my way to the office I popped in to MD's place. He had been raided during the night. I had to inform MP and take some cheques to deposit into his account. Neither MD nor I yet knew all of what had happened the previous night.

The police had been busy. They had raided Manuel Isaacs and Coetzee Naicker and picked MP up. They also went round to Ebbie's but there was no one there. And they were looking for me, as 'Desai', all around the Grey Street area. Desai is a clan name for the *anavil brahmin* and my first passport had me as 'Babenia, alias Desai'. Also they did not know where I actually stayed.

After leaving MD's I went straight to the office. Van Dyk and Schoon were at the office.[11] Waiting for me. It was just before nine in the morning. I was being detained. They let me go into the SACTU offices to give the cheques to Emma which gave me the chance to whisper the news to her.

---

[11] Both policemen who would later acquire public notoriety for their alleged involvement in 'hit squad' activities.

The two SBs took me to Smith Street police station, parked the car and left me inside with an African SB. After about an hour they came back and told me to take them to my home. My heart sank! All the stuff which Siva was to have taken to Kloof was still inside!

As I knew, there on the table was the big toilet roll carton. They pounced on it with excitement. Then they searched every corner of the room. They found a small box full of match ends and a tin of nails on top of the wardrobe. I told the landlady that I was giving up the flat.

They made me carry the carton to the car and put in the boot. From there they drove to Wentworth police station. I had to take my box in with me. There I met two Sabotage Squad cops, Lieutenants Steenkamp and Prins. They started firing questions at me but I just looked at them.

Lt Steenkamp phoned and an SB from the Political Department came. The cop came in, looked at me and just said "Ja, die man is Babenia."[12] My world ended. That was all they wanted! They had identified me and now they could get me. They said, "Dankie! Jy moet gaan!"[13] and closed the door and curtains and fell on me like hungry wolves. I was kicked, punched and thrown to the ground and jumped on. They dragged me by the hair and started kicking me. Prins got hold of my testicles and started twisting them. I was in severe agony but I remembered that Sonia's husband Reggie was teaching in a nearby school. I started to scream as loud as I could so that Reggie might hear.

"They are killing me! They are killing me!"

They beat me like this for what seemed like ages.

As Steenkamp and Prins rushed out somewhere they called Vermeulen in and told me to wash my blood-stained face. Vermeulen asked an African SB to make some tea for me. I sat down in the corner and drank it.

I started cursing Siva! It was his stupidity that got me caught red-handed holding the baby. As I found out later, I was the only one actually picked up with stuff in possession. My box contained everything a saboteur needed. When I thought about that I cursed Siva even more.

I also cursed the comrades who had a room in Fountain Lane behind Atlas Garage. Ronnie was sitting on these comrades to give us the place as things were becoming dangerous. It was bad of me to keep the stuff with me. The Fountain Lane room was a safe place

---

[12] Afrikaans for "Yes, this man is Babenia".
[13] Afrikaans for "Thank you! You must go!"

and we could have hidden our stuff there but no, there was a couch there and the comrades wanted to use it for their debauchery. Hell man! Sex was not that important at a time like this!

Earlier I had found out that a Muslim friend of mine, who actually came to the trial with Rasoolbibi when she gave evidence against me, had a spare room quite close to my place. But nobody had any money to rent the damn place.

We were always strapped for cash. So much so that somebody told Ronnie that Phyllis Naidoo's sister Cynthia worked as a clerk for Kingsgate Clothing. Every pay day, which was Wednesday in those days, she would go and withdraw money from a bank. Ronnie tells me to track her movements every Wednesday. I did this for about a month. Then one day I went to the factory and found out that the boss's son actually went to the bank in his car. The plan had been to chloroform Cynthia, take the money and take her and leave her at Springfield sports grounds.

There was also a suggestion that we use one of the warehouses of the Indian merchants. We could have hidden stuff easily in these places and no one would have found us. These fellows had storerooms in funny places and with lots of nooks and corners and things. And there were many merchants who gave money to the NIC every month. It should not have been a problem to organise, but when MP and MD were detained the whole structure just fell away into nothing.

So there I am sitting cursing and swearing. I was really pissed off with Siva.

Steenkamp and Prins came back after about three hours. They wanted to know about a meeting held in Kloof. As I knew nothing about it they started kicking me again.

Then Steenkamp read out list of names.

"MP Naicker, Coetzee Naicker, Ebrahim Ismail, David Ndawonde, Manuel Isaacs, David Perumal, Sunny Singh and Siva Pillay."

It seemed clear to me what was happening. 'Zed', Moonsamy, 'Dip' Doorsamy, Billy, Curnick, Solomon Mbanjwa, Mathews Meyiwa, Zakhele Mdlalose and Joshua Zulu were already in detention. Somebody was playing a long-playing record. I knew it had to be Bruno. He was the only one still out who knew all the comrades on the list.

Later I realised what had happened. Steven Mtshali was the first to be picked up. On the Friday. And he coughed that same day. So the cops were waiting for Bruno on Saturday when he was near Kloof station waiting for Siva and the powders. Then they must have worked on Bruno. The raids started. All they had to do was pull the thread. I was certain it was Bruno.

As I heard later, the cops had trailed Bruno to some African place out Kloof way. Bruno had shot his way out, on the way collecting a gash on his head. When they eventually picked him up they threatened him:

"Ja! Bruno you going to swing for killing one of our chaps."

Bruno did not know if he had or not and he broke down completely. Four days later we were inside.

I knew we were in for it.

That afternoon Prins and Francois Steenkamp started with the beatings again. I was all over the floor with my nose bleeding again. I must have lost consciousness because I found myself huddled in a small bundle on the floor in the corner looking up at two walls. When I saw my position pain slowly started all over my body. Steenkamp and Prins returned. Steenkamp brought a chair and sat in front of me. He held my head between his palms and asked how was my pain, I did not reply. He then started banging my head against the wall in rapid succession. He then put a cigarette in his mouth and started banging my head against the wall again. He let saliva drip through his mouth and made gurgling noises. To me all these cheap tricks were useless. It was cheap psychology. He then started snarling and the cigarette fell from his mouth. I picked it up.

"Lieutenant, your cigarette!"

"Fuck the cigarette."

He started banging my head harder. I lost consciousness. When I woke I found myself huddled on the floor again.

Later 'Fats' Grobbelaar and another SB drove me to Greenwood Park police station for the night. On the way I asked Fats to stop at a cafe and get me some food. I had not eaten the whole day. I gave him money for two rounds of sandwiches and a pint of milk. I ate them on the way to the police station.

Before lock up I demanded a mattress and lay down. I started chaining together the events of the day. Steenkamp's list drew my attention. Apart from David Ndawonde, all the other names were Indian. Who gave the names? It must have been Bruno. He knew us! The bastard! He sold us out! I started cursing Siva's stupidity and Bruno. They cooked my goose and the rest of my MK comrades with all the stuff they found. I walked around the cell. Tiring of this I read all the names on the cell walls. The obscene language told me of another world. In one place I saw 'Viva Castro! Viva Castro!' Try as I could, I could not forget Wentworth. Sigh after sigh came out. In the end I fell asleep.

In the morning the door and grill clanked open and an Indian policeman brought porridge. He said he'd prepared it himself. I was madly angry at his soft approach.

"Take the fucking thing back! And don't give me that sweet-talk."

He left the porridge. I started reading the swearwords again. 'Bushy, you bastard, you sold out!' 'I was here, Siga.' 'Police are dogs! But licking their boots are hogs.' 'Dan, I'll kill you!' 'Hammer and Sickle, our Salvation!' 'Boonga! Why your wife left you? You should have killed her!' But the one who wrote about Cuba drew my attention most. The chappie had a very good handwriting. The rest was rubbish.

It was the 6th of August, 1963. I was detained on the 5th. Others detained on the 5th were M P Naicker, Ebrahim Ismail, MP's brother Coetzee, Manuel Isaacs and David Ndawonde.

In the morning the SBs sweet talker came. This time it was Dalzell and he kept on about how very sorry he was that Steenkamp and Prins had beaten me. He said he did not like it.

Through all of this he was always phoning his wife, just to hear that she was fine. I knew why he was doing this. It was a prevalent attitude amongst the SBs at that time. Steenkamp would change his residence often. They were shit-scared that we would eliminate them. But they were never on our programme. But I do know that Eleanor, for some reason or other, kept track of Steenkamp's house movements.

Steenkamp's favourite man in the force was a witchdoctor. One day he told me that he wanted to catch a big jackpot and resign from the service. He told me it was his dream.

In 1963 things had hotted up to such an extent that MD had drawn up a leaflet giving guidelines as to how harsh the state of repression was going to be when the ninety day detention clauses came into full force. It had been widely circulated and I had read it. But I only realised the importance of this leaflet when I was picked up.

On the weekend before my detention I knew things were bad. But we never really knew anything because we never had the chance to meet and plan things and clear up little odds and ends. So when we were detained we were all alone.

When you sit in your cell in solitary you try to find some meaning for your predicament. Some can say "I will not talk!" but sooner or later you are beaten and you talk. And you need to talk! The only way you can find some scraps of information to feed your brain on is by talking. And the only ones who will talk to you are the SBs. So you try and listen to their questions and their responses to you to gather things around you. You are yearning for some knowledge which can give you safety.

So the SBs are in powerful position. They controlled you. You need to talk but you are scared and vulnerable because you do not know how to look at what the police are saying. Is this or that true? What are they planning for me? But you have to rely on them.

This is why those very first days in detention are so crucial for the police. Because soon you find that all you have really done by chatting is to give the police even more than they had when they take you in. This is a terrible thing to realise. Then you are finished.

I wish we had known more about this before we went inside. We were unprepared. And I think we believed that the cops would play by the old rules. While some of us had previous convictions for political offences, like going into 'Europeans Only' facilities, most of us had no previous convictions. I had been in jail in India, but that was a different story. Most of us had only really met up with the police on the streets during demonstrations, not inside jails under interrogation. The new era really only came with the stiff banning orders they had handed out earlier in the year.

But we also had some toughies amongst us. People who were struggling at.the bottom parts of life in grey areas in so far as matters of lifestyles were concerned. But a lot of us were just regular guys.

During all this time the only thing I tried to hang on to was that I would only incriminate Bruno. But it never works that easily. I also offered to show the police where the dynamite was.

But then came the 'pointing outs', which the cops were to use vengefully against us during our trial.

The night of the 6th, Steenkamp and Prins took me out. They stopped near Natal 'Varsity and picked up a photographer with a flash camera. Then they drove to Treasure Cove beach where we had buried dynamite. We got out and Prins tells the photographer to stay in the car. They asked me to lead them down. It was a slope and I had to watch my footsteps. I showed them the spot. I could see that it had already been disturbed. A little hollowed out. They asked me to dig. I dug and pulled out the rusty tin. I pulled it out slowly! There was only one stick in this tin. They called the photographer and he took shots of the things.

On the way back Steenkamp was terribly scared of the dynamite so he drove real slowly. We reached Wentworth and Grobbelaar took me to Greenwood Park.

Later Prins and Steenkamp took me to the place in Cato Manor where we had experimented. That evening we went to 115 May Street.

I was talking to the police. I yearned to think about normal personal things and to make contact with my life as I knew it. I spoke to the cops about money, horse racing and things and asked if we could go by to my old place so that I could ask Moodley for some money. Moodley was renting three rooms and a kitchen in the same passage as my old room. I also wanted Moodley to pay the maid who worked for both of us. I needed to do these normal things. As I realised later, it was a silly thing to have done.

There they found some bound copy sequences of *New Age*, volumes of Mao Zedong's writings and some books that MP had given me. Later I found out that a lot of personal things, like photographs of my children, their birth certificates and my cricket photographs had disappeared.

Three days later I had to point out the Victoria Street bridge, where we had blown the line up. They also asked me to show them the Fountain Lane flat near Atlas Garage. They seemed to know all about it already. All this time I was in a balaclava so nobody could see me. Then we went to Wentworth police station.

There Steenkamp told me not to answer any questions from other SBs. It looked like he wanted to take all the credit. This suited me fine! Grobbelaar swore at me when I refused to answer questions and told him why.

On the third day I was taken to 138 May Street. I asked Mrs Rasoolbibi to hand me the box that Bruno had brought. I did this because she was in no way involved in our activities. Besides there was every possibility that Bruno would show the cops. It was better that I did it. The cops put the box in the boot. The next time I saw that box was in court. Then, inside the box was a threading gadget which, along with some four inch pipes, I saw for the first time.

Then I was taken to Wentworth where I made a statement. It was about a page and a quarter long. I said that Bruno had recruited me into *Umkhonto we Sizwe*.

That afternoon sitting in Steenkamp's office I heard screams from down the corridor. It was David Perumal! I told Steenkamp to bring David in. I told Steenkamp that I wanted to tell David to speak the truth. David came in with his face all swollen and crying. I winked at him and told him it would be okay. They took him away but no more screams came. Perumal gave evidence in our trial but it was not that damaging.

Then Prins and Steenkamp did a strange thing. They took me to a place behind the Ropes and Matting factory. They started telling me that I should have followed the Gandhian policy of non-violence. They kept rambling on and I was getting more and more curious about the place where we had parked. Up to today I do not know why they parked there. I had known of NIC members working in Ropes and Matting but none were members of MK.

Later Grobbelaar took me to Dan's shop so that I could collect the tin of aluminium powder. I had told them about it. Grobbelaar left me in the car and went and spoke to Dan who panicked and got flustered. They detained him. His dad was there crying and pleading with the police as they drove us away.

Dan was an NIC member in the Greyville branch who knew nothing of our MK activities so it was imperative for him to be saved a beating. A couple of hundred yards down the road I turned to Dan and asked him whether Siva had been to the shop last Saturday. Dan looked very relieved. He said he thought so, because one day Siva had come and while Dan had been busy elsewhere in the shop, Siva had left and the tin had gone. As I found out later, Siva had taken it to Bruno's girlfriend's place. The police had already picked it up on the Sunday. Dan was okay. He spent three days inside.

Another SB, Erasmus, was told to drive me back to my lockup. We all knew him as a pleasant guy.

"Babenia, it looks like they fucked you up! Your cheeks are all swollen up. You are lucky to go inside the Wentworth building. We from the political section of the Special Branch cannot as we are not from the Sabotage Squad. I had to wait for you outside like a dog to take you to the police station. It's a funny world!"

Thereafter he kept quiet and drove me to Durban North police station. I told him that I was being kept in Greenwood Park police station. He swore at the SBs stupidity and drove me to Greenwood Park police station. There I met Joshua Zulu of Georgedale.

I stayed at Greenwood Park police station for eight more days. On the ninth day the SBs came and took me out of my cell. I had no spare clothes but about eight Rands, which I collected from the station commander. I was put into a van. There were Sunny Singh, Zakhele Mdalose, Phungula and Siva. I only knew Sunny and Siva. Also inside with us were the SBs Nayager and Pat Moodley: the two who were always watching Lodson House and Lakhani Chambers. We were taken to Wentworth and finger-printed and then off to Point Prison and lodged in B section.

Here I spent seventy eight days in solitary. We patiently awaited the day we would be charged.

The End

Real problems started in Point Prison. Real problems. Each of us was on their own, selfish and scared. We had not yet become one.

There was too much dust in the air. You could hardly see yourself.

You sit alone in your cell and you hear the grille opening down the corridor. Then another cell opening and closing, shutting someone else up.

"Who are you?"

Silence. It was terrible.

"Why do you not talk?"

Silence. People were too scared.

In the cell next to mine was Phungula. The cell on the other side of me was vacant. In the next cell down was David Ndawonde. Across the corridor from me was Sunny Singh and on either side of him, Mdalose and Simelane. We were all in it together but I only knew David, Mdalose, Simelane and Phungula by face. No one really knows who the others are, what you have said and whether you are already an *impimpi*. It was terrible. You could talk as much as you wanted. There were no cops to stop you. But no one spoke because we did not trust each other. When David Ndawonde came in he would not answer any of us.

Later they brought Billy from A section into the vacant cell next to mine. I do not know why. Possibly because they did not want Billy to be close to Ebbie. During exercise time when the cell doors were left open, Billy would often walk around and look into my cell.

When you get out into the sun for exercise time you can at least see who were in the other cells. But that does not help much. We would just sit quietly by ourselves smoking. At least they allowed us to take our tobacco outside. At Point Prison the warders never raided us. I had a good stash under my toilet pan.

During exercise time on the second morning Siva wanted to know from me what statement I had made to the SBs! I told him, but he jumped the gun and said I should have denied saying that the stuff they found at my place was mine. I got angry and shouted that if he had only kept his appointment nothing would have been found. But he kept on at me.

This went on for days. One day Phungula got very angry with Siva and told him to shut up and stop making life miserable for the others. Comrades became depressed with all this loose talk and doubting. Things became even worse when David Ndawonde came because Siva started talking about me to David.

David started looking at me with suspicion. He could not keep it bottled up and he eventually came out asking me why I did not deny that the materials were mine? I got heated and told David all about Siva's nonsense. I was angry, so David kept quiet.

'Zed' and George Naicker were really the only ones above playing funny games. However looking back I can say that there were things happening to all of us during our detention which nobody can fully understand. It was horrible.

After that it slowly became a habit of mine to go out late for exercise and to be the first one to return to the cells. I wanted to get away from Siva! In the very tense atmosphere we were loosing our senses. You start thinking about what the SBs said and start believing them. This even though you know that they are your enemy!

"Babenia they used you!" "You were a fool to believe their sincerity!"

In an encouraging atmosphere you will not have these doubts. Then comrades can encourage each other, talk about all the mistakes and agree to face the future together.

But the situation was exactly the reverse. I often stood on my cistern, looking outside. I could see seagulls and the sea. I started hating everything and everybody.

But at times I would watch the ants crawling and try to count them. One day I saw a crumb of bread lathered in jam floating in the pan with the ants trying to retrieve it. All of a sudden I started laughing loudly! Then the next moment I felt guilty. The ants were my friends. My only friends in that six by three foot cell! I slowly got the piece of crumb out and placed it in a corner where some ants were running around. I helped some of the others out of the cistern and watched as they carried the crumb away.

From then onwards I would always break up some bread into very small pieces so that they would not have to struggle too hard and watch as my companions went about their business.

A day or two later while lying down I started thinking about my six-year-old son. In my days of freedom his mother used to bring him and my daughter around to visit me. One day I sent him to the shop to buy some sweets. He strolled back in after about twenty minutes. I was already dressed and waiting to go and teach. I lost my head and smacked him on his legs. He pissed himself wet! This incident came into clear relief in my mind and I deeply regretted my behaviour.

It did not help! I found that I could not breathe air into my lungs and I was sweating. I started banging on the cell door. Sunny asked me what was wrong. I told him and he started banging on his door as well. The head warder came and Sunny told him I was ill.

Soon the district surgeon came, took my blood pressure, pulse and temperature. He said that I should not worry and to take things easy! He told me that he was going to give me something special to take every night before bed. He told the head warder to make sure I took a pill each night. I felt relieved!

I do not know how to describe this syndrome! The only way I can is to describe it as a rejection of cell mates and an acceptance of the enemy. You get caught between accepting and rejecting. Warders are told not to converse with ninety day detainees. One would like to talk to them but the law stops you! I needed a special letter. That is what I asked for. After about five days a warder brought it to me.

In the cell I sat and planned my next move. I had my passport at Iqbal's place. The only thing I wanted was to get out and leave the country. I knew that at times like this my brother would help with money.

On the 26th of August 1963 I sat and wrote to John Vorster, the Minister of Justice. I said that I had pointed out certain places to the police and was willing to help giving other evidence. The head warder took my letter and gave it to Prins. That was that.

I felt relieved. I needed to get out of that wretched cell and away from Siva! How can you deny something that is in your room? That bloody idiot!

This was a political miscalculation and a cowardly act. My senses were out of control but deep down I knew I could probably never do it.

I never knew whether my letter was ever sent. Looking back I can see that it never was. At the time I fretted about this. I started to write a little note to the SBs. On the back of a *Du Maurier* cigarette box, I asked them about my clothes in the SACTU offices, about my racing winnings; only a couple of Rands that I had left in the NIC offices when I had been detained, if my house was open, for some fiction or cowboy books, and if I could be tried under the Explosives Act and be paid by the police. And if they had sent my letter to the Minister. I gave the note to Wessels.

I gave them three names: Ronnie, Ebbie and Siva.

Another Past

But this is all wrong. All I do really know about that little cigarette box are three things. This is for certain. I did write it. Then, that someone tore off a small piece at the bottom. By the time it arrived in court there were important things torn off. What I do not know. Now, it doesn't make sense because there was something else written there. I didn't tear it. Who tore this I do not know. Then, the damn thing did get into the SBs hands and so it went to court. While Combrink embarrassed me about it in court, there was nothing on it that they could actually use. It was useless, apart from humiliating me.

We were going fucking nuts in solitary. If I try and look back over the whole thing I think that it was a note that I wrote to try and order things in my own mind. To clarify things. Whether I intended to actually give it to the SBs or whether I just needed it for my own head I cannot say. I still do not know if I actually did give it to them.

To me the word Ronnie was because I wanted to know if Ronnie was in detention. I needed to know this. That first day of detention, Grobbler asks one of the SBs, "What about Ronnie?" and another says "Don't worry about him. He is my baby!"

Ebbie. I wanted to know if Ebbie still had a key for my flat. You see I had a calendar hanging in my room. Behind it I had pinned a small note. About ten or twelve lines. I wrote these before my detention. I didn't know what I was doing. But I knew I was going inside. Rasoolbibi was meant to take my furniture away when I was detained. The police never said anything about this note. I wanted to know where it was. I think.

Ebbie might come back and pick it up. And Ebrahim and I had keys for the house. Ebbie was with me in B section. And I wanted to know if they had gone and planted things at my place.

And Siva, I wanted out of that damn cell and into A section.

Why did I write it? I was going nuts. And it is so long ago I cannot remember. So now these are things that torture us. You get that? And if we had sane people living with us, like Sunny, no problem.

Like Sunny. We used to transfer, you know, handmade bread my sister-in-law used to send my niece. Sunny, at least he was detained three days after me. The bugger was still running around. He says "Look we can't go, you can, you are the niece." After two days they start sending me the food.

When the cops come and give me the food, they give me the name of the person who gives it. They don't let the *laaitie* in. So then I say I have some clothes. I had some underwear and things like that. I managed to give, amongst my dirty clothes, a handkerchief full of blood to be given to them. I don't know if they got it. It is too late now. Far too late. Whether the SBs took it or not I don't know.

Back to the End

On October the 21st the cell doors started clanking open and all of us were taken to a large hall. We heard new voices. They had nineteen of us.

Comrade George Naicker said,

"This is it."

And he was right.

From the hall the SBs took us, one by one, into an office to be formally charged.

In the hall waiting our turn we started embracing one another and joking. It was now that we finally became one. Through all our time in detention we had not really trusted each other. We simply did not know enough. Now with us all together we were strong. My letter to Vorster meant absolutely nothing to me now.

"Hey, George! You silly fool, we thought that you were gone to the Soviet Union!"

"Aye, when were you picked up?"

"We thought that you comrades were out of the country."

"I was arrested in September."

"Aye, comrades, they knocked the shit out of us."

Though we were being charged we were happy to meet as cadres. Not everyone knew everyone. Questions and answers drowned each other.

"Aye, Duma where were you kept?"

"George, we thought you were in Moscow! Aye, where is Bruno? Is he going to be a state witness?"

"I was locked up in Sydenham! It was hell there!"

"Where is Steven Mtshali? David Perumal is not here! Was he released?

"Are any more joining us?"

"No! No one else is joining us. They have become Tshombes."

"Where is Coetzee?"

When my turn came Prins and Steenkamp ask me who I wanted as my defence attorney. I said Rowley. Of course! Then Prins says that the Attorney General had decided not to use me, but that they could arrange for me to be tried separately and that they could arrange for a lawyer. They said maybe I would get a suspended sentence.

I knew what was going on. My hallucinations had gone and I was seeing clearly. All the dust had settled. They would try me first, throw the book at me, get everything down in the court record, convict me and then use all the evidence presented in my trial seen as legal fact to be used against the others later. They were playing for very big stakes and using me completely. I told them to fuck off.

They were angry that their little ruse had failed. That is when they got very pissed off and told me that they were going to throw the book at me. Which is what they did.

Eighteen of us wanted Rowley Arenstein to be instructed to represent. Siva Pillay wanted G S Naidu.

To our surprise Rowley was already there. As soon as the Special Branch left, Rowley asked the jailer, Mr Horne, if he could see us. He met each of us, encouraged us and said that he would be the instructing attorney, with Hassan Mall and M D Naidoo as defence council. All were Party members. We felt good. And Rowley gave us each a box with sandwiches, cigarettes and *bhajia*. Each of us took our box to the exercise yard and for the first time I ate a good meal.

Then we were locked up. We carried on talking excitedly and making a din. That night, Mdlalose's voice came through. *"Mayibuye, Mayibuye, Mayibuye i-Afrika."* The din died down and all started to sing. In all our trials and tribulations we had become one. This was the oneness that we always clamoured for in our struggle.

Soon the state placed another obstacle in our way. They decided to hold the court case in Pietermaritzburg. This was so that our chosen defence team, and particularly Rowley, then banned and restricted to the Durban magisterial area, could not be with us. This put us in an awkward position as we had full confidence in our defence team. In protest, all the accused decided to go on a hundred hour fast. Telegrams were sent to John Vorster and they were ignored. The Nats were fond of ignoring lots of things.

With bitterness we went into the trial to hear dozens of state witnesses speak half-truth and lies.

Rowley nevertheless did have a good influence over the court proceedings. It was on his advice that Mr Gurvitz and Mr Thirion from Johannesburg were selected as our defence council. Thirion, who was a good United Party supporter, had worked with Colin Rees in the Attorney General's office. Both were public prosecutors. Rees and Thirion had never got on and, as well, Rees had been promoted over Thirion's head. Thirion then set up his own practise. He really proved his mettle in the battle of wits with Rees. He was our ace council. Andrew Wilson was a junior council with Thumba Pillay the instructing attorney.

We sang freedom songs all the way to the College Road Supreme Court. Sympathetic lawyers told us that we were lucky to have the Judge President of Natal, Justice Milne presiding over our case. We would get a fair trial.

We stand up when the Judge comes in with his two assessors, Mr P C Tweedie and Mr A J Turton, Natal's Chief Bantu Commissioner. The case goes down in the law books as *'The State vs Ebrahim Ismail and Others'*. The Registrar, a Miss de Villiers reads out the indictment. We are being charged for conspiracy, being members of a banned organisation and carrying on its activities, twenty seven counts of sabotage and one for being in possession of explosives. They spelt some of our names wrong. The twenty eight counts as read into the record were:

COUNT 1 alleges that on October 14, 1962, between Durban and Verulam E Ismail, G Singh and N Babenia placed an explosive and/or inflammable substance in a railway passenger coach.

COUNT 2 alleges that on October 14, 1962, at Georgedale, M B Nkosi, M Meyiwa, J T Zulu and Z Mdlalose cut railway signal wires and/or signal cables.

COUNT 3 alleges that on October 14, 1962, at Madelene Building, Durban, R Kasrils placed and ignited an incendiary bomb against the door of an office in Madelene Building.

COUNT 4 alleges that on October 14, 1962, in Stanger Street, Durban, accused unknown to the prosecutor placed and ignited an incendiary bomb against the door of the Bantu Commissioner's Office.

COUNT 5 alleges that on October 14, 1962, at Kwa Mashu, Durban, R Mkwanazi and A Duma placed an incendiary bomb at the Bantu Administration Offices.

COUNT 6 alleges that on October 17, 1962, at Kwa Mashu, J Mpanza, R Mkwanzi, A Duma and R Mpanga placed and ignited an incendiary bomb under the offices of the Superintendent, Kwa Mashu.

COUNT 7 alleges that on November 1, 1962, at New Germany, B Mtolo, G Naicker, B Nair and R Kasrils affixed and detonated charges of dynamite to a line pylon.

COUNT 8 alleges that on November 1, 1962, at Sarnia, G Naicker, B Nair and R Kasrils affixed and detonated charges of dynamite to a power transmission line pylon.

COUNT 9 alleges that on November 1, 1962, at Montclair, B Nair, E Ismail, K Moonsamy, G Naicker and R Kasrils affixed and detonated charges of dynamite to a power transmission line pylon.

COUNT 10 alleges that on November 19, 1962, between Cliffdale and Ntshongweni Station, B Mtolo affixed and detonated charges of dynamite to a power transmission carrier.

COUNT 11 alleges that on December 5, 1962, at Umlazi Bridge K Moonsamy, K Doorsamy, and R Kistensamy affixed and detonated charges of dynamite to a power transmission line carrier.

COUNT 12 alleges that on December 9, 1962, at Alice Street, Durban, E Ismail and G Singh placed and detonated charges of dynamite at the office of Mr Kajee.

COUNT 13 alleges that on December 9, 1962, between Cliffdale and Hammersdale, M B Nkosi, Z Mdlalose, J T Zulu, T Meyiwa and B Mtolo affixed and detonated charges of dynamite to the legs of a power transmission line pylon on both sides of the railway line.

COUNT 14 alleges that on December 12, 1962, at Kwa Mashu, B Mtolo, N Babenia, R Kasrils and B Nair placed and ignited an explosive and/or inflammable substance (pipe bomb) in the bedroom window of C Mbutho.

COUNT 15 alleges that on December 12, 1962, at Kwa Mashu, B Mtolo, N Babenia, R Kasrils and B Nair placed and ignited a pipe bomb in the window of a room of W Dhladla.

COUNT 16 alleges that on December 12, 1962, at Kwa Mashu, B Mtolo, N Babenia, R Kasrils and B Nair placed and ignited a pipe bomb in the window of a room of L Makwaza.

COUNT 17 alleges that on December 23, 1962, in West Street, Durban, R Kasrils and N Babenia inserted and ignited a pipe bomb into the airmail letter box of the Main Post Office.

COUNT 18 alleges that on December 23, 1962, at Victoria Embankment, Durban, E Ismail affixed a pipe bomb on to a communication cable.

COUNT 19 alleges that on January 8, 1963, between Durban and Port Shepstone, South of Karridene, R Kasrils, A Duma and B Mtolo affixed and detonated charges of dynamite to a railway line.

COUNT 20 alleges that on January 11, 1963, at Durban, N Babenia placed a pipe bomb in the letter box of the Central Mercantile Corporation and/or Nichol Square Holdings (Pty) Ltd.

COUNT 21 alleges that on January 15, 1963, at Montclair, K Moonsamy, K Doorsamy and R Kistensamy placed and detonated charges of dynamite in the telephone communications cable chamber.

COUNT 22 alleges that on January 18, 1963, at Durban, M S Mapumulo placed charges of dynamite and/or some other explosive and/or inflammable substances at the building of

Drakensberg Pers Ltd., and ignited and/or detonated the said charges.

COUNT 23 alleges that on January 2, 1963, at Greenwood Park, Durban, R Mkwanazi and J Mpanza sawed off three wooden telephone standards.

COUNT 24 alleges that on February 10, 1963, at the Point Durban, J Mpanza placed a pipe bomb in a Durban Corporation beerhall.

COUNT 25 alleges that on March 21, 1963, in Durban, at Victoria Street Bridge, E Ismail, G Singh and N Babenia affixed and detonated charges of dynamite to the railway lines and cables.

COUNT 26 alleges that on April 7, 1963, at Durban, M Mkwanazi and M S Mapumulo prepared and threw explosives and/or inflammable substances incendiary bomb on a moving passenger train near Duffs Road Station.

COUNT 27 alleges that on June 21, 1963, at Durban, A Duma, M S Mapumulo and M D Mkhize affixed and detonated charges of dynamite to a signal control box near Duffs Road Railway line.

COUNT 28 alleges that during the same period in pursuance of a common purpose, the accused unlawfully possessed explosives— 2,500 ft. of cordtex, 270 cartridges of dynamite, a quantity of fuse, a quantity of detonators and a quantity of potassium chloride—in or on various premises.

The state decided that we were to have a summary trial with no preliminary investigation. And they refused to provide our defence team with a detailed outline of the cases against us.

One of the main issues was that of common purpose in association. And quite what was this common purpose? Here the state tried to cover themselves by framing a set of alternative charges. These were worded so broadly that if they could not pin us down on the main charges, then they would nail us on these. One of these alternative charges said something like we had 'incited, instigated, aided, commanded and procured' a whole lot of things in 'pursuance of a common purpose'.

When they did this we knew we were in for a big ride. However only George Naicker and I were actually convicted under the alternative charges. This I have never understood.

In one of the other additional counts they tried to name this organisation to which we belonged. They kept all their options open by listing a whole list of possible names. Like the 'Regional Command of MK', 'Natal Regional Council', 'Regional Council of MK', 'Spear of the Nation', 'The Sabotage' and so on. It was ridiculous.

In jail Billy, Kisten, Ragoowan and myself were in a cell together. They were still separating the Africans and the Indians. Just for jokes we called ourselves the 'High Command.' The other chaps would chat away and then say "And what does the High Command say to this?" It was good stuff; a harmless absurdity. But once we were in the 'High Command' there were no problems with me and them.

It was tough and bizarre at Pietermaritzburg. The warder 'Poison' would open the big door with the grille to the hanging chamber. We were in the death cells. And he would show us the trap-door and the rope. He said the last time they hung someone there was in the twenties.

We all pleaded not guilty.

On Monday when we went to court we found a young lady stenographer who was pleasant with us and greeted us when we were brought into the court. Someone must have noticed the old lady's antics and fired her.

Steenkamp, who was in charge of our investigations was really shitting himself. He had an illusion that MK would get him. Whenever a chair squeaked Steenkamp quickly looked back. Thirion was always moving about giving Steenkamp jitters. It amused us a lot.

There was also much hilarity in court when Steven told of the room above the Atlas Garage in Alice Street. This was a room used by comrades for liaisons with girlfriends. Steven is standing there telling the judge where people would put the condoms after finishing their business. "What business?" asks the judge and everyone packs up.

South Africa or England was playing Australia in Australia. I was very interested in the scores and I usually asked a defence team lawyer to get the score from the *Natal Mercury* reporter. He got so used to my request that he would pass the score to the defence to pass it on to me.

The fun was best when the state called *Khosan* Kajee to give evidence on the dynamite attack of his office in Alice Street. He rattled away and said that MK often made threatening calls to him. When asked why by the prosecution, he said that he was called a 'S...T...O...O...G...E.' The way he dragged the last word made me laugh out aloud. I laughed so loud that the whole court could hear it and the funniest part was that I could not stop. The court orderly

came and told me that if I do not stop, I would be charged for
contempt of court. With tears in my eyes I gagged my mouth with
my handkerchief. It was the only way I could stop. Gurwitz also
rode into Kajee.

David Perumal looked very scared when he gave evidence
against us for the state. He only had around Standard Six education
and when we came to trial David was only nineteen years old. In
court you could hardly hear what he was trying to say.

And then of course good old Ronnie. Ronnie's name was mentioned so many times. The judge would always ask the prosecution,
very dryly, "Is he the bird that flew?" I think he found it funny.
Ronnie was in Dar-es-Salaam.

It was also funny when Combrink wanted to bring some dynamite into the court. He asks Milne's permission. Milne looks startled
and asks why he needs permission. Combrink tells him it is an
explosive. Milne asks if it might go off in his court because he would
not be happy with that. Combrink says they will handle it carefully.
After they had finished proudly showing the stuff off, Combrink
and Milne decide that these exhibits should be kept locked away in
a cell. Milne asks Gurwitz if he has any objection to this!

But it could get quite tense. Kisten Moonsamy's father, who was
about ninety-five with failing eyesight, was called by the state to
identify certain exhibits: tools. After that the state asked him to point
out his son. He told the court that from the witness-box he could
only see blurs. He was told to leave the witness-box and point out
his son. The old man left the witness-stand and came towards us. He
peered at Ebrahim and shook his head, then at Sunny and shook his
head, then me and Billy. When he came to Kisten, he peered and
said that he was his *kanna*. Kisten lost his head.

"'Ginger' Grobbelaar! You bastard! I will get you! You hear that! I will get
you even if I get twenty years!"

The court went silent. I patted Kisten and said "Don't worry Zed!
I am with you!" This was the only way to calm Kisten. There were
tears in his eyes. During lunch break he said the same thing to the
SB Nayagar.

Many years later, just before Kisten was released we heard that
Ginger had shot himself. Nayagar had also died.

M P Naicker's brother Coetzee gave evidence for the state. He
came in holding his stomach and started lying that I was present at
two MK Technical Committee meetings at Botanic Gardens. The
damn fellow lied and instead of pointing to Kisten, who he knew
had been there, he pointed at me. He also made a fool of himself
when he said that he was a leftist in the Natal Indian Youth

Congress and admitted that he was as fascinated by politics as Americans were by sport. Coetzee also had a tough time saying why he took a cheque and cashed it into his own account when it was not meant for him. He was unemployed at the time. There was something fishy about that cheque.

Bruno's evidence was also all tangled lies and it was thrown out. A lot of the things he said about me were lies.

But we could not break Solomon Mbanjwa. But he also lied. Like about me. He said he only knew me as an ordinary NIC organiser. That was a lie. We had had dealings as MK cadres!

M H Wessels never lied.

When Steven Mtshali gave his evidence for the state, the fellow described how I put the kettle water on the hot plate and when it boiled how I put the tea leaves in the kettle and then added milk. And how I used the strainer to pour the tea and every minute detail of my movements at my North Street home. I know I like tea but it was bizzare. To every answer, he added, *"Yebo Nkosi!"*[14] The old lady stenographer encouraged him by nodding her head.

When Schoon gave evidence about me he got into trouble from Milne. Schoon had not given me any receipts for the things he took from my rooms. And their documents listing what they found at which places were all incorrectly marked. But the biggest thing was that the lists of powders, capsules, tools and things were so long. I did not have that much stuff. The cops have to have added to the evidence. They said they found this big carton full of things at my old place in May Street. They may have found some odd things there but by the time I was arrested I had taken most of the stuff to North Street. I should never have asked them to take me to Moodley's for that money. I thought they were being kind! They planted me! I only realised much later why I think they did this.

After the state led a lot of evidence, the 'pointings out' and things, there was then a trial within a trial over whether to admit the statements that twelve of us had made to the cops. The cops swore under oath that we had all made these things under sound mind and sober senses! They were allowed.

Joffe, a progressive lawyer from Johannesburg who was representing the Rivonia trialists came down to Pietermaritzburg and spoke to Rowley. Some of us who were in it up to our necks should plead guilty and thus give the chance for others to get off. Rowley told Thumba Pillay, who contacted our defence team. This was in

---

[14] Zulu, "Yes, my King! (Or chief)."

early 1964. The cops had lots of evidence and our defence team had to change tactics anyway.

Six of us had to change our pleas.

At this stage in the trial it is normal for the defence to assess the State's case and thus tender application for discharge. Usually, applications for discharge would be made first and then any changed pleas would be tendered. Gurwitz suggested that for convenience, the defence would propose to tender the changed pleas first and then make the applications for discharge. That is how we pleaded guilty.

Ebrahim admitted guilt on four counts, Billy to fourteen, Riot for three and Comrade Msizeni Mapumulo on two. Naicker pleaded guilty for being in possession of explosives. I admitted guilt on five counts: 1, 17, 20, 25 and 28.

Gurwitz came to me and said that the prosecution was not satisfied with my plea of guilty to five counts. I told Gurwitz no ways more. He just looked at me. So I went to Thirion and he understood. I told Thirion that the cops can go to fucking hell.

Milne then asks Gurwitz if, because of the serious nature of the charges, it would be proper for the court to just accept these changed pleas. Gurwitz replied that even in spite of the fact that this was a summary trial he thought it would be fine to accept the pleas. Milne said no, the State would still have to prove its cases.

On the 7th of February Gurwitz applied for the discharge of two comrades, Kirsten Doorsamy and Ragoowan Kistensamy and the dropping of some charges against four or five others. The State then abandoned its case against Ragoowan. He was discharged.

Then Rees announces that he is not happy about my pleas. The state intended to push for my conviction on additional charges. It was amazing. He read out the list of these other charges. Counts 3, 4, 5, 6, 7, 8, 9, 10, 11, 12, 13, 14, 15, 16, 18, 24 and 27! Twenty two charges in all! I can laugh about it now!

I now know why the bastards wanted me so badly.

I had a tough time. I had left myself wide open. Combrink wanted to rub it in. I got fucking cross with him while I was in the witness-box. I was making a blue by doing this! And he got angry with me. There was too much pressure and I did not answer things like I should have.

But I stuck to my story that Eleanor Anderson had shown me the explosives and told me to take the tin with more than a hundred or so sticks of dynamite and rebury them. This so that if anyone who had known where they were was picked up, they could not take the police to the spot. I said that Eleanor asked me to tell Absolom Duma where I reburied the stuff. However I had failed to contact

Duma and had instead told Siva where the stuff was. This was all lies. Completely! What I was wanting to do was to get Siva out of the mess that he had created himself. I was taking on the task that had actually been allotted to Siva. If that had come out it would have meant not only that Siva was an MK member, but that he was part of the restructured MK. In my evidence I always denied that Siva was an MK member.

We rehearsed this whole fabrication: Billy, myself and Siva. We never told our lawyers about this. But Siva was never able to follow what I was saying. After repeating things several times he kept on contradicting what I was to say. Then Billy decided that Siva should not go into the witness-box and told me that I must try my best to get him out.

The gist of my line was to play my role up and to show how undisciplined I was. When Combrink cross-examined me he went for me and made me look really foolish. Just because I had failed to contact Absolom, I asked a non-member of *Umkhonto we Sizwe* to do something and thereby I jeopardised the whole of our operations. But what he really wanted was for me to say that Siva was a member. That I never did. He also humiliated me about the letter thing.

A Different Story

For a long time I have remembered parts of this story, which it certainly was, as if it really happened.

About five days before my arrest Eleanor Anderson took me out to the Bluff and showed me where our tins of dynamite were buried. There were two tins. One was rusty and only had one stick of dynamite left in it. The other tin was heavy and shiny with lots of dynamite in it. Over a hundred sticks of the damn stuff. Ronnie wanted me to bury this tin in another place nearby. Next to the 'zig zag' tree. I had to show Absalom Duma where it was buried. The nearly empty tin was left in its original hole.

I did see Siva on the Sunday, sitting in a cafe in Grey Street. He refused to answer my questions. All he did was to start smiling. He said he would come by the NIC offices early the next morning, a Monday. But I did take him out to the Bluff and showed him where the big stash of dynamite was kept. I told him to tell Duma where it was.

I was feeling all alone and sometimes quite panicky. I had lots of mixed feelings. I was cross with Ebbie for pushing me out. But that Eleanor should come to me and give me the dynamite task? That meant Ronnie trusted me! On that Thursday there were only two people in the whole world who knew where our only main supply of dynamite was.

By this time about half of our cadres were inside. But no key people yet. Ronnie knew something would happen soon. So he was restructuring to avoid the possibility of everything falling apart if someone coughed to the police. In fact Eleanor actually said this to me out on the beach. Someone who knew where it had been buried could get taken in, break and the police could play around with them. Up until that time I did not know where the dynamite had been hidden.

I was feeling excluded and bitter but here I was right at the centre of it! Maybe it was too much for me. Maybe I wanted out. I did not contact Duma. And I was worried that I could get taken in soon. So I thought let Siva get the message to Duma. They knew each other and stayed close by to each other and Siva was in the same cell as me.

This was a mistake. It certainly was an ill-disciplined move on my part.

But it never happened like that. I remembered it so because I said some of these things during the trial.

Back to the Trial

Part of our defence case rested on trying to throw holes in the thing about common purpose. So Thirion and Wilson stress the idea of adventurism. So when Curnick takes the stand Wilson leads him on about how the Regional Command would have to discipline Ronnie for letting the cells get out of hand and do things which overstepped the mark. Ronnie was out so that was okay. Curnick tried his best.

There was this funny side to this ploy. Thirion goes on and on about whether the Regional Command gave specific instructions and if they ever knew how operations had gone. At one point he asks Curnick if he ever heard a report back on the success or otherwise of count 21. That was the dynamiting of the telephone sub-station at Montclair. Milne breaks in, saying that surely we all know it was successful! Thirion says no, that is not the point. We must find out what Curnick knows!

This thing about sub-stations was funny. When the chaps used to go the Fountain Lane, they used to call the woman who they have there 'sub-stations'.

The lynch pin in our operations was Ronnie. He was the comrade between the Regional Command and the cells. If the cops had got Ronnie then we would have really been in shit.

So for the cops to prove their case there were only two other people who were crucial. Bruno, as the head of the Technical Committee. But by now Bruno was theirs. And so, . . . me, because I was on the Technical Committee. If they could get me on all those charges then they could show conspiracy. They needed me guilty on the lot.

During my detention I had fucked up. They never wanted me as a state witness. They had Bruno. They needed me in the dock. That is why, even when they charged me they played around with me, suggesting a separation of trials. They were trying to entice me. What would have actually happened was that they would have flung the book at me and got all the evidence of how bombs and things were distributed throughout the cells. Then they would get the others later. And they needed to plant lots of stuff on me so that it would show how organised and concerted we were.

And they hated my guts. I had messed them around. They were furious about my not showing them the big stash of dynamite. They questioned me at length about this. They really thought I knew where it was and had deceived them.

Anyway it is not important now. There is a lot that happens in these circumstances and it is a long time ago. We were in it up to our necks and they got us. The struggle does not happen cleanly and according to order. It is always messy and brutal. So be it. That was that. But they spelt my name wrong. It was not me, but I was going to sit.

Judgment Day

The trial continued for fifty six days and eighteen of us were found guilty and sentenced thus:

EBRAHIM ISMAIL: Counts 1, 9, 12, 18, 25 and 27 of the main charge. Sentence: 15 years.

GIRJA SINGH: Counts 1, 12 and 25 of the main charge. Sentence: 10 years.

NATVARIAL BABENIA: Counts 1, 17, 20, 25 and 28 of the main charge and counts 3, 4, 5, 7, 8 and 9 of the second alternative charge. Sentence: 16 years.

BILLY NAIR: Counts 2, 3, 4, 5, 6, 7, 8, 9, 11, 12, 21, 25, 26, 27 and 28 of the main charge. Sentence: 20 years.

KISTEN MOONSAMY: Counts 9, 11 and 21 of the main charge. Sentence: 14 years.

GEORGE NAICKER: Count 28 of the main charge and counts 7, 8 and 9 of the second alternative charge. Sentence: 14 years.

KISTEN DOORSAMY: Counts 11 and 21 of the main charge. Sentence: 12 years.

CURNICK NDLOVU: As for accused no. 4. Sentence: 20 years.

RIOT MKWANAZI: Counts 5, 6, 23 and 26 of the main charge. Sentence: 10 years.

ALFRED DUMA: Counts 5, 6 and 27 of the main charge. Sentence: 10 years.

MSIZENI SHADRACK MAPUMULO: Counts 22, 26 and 27 of the main charge. Sentence: 10 years.

MFANYANA BERNARD NKOSI: Count 13 of the main charge. Sentence: 10 years.

ZAKELA MDLALOSE: Counts 2 and 13 of the main charge. Sentence: 10 years.

MATTHEWS MEYIYA: Count 13 of the main charge. Sentence: 8 years.

JOSHUA TEMBINKOSI ZULU: Count 13 of the main charge. Sentence: 8 years.

MDINGENI DAVID MKIZE: Count 27 of the main charge. Sentence: 5 years.

DAVID NDAWONDE: Count 28 of the main charge. Sentence: 8 years.

SIVA PILLAY: Count 28 of the main charge. Sentence: 8 years.

For years and years I have often looked back on this period. It was such a short time really. It was just a little over two years. Sadly my feelings for this pivotal point in my life have often been ones of betrayal and shame. It is only now that I look back with pride. We did change South African politics for the better.

We were soon on off to Robben Island. The day we were sentenced was my birthday. What a cruel present!

PART THREE

CAST IN STONE IN A HELL HOLE

Robben Island, 1964–1980

Robben Island
certificates

ROBBEN ISLAND

Institute Education

of

Council Literary Award

First Prize

This Certificate is awarded to

N. BABENIA

having presented the most outstanding Short Story

At the Open Level of the

1974 Literary Competition

_____
Chairman of Adjudication Panel 1974

_____
B. Sc., S.T.D. (Dip't level), Hons Esc., B.A. (S.A)
CHAIRMAN OF COUNCIL

24th March, 1974
DATE

Robben Island Academy Of Fine Arts

Presents this

Certificate to

N. BABENIA

having presented work ranked

POSITION 2 (RIVER SCENE)

at

The exhibition held on 28th June, 1973.

ADJUDICATORS

1. _____
2. _____
3. _____

_____
CHAIRMAN

Veterans of Umkhonto we Sizwe presented to the organisation's last rally, Curries Fountain, 16 December 1993 *Left to right:* N. Babenia, M. Meyiwa, Miss M. Mfusi, B. Ngcobo, M. Mzimela, R. Mkhwanazi, Cuno, P. Kumalo, Z. Mdalalose (Associated Press and Daily News)

Leeukop Prison

The day we were convicted the Boers declared war on us. They wanted to break us and then fight us.

Having received our sentences, we left the courtroom and returned to prison, now for the first time as convicted prisoners. We got our prison cards and were taken to our new empty cells. All our food rations, which we had received from well wishers during the trial had already been taken away. We were now *bandiete*.

That afternoon the chief warder comes around with Sgt 'Poison', who issued us with new clothes but all the sizes were out. George Naicker, a shorty, get some pants that reached up to his chest. Later 'Dip' would try to alter them.

I lay down that night with thoughts flooding past. "We had really shocked the Boers." "They had become scared of us." "Eleanor knew the SBs addresses, she would get them!" "Shit! The stuff we lost to the cops . . . detonators, dynamite, fuses. . .!"

I thought of the Technical Committee and Bruno's inefficiency. How Ronnie had come to me fuming. How key Ronnie became and how he could play funny games with us! Such a passion for life! How I showed them how to make a pipe bomb!

I thought of the risks we had taken. We were just lucky that we lost no one and killed nobody. I thought of the judge remarking on how Curnick seemed to be an efficient regional commander.

Maybe it was not so bad. With a smile I dozed off.

Early the next morning we learnt that we were off to the place *New Age* had told us so much about. Dejected, the eighteen of us were put into leg-irons and handcuffs, shoved into a big truck and, with an SB car behind us, we set off for Leeukop Prison.

All politicals had first to be processed at Leeukop before being sent off, often for forever, to the Island. Leeukop was to be our first rite of passage.

We stopped off at Ladysmith Prison for lunch. There we saw 'Mr No' again, climbing out of the SBs car. At Point Prison he was the bloke who came around to ask if we have any complaints. He only ever had one retort, "Nee!" Silly fool. He got such satisfaction from saying 'No!' Now, it seemed as if he did not want to let us go.

Near Heidelberg Prison, the SBs car passed us. Curnick managed to spot Solomon Mbanjwa sitting on the back seat. Solly had given evidence against us and now who was he going to rat on now?

At Leeukop that evening we were herded out of the van like cattle and the warders' howling started. It never really stopped for years and years. Amidst the shouts and cracks, our leg-irons and cuffs came off, we got some cold porridge and then were locked in a big cell smelling of old blankets. We were exhausted. Nobody said anything. We all needed to be alone. What could we have said?

Next day, during the breakfast running, spilling, shouting, beating and eating, one of the kitchen cleaners warned us of the marathon we were to run. We were all quiet. Horror's advance tormented us! There was no way out of having to undergo the rituals to suppress us into *bandiete*.

After breakfast we had to exchange all our new clothes for ill-fitting sets of old smelly ones. We were up against a wall. A chief warder wanted to know who the boxer was. We all kept quiet. He went to Sunny Singh and started to handle him. We all shuffled around and looked down. He thought we were threatening and moved away, eyeing us all. The rules were not yet in place.

Stupid bastard, he was totally misinformed! He was actually looking for Riot Mkwanazi, an amateur boxer.

During the Christmas trial recess we had been taken to Durban Central so that we could have access to our relatives. As the trial was being heard *in camera* we could have no chance to see friends whilst the trial was going on. On the day before the recess expired the SBs came early in the morning and wanted to take us back to Pietermaritzburg. I do not know why. Maybe it was to block us from getting our ironed clothes and last parcels. We heard later that there may have been a plan to spring us.

We resisted and refused to come out. Even the chief warder, who had been good to us during the recess could not persuade the SBs. The SBs even refused to allow us to contact Rowley.

So we had to come out. When we saw the warders and the SBs lined up in front of the gate we smelt a rat. The black warders had just come off night duty and they wanted some action too but the chief warder told them to back off. Billy went forward to the grille to speak with the SBs. But then the SBs poured through the open gate with the huge six-footer cop at the front. All hell broke loose. Besides Siva, we all got stuck into them, using hangers, plates and whatever. In all this Riot had got hold of the big cop and held him against the wall while Matthews Meyiwa started flattening him badly.

In all this Curnick shouted to the chief warder that we were willing to come out into the yard. It soon subsided and we were marched to the car park and the vans with doors open waiting. In between the lines of vans, the cops got their revenge, beating us with their batons as we climbed in. I was last, with the other comrades having to pull me in as the cops put lumps on my head. Later that day I fainted and was taken to Grey's Hospital for X-rays.

Clearly news of this little episode had spread amongst the cops who were keen to know who had sunk the six-footer.

But it was hardly the time to savour victory. Later that day we were marched off to see the Prison Board. The head of these five officials was a Lieutenant Colonel. He looked at us with a wicked eye and raved.

"You want to overthrow the Government! You want to bite the hand that feeds you. You want to go for military training! . . . You want to go to Tanzania. . . Egypt and Moscow! . . . You want to come back and ki. . . l. . .l us whites! Now we are going to send you overseas . . . in boats . . . not Tanzania . . . not Egypt . . . not Moscow but to . . . R. . .O. . .B. . .B. . .E. . .N. . . Island . . . and free of charge!"

He raved about whites being a superior race and went on and on. It was all crap to us, oozing out of a foul mouth. We kept our silence and let him rave on. The words meant little to us anyway. It was our silence which kept us quiet. Some months before, even before the trial I suppose, we had lived with courage and dignity. Now, we had not yet found a way of getting our soul spirits back again in our new lives. And we knew what the next ritual was.

Off to the hospital for a medical. But first you must strip and run around the prison yard, faster and faster. . . If you are slow, you are beaten up and called 'Kaffir', 'Charra' or 'Koelie' and 'Boesman'. Warders standing in the four corners of this torture yard hitting us with the leather strap of the baton every time we passed them. And all the time Sergeants Magalies and Khumalo will yell at you to run faster. Running naked, your private parts are flip-flopping between your thighs. The faster you are made to run, the faster they are flip-flopping. As if this humiliation is not enough, you shall hear crude comments like, "kyk die kaffirtjie se groot piel!"[1]

Then we are playing the medical ritual. Naked, in single-file you are to line up facing the wall, touching your toes with wide-stretched legs. There is a criminal prisoner with a substance like jelly made from green soap in a bowl or tin waiting in attendance. A medical orderly puts on surgical gloves. But do not see this. Don't look sideways or you will get beaten. If someone before you screams, do not flinch or try to look. You must wait for your turn, bent, touching your toes.

When your turn comes, the orderly will dip his middle finger in the bowl and shove the finger crudely in the anus and then bend it as if it is a periscope looking for enemy ships at sea. It will be excruciating but do not try and bend your legs or stand up. You will be cracked open. Comrade Duma screamed and look how the batons fell on his head.

---

[1] Afrikaans for 'Look at that little kaffir's big penis!'.

When it is their time, the search party will leave. Quickly, with the finger nearly bent double. A spine-chilling pain runs through the body, your knees buckle with pain and as you collapse the batons will come. Later you will find that you could be bleeding.

Then the District Surgeon told us that we had no ailments, checked our breathing and in no time you are away.

After lunch in the prison yard you will go to reception and receive your prison card. Then you will get an old blade to shave while a convict will use sheep shears to take your hair away.

Then a Lieutenant, a chief warder, two white Sergeants and an African Sergeant, Khumalo again, come. It is time to shower. Try to get clean and remove the sweat, pain and memory. The small *stuk* of soap that never lathers might help you. There will be no towels. You will have to run around the yard and dry yourself. The warders will emerge and the beatings continue. I ran around about five times and then my legs gave in. I was out cold. When I woke up the running had stopped and there was water all around me. It was still only the 2nd of March 1964.

Evening *paka* was called. We ran to the gate and lined up in twos. The warder let us through and you run, five yards behind the comrades in front, for the porridge amidst the howling of Sergeants Magalies and Khumalo. On the run you will have to pick up a plate of porridge, run again and pick a mug and dip it into the churn of *puzamandla* or coffee. If you are slow Magalies or Khumalo will push you from behind and you will go without coffee or even that *puzamandla* mess. And the porridge, which will be on the floor, spilt, is behind you. If you have your food, you must run away fast remembering that it is difficult to balance the hot plate of porridge and a mug of hot liquid. Comrades who have been at Leeukop for a while give lessons to new comers and after a day or two you will manage.

The main thing to remember is that even if you can manage, the whole thing depends upon Magalies and Khumalo. If they do not want you to have your meal they will 'vinnig loop!' you and you will find yourself sharing a comrade's meal.

This was the first time we had seen our other comrades. Someone amongst us pointed out Dennis Brutus. They all saw comrade George loose his coffee and when Sergeant 'Steel Rims', another bastard, pushed me badly, I lost my porridge. I was sad and just walked back to the cell. We were in Cell Seven, which had just been cleaned up for us. We just had bed rolls and blankets and toilet pans.

Later when comrade Jacob Zuma came running by he pushed his plate of porridge to me and also a parcel of tobacco. 'For Curnick' he says. Soon along runs comrade Edward Mkhize who tells Curnick to empty the toilet basin around 6 o'clock that evening.

After food the kitchen staff come and take away the mugs, spoons and plates and you are locked up for the night.

Before the night warders come, we hear a "Hello". It was Jacob. Curnick had cleared the basin. The telephone line was now open. It works very well. You don't need to dial, all you do is speak into the bowl and then put your ear into it to hear the reply.

"Hello comrade!"

It felt good.

Zuma wanted to know about our sentences. Curnick told him that Bruno and Steven had become Tshombes.

Zuma wanted to know about the comrade who had collapsed. My name went through and Zuma advised us to run as slowly as possible because the warders usually make new arrivals do twenty or thirty laps. Comrade Zuma said he was closing the line and would call Curnick again the next day at the same time. He would only ever speak to Curnick.

Same with the kitchen convict when he came the next day with more tobacco. Only ever to Curnick.

Calling again the next night Curnick tells Jacob that the Ladysmith ANC trial had not yet started and that it was only during the last days of our trial that he had heard that they were to appear in Ladysmith and be formally charged. Curnick said that during Christmas recess he had met the Ladysmith comrades: Stephen Dlamini, M P Naicker, George Mbele, Sello, Msizi Dube and others at the Durban Central Prison and that they were in high spirits. They would join us soon.

We all sit quietly as Curnick makes the *zol*. The comrades had become experts in tobacco, to satisfy their craving, and even in getting newspapers. It all came from the common prisoners. Each smoker takes three puffs on the *zol* and passes it on. If there is still anything left after all have had, then it will be decided collectively how many puffs on the *stompie* we can each have a second time round.

At around ten we were all asleep.

Nothing out of the ordinary happened until around the 8th. We came out for exercise and saw quite a number of new faces. They did not look like political prisoners. Curnick managed to find out that they were long term prisoners from a Transvaal prison and were being sent to Robben Island. He added that according to the two leaders, Stephen Phegu and Caxton Mogorosi, life for them in the Transvaal prison became unbearable so they decided to form a political front called National Liberation Front; a front of two organisations. Those who had leanings towards ANC joined the ANC and those who had leanings towards PAC joined the PAC. These two organisations formed the NLF. They wanted to get away, so they decided to hold political lectures and were thus caught as politicos and were being sent to Robben Island. We warned comrade Curnick to be careful of them. He knew already.

Prison by Prison to Robben Island

Long before sunrise on the 10th of March we were woken up and told to 'get ready!'. The guards were in a filthy mood, cross about having to be up so early. The batons were speaking coarsely. One got to sense these things quickly and adapt sharply. And we knew this was the big day. The roll call had fifty one names. C Section was off to the Island. As the present worsened so the future bore down.

In twos, holding onto our meagre belongings, we went to the yard where we got our handcuffs. One to your wrist and the other to the comrade beside you. So too with the leg-irons. I was with Zuma. We hardly made a comfortable pair, Babenia the shorty and the tall, well-built Jacob. Try as we might, we could hardly keep a rhythm in step so, as we hobbled to the vans, all my bruises and scabby cuts from the last chaining started biting open again.

There were twenty six of us in our twenty seater *Meleko*. Crushed in on the seats and floor we started getting bad tempered. But as we got going we calmed down, started introducing ourselves and chatted about the past. All this while one of the NLF chaps got to work with some string opening handcuffs. As *bandiete* they were old hands at working the cuffs, but they could not manage the leg-irons. Soon quite a few of our guys became experts with the handcuffs too. Whenever the lorry stopped we quickly clamped ourselves shut again.

When the sun came out there they were. Two cars full of SBs, one driven by 'Fats' Grobbelaar. When we stopped at Kroonstad Prison for us to piss they got the coffee flasks filled. It was ominous to see the Kroonstad Prison. It was a huge new complex with cells for both men and women. Clearly the state knew what its future needs would be.

Sometimes life gives you little surprises when you hardly think you are first in line for happiness. Such was Colesberg Prison, where we stopped for the night. Magalies left us and a very polite young Lieutenant and his warders took over. They freed us from the shackles, handed out towels and about six new small Lux toilet soap cakes and allowed us to shower and freshen up. Then came a good warm supper after which we were taken to four large, clean cells. Although the main grille was obviously locked the cells were not, so we could move around. And no 'Kaffir!', no 'Koelie!', no 'Boesman!' And no batons. This was something new and some of us hoped that it would be nice if we were dumped here. We were too tired to converse so we went to sleep.

On being woken up the next morning we had a chance to wash, enjoyed some good hot coffee and porridge and then went into the shackles and vans.

As with moving, pleasures can be an extremely harsh thing to endure. Just when one comes to terms with brutality one gets the surprise of humanity thrust upon you. Your defences are thrown, desperately seeking calm and rest but resisting knowing its deceit. Oh!, where was the known Magalies? And then you fully realise that whilst the State owns you, the *bandiet* is in all other ways entirely and infinitely stateless.

Soon we were in fact roaring along through the *platteland*. A blitz of a lunch at Beaufort West Prison. Just bread, brown for a change, tossed into the van where we sat and ate. A brief stop at Victor Verster Prison. We remained inside the van and the warders had coffee while they notified Robben Island of our imminent arrival.

Then the speed picked up. Maybe for them time was running out for we hurtled down to the Docks, were hustled out of the vans, counted and pushed into the boat called *Izzy*.

This was a tricky part. With the boat lurching around, we had to get on and clamber down the narrow ladder onto the wooden benches in the hold. Shackled two-by-two you must try as best you can to hold your comrade's shoulder, steady yourselves and then hop across and down as the chains bit fiercely.

Some of us fell but eventually we were all inside. The warders poured in too, batons wielded and shouting "Stilte! Stilte! Julle Kaffirs!"[2] When they saw Indian comrades huddled together on a bench, they saw red. They rushed along, "Julle Koelies! Wat soek julle hier? More julle wil sien! Julle gaan kak!"[3] As the boat moved out all but one of them went up. The one stayed at the foot of the ladder just hitting his baton against his hand and waiting like a hungered puff adder. He wanted us.

We stayed quiet but inside our hearts had left us. Our journey was coming to an end. It was a bad and demoralising feeling.

---

[2] Afrikaans for 'Silence! Silence! You kaffirs!'
[3] Afrikaans for "You Coolies!, what are you doing here? Tomorrow, you will see! You will shit!"

First Tastes of Hell

How do you try to look forward to time? 'Sixteen years' is hardly the answer. And we knew nothing of the Island. So your horizons disappear into meaningless confusion, with no shape, depth, smell or feel. And yet our lives were so banal. So, we were to live and become a routine where differences came and went.

The boat arrived. We limped out and felt the force of clear skies and vast seas. There was jubilation amongst the ranks of warders, two of whom stood on the concrete jetty, rifles slung cockily across their arms. The taunts and baton blows pushed us into lorries and to the Prison. Pushed into five lines we stood in front of A Section and spotted many prisoners peeping through the windows. We saw many palms raised. There were obviously a lot of PAC comrades here already. Zuma spotted a fist and I saw his eyes moved, acknowledging the sign.

A Lieutenant came with a storky bow-legged chief warder and addressed us in English.

> "You people have been sabotaging outside. We know that you people are dangerous. Your record speaks for itself. We are going to knock your ideas out of your head. We will deal with you and break you! Do you understand! We will break you!"

He then said something to the head warder in Afrikaans and left.

Our leg-irons and handcuffs were removed, and then we were taken to B Section. The whole fifty one of us were shoved in B1. It was icy cold. And the whole place smelt of new paint. What we had seen outside now became clearer. This block had just been finished and another whole two blocks were being built. They were preparing for the influx of political prisoners. The buildings seemed like huge monuments to victory.

Each of the blocks was in an 'H' shape. There were four cells to a section with toilets and open bathrooms adjoining the sides. Two warder's offices lay opposite each other in the passage. The passage divided the cells and one could not communicate very well in this 'H' shape. There were four grilles and four doors between the passage and a main grille in front. About sixty five prisoners could sleep in each cell.

Besides this we had the *zinktronk* where some 'A' and 'B' group prisoners were kept. It had about two wards, a dispensary and an office for medical staff.

Porridge and cold coffee and some piss-like soup arrived. We left the piss to itself. Then we lost our old prison clothes and naked, we were told that we would receive our Robben Island suits the following morning. After some *zol* which the NLF guys had managed to get, the eight o'clock bell rang and the lights went out.

At five o'clock the bell shrilled through us. Solemnly, obediently and scared and quiet we pissed, washed, rolled up our blankets and waited. Each one of us kept apart and wanted our own clothes.

When they came they knew what we wanted. They were all powerful, curt and abusive.

"So! Julle wil klere he'. Julle kaffirs dink ons werk vir jou! He'? Dit sal die donderse dag wees."[4]

The grille door slammed closed again.

But soon a couple of criminals came in and gave each of us short pants, a khaki shirt and a *baadjie*. The shirts and short canvas pants had several patches on them. Some pants were so small that the abdomen buttons could not be closed. We quickly changed the pants with the others and somehow managed to partly cover our naked bodies. Indian comrades were given hats, old and new, and the African comrades were given caps. We were also given assorted sizes of sandals for our feet.

Then we were led out, given coffee and pap and hunked down in the yard for our first breakfast. The criminals soon drifted into sight, sizing us up. They ambled between us leering with weasel eyes, their shorts pulled so far down their bums stuck out. They were looking for *laaities*: wives. The choicest would be those of us with good looking boyish faces and fat bums. The Afrikaner warders rejoiced and encouraged the criminals to indulge in sodomy and taunt us.

The common law prisoners shared the cells with us. In fact just before we arrived the authorities brought a whole herd of them to the Island. These criminals ordered themselves into gangs and members of the same gang would always stay in the same cell together. This in order to protect themselves from the other gangs. The most prominent gangs were the 'Big Fives' and the 'Desperadoes'. Then there were the '26s', the '27s' and the 'Springboks'. The Springboks was a small gang who kept to themselves and were always on the lookout for a chance to escape. The 'Big Fives' were the most notorious and always fought to maintain their superiority over the others. They were the worst sort of pimps who would sell their mothers for a small favour.

Soon we were running in fours to reception. Lombard, a warder named 'Rooi Nek',[5] howled at us and encouraged the criminals to harass us. One of them tried to tackle Kisten, but this working class

---

[4] Afrikaans for "So! You want clothes? You kaffirs think we work for you. That will be the damned day."
[5] Afrikaans for 'Red Neck'.

comrade just balled his fists and moved forward. The criminal moved away.

One by one our names were called and as we ran inside the wood and iron building Rooi Nek would grab you by the scruff of your neck and kick you up the stairs. When you came out, after getting your prison cards, you would fly out with another kick. We soon made a wall to catch the flying comrades.

Somewhere in all this confusion along comes comrade George Peake. He was a Coloured People's Congress leader and had been a Cape Town city councillor. He had the place taped! The criminals take one look at him and leave. He clearly had a latch onto them and they treated him with great caution. When we were later locked in the cell for lunch George sent a criminal with some tobacco and brown paper for us.

During all this commotion, as we are being hurled this way and that, I managed to speak to George. I had never met him before, but I knew and respected him greatly. I told him how I had fucked up in detention and had coughed. He was wonderful.

> "Come on Babenia! You are here with us. All that is long time ago. You have always been with us. You have never been a Tshombe! You are one of us. You can see it through, do not worry!"

I felt very relieved. It had been one of those things which I had never really spoken to anybody about. It had been one of the silences amongst us all. I needed to know how things would be on the Island.

But we were still not quite into things. For while we sat around smoking *zol*. There is a helluva beating and blood letting going on outside in the yard. We just hear it. People are being badly beaten.

But soon the warders are beating us. Into fours we go and into the prison yard. We were to pick up large stones and boulders and throw them into a hole near the old hospital. Soon it was clear that they did not just want the stones. They needed to get the stones so that they could get us. Along the route they waited with batons while others hand picked our rocks for us. In the interests of speed we get beaten. By the time one reaches the dump hole one has already received about six or seven baton blows on one's buttocks and back. At the dump hole stood a young warder of about seventeen, well-built and with the ferocity of a wild animal. Before we threw the stones or boulders he beat us with something sounding like all his might. His name was Karnakemp. I think this is how you spell his name, but I wouldn't know because I never saw it written down. But I will never forget that man.

Puny little George was told to carry a boulder which must have been all of three times his weight. It just sat there. He couldn't even move it. When Mbata tried to help, he was beaten and told to carry on with his work. Batons started raining on George but he kept on trying to move the boulder. He managed to roll it slowly along. By the time he was at the hole his hands were already bleeding with blisters which were not there a few minutes ago.

Comrade Dennis Brutus was in similar condition. His gunshot wound had not ever really healed properly and now with the strain and bruising it opened again. And Karnakemp kicked him in the stomach. He fell forward and Billy dropped his own stone to help Dennis. For this Billy was dragged to the ground, beaten and his Bible lay in tatters.

I only managed about six or seven dizzy steps before I collapsed. Warder Jan Kleynhans tried to pull me up but I was out. A head warder apparently shouted to get some hospital cleaners to bring water. Teezar was the one whose bucket of water brought me round.

But as they took me to the hospital, Kleynhans needed more. He asked me whether I had 'signed', meaning that I was not willing for work. I had no idea what he meant and anyway I was finished.

The other comrades were amazed at what we were going through. When the chief warder, who had been watching from a distance, came closer some of them tried to complain. But the warders closed ranks and no one but us seemed in the slightest bit perturbed or pained.

However later on we realised that when I went out cold the beatings stopped immediately. The signal was just the unspoken presence of the chief warder. Not that they should not have beaten us, but that they had found our limits. Through these ways they began to know us. It was our first real experience of what was known as a 'carry on'. They knocked shit out of us. So now it was time for *phaka*.

The next day at role call a lot of us fell into the *siektespan*. The medical orderly just looked at us and put mercurochrome on the cuts and blisters and sent us away to be part of the *losspan* which was supposed to be for lighter manual work. Poor old Ebbie, he gets told to push a wheelbarrow and so he shows up his bandaged hands. First he gets some clubbing and then his prison card gets taken away. He lost one meal.

That lunch we sat around with comrade Billy Malgas. He introduced us to other comrades like Jeremiah Francis, Gloria Mdingi and Andrew Masondo. They also explained some things to us. All political prisoners, whether of the ANC or PAC were called *Poqos* by the warders. Criminals they called *bandiete*. And we had to watch out for the 'Kleynhans group': the warder team under this bastard. They were in charge of the New Quarry. This was where we got the stone to build the new cells for our soon to be arriving comrades. The regime was getting us to build monuments to their own successes.

That afternoon at supper time we met up with Reggie, Shirish Nanabhai and Indris Naidoo. They were under Delport at the Old Quarry.

Over that first weekend we spent a lot of time just being locked up. A horrible realisation came by. Nothing had ever been explained to us, nothing formal ever said. No rules had ever been spoken to us. We had not been told to understand anything.

It struck me clearly that first Sunday. We expected an officer to take the inspection whereupon we would voice our complaints. But chief warder Theron just passed us by completely. We could do nothing about it? That day we never left our cell, just sitting there waiting for breakfast, lunch, supper and lights out. We planned to complain the following week and selected six spokesmen to put our complaints and protests.

But it was that speaking can allow for argument where none could be tolerated. Or, also, that you could not put such power into words. Everything had to be unspoken and you just had to be beaten into learning their daily routines. It was the shouted and screamed words which you must immediately train yourself to obey and feel like a dog. You must never avoid.

And before we had even touched ground we were working away at the most painful pace. I felt like I had never been anywhere else. How long had I been here? And I felt like time never ends.

The Longest Day

The morning of the 16th of March started normally enough. But soon this day was to turn into a nightmare. As we did our morning chores we knew we would be going out to work. But where? There were always a number of different spans. The Quarry *span*, known as the *bombela* span, the *landbouspan*, the *steenmakerspan*, the *kalkspan*, the GI Store *span*, the *dokspan*, the *houdspan*, the *bamboospan*, the *losspan*, the Lighthouse *span* and several other smaller *spans*.

An ominous indication of things to come came with the warders chasing us back to the cells after washing. We had to go and collect our sandals which we had to keep outside our lock up. While we had been cleaning, the night warders had mixed them all up. Shit! We just grabbed. "Sorry com! You know how hot it is!"

After breakfast everyone is there lined up four deep and we hear Theron giving the *quarryspan* to us. The last of the *spans* to move out, we passed the old jail and walked on quite a distance and then took a left turn and saw the sea.

This was the new quarry. Before the quarry could really be worked, it had to be prepared. Part of this job entailed building a dyke out into the sea and around so that we could get at some good blue stones that were sticking up from the sea. This job was given to us new arrivals. All the rubble was dug out around the blue stones and dumped into the sea in a semi-circular shape. The dyke was meant to keep the sea water away from the blue stones. It took us about six months to build. Then the pumps would pump the water out.

Us new drafts were told to take the wheelbarrows with spindly, creaky iron wheels. Others were taken to a hole and told to pull out big stones to be loaded on the barrows. The 'Big Fives' did the loading.

The Big Fives were one of the notorious criminal gangs which operated on the Island. They were a real bad bunch who had allied themselves with the Kleynhans brothers.

We had to push the barrows through the line of Kleynhans' warders. As we moved along each of them would let fly with the baton. At the end of the journey was a small incline where Karnakemp waited for us. He was a dirty mouthed brute who could only find himself by getting at us all the time. Baton flying around he would scream "Ek's nie jou 'Sir' nie, ek is jou Baas!".[6]

Actually none of the warders wanted to be called 'meneer' or 'sir'. We wanted to use those words but not them. 'Baas' was what they needed.

Once you passed Karnakemp we had to tip the stones into the sea and go back for more. The Big Fives would be waiting. Come slowly and they would leave their spades and beat us. Or they would overload the wheelbarrow so that we could hardly push it. Shits like Teeman and Meintjies would then run to Jan or Piet Kleynhans and say "Baas! Baas! Daai kaffirtjie wil nie werk nie!"[7] Piet and Jan will rush to us and ask "Wie wil nie werk nie?"[8] Piet and Jan would then sit on the wheelbarrow and ask us to push. If we tried and the wheelbarrow fell from our grip they would fall on us with their batons shouting "Julle wou ons seer maak! Julle wou ons dood maak!"[9] We'd then get our cards taken away for three meal stops.

---

[6] Afrikaans for "I am not your 'Sir', I'm your 'Master'!".
[7] Afrikaans for "Master! Master! Those little kaffirs don't want to work."
[8] Afrikaans for "Who will not work?".
[9] Afrikaans for "You want to hurt us! You want to kill us!"

As time went the warders got us to push faster. Inevitably you would push the wheel into the ankles of the comrade in front. Karnakemp the sadist liked to see this. On the painful impact, comrades crashed and then quickly tried to get going again. He could bear down on us with all his might. Once he even pushed an exhausted George into the sea and we had to pull him up.

As we dashed around, 'Zed' gasps to me "Natoo, they are going to kill us!" I had tears in my eyes and was limping with only one sandal. Riot, just behind me, was also crying. It was such a quick glimpse into tragedy. But next moment we heard Piet shouting "Wat doen daai twee Koelies daar?".[10] Quickly we took up our wheel-barrows and went our separate lonely ways.

Sometime in the middle of this first morning some Big Fives brought a water churn and a tin cup along. Each of us was given a quarter cup of water to drink. If we asked for more Teeman would say "Julle moet jou pis drink!".[11]

We would keep asking friendly warders the time. Their replies always chilled us. It seemed that the day was never going to end. We must surely be dead soon? I salute all of us who managed to get through that first day.

We went for lunch at midday. Nobody spoke, each having his own thoughts and protecting them. A criminal named Gumbi, who tried to help us when our wheelbarrows wouldn't move, made a few *zols* and told us to smoke and forget about what had happened. He told us that the young amongst us should at all times stay with the older folks, even if they are sent to the shed by the warders. The Big Fives would persuade Piet or Jan Kleynhans to send one of the youngsters to the shed and there the Big Fives would bugger them. We had quite a few youngsters in our draft of fifty one. Siva Pillay, Girja Singh, Zuma, Caiphas, Nene, Owen Damoi, Solomon Morewa and Charles. None of them, right throughout their sentences, ever became a victim.

By the afternoon the warders cooled down a bit and it all ended at around 4 o'clock. We hobbled back, got counted and had *phaka*. There, Reggie, Francis and Indris consoled us, saying that we should just bear it for the next few days and then we would be okay. It wasn't great news but at least they were saying it.

After lock up we had a meeting. What to do about the Big Fives? They had given us a fright. If they are the Big Fives how were we to let them know that we are the 'Big Fifty Ones'? We also discussed the beatings. They could not carry on. We swapped wounds and

---

[10] Afrikaans for "What are those two Coolies doing over there?".
[11] Afrikaans for "Drink your own urine!".

everybody was shocked at how my back and buttocks were like a washing board with purple welts. It was the same with comrades Brutus and Zuma and others. We would have to raise this next Sunday. The *zols* came but there was only enough for two pulls each.

Going Alone

The next day a lot of us reported for the *siektespan* and off we went to the hospital. After getting some ointment and stuff we were being taken back to the cells for lock up when we see the Lieutenant and chief warder Theron walking towards us. Dennis and I decide to act quickly. We complain about the beatings. As the officer listens, Theron chips in wanting to know if we could identify the warders. "Ja, it is the Kleynhans brothers and Karnakemp", Brutus said. He looks towards me and I nod in agreement. The Lieutenant said he would investigate and then turns to Brutus: "You must remember that it is through you, we are barred from the International Olympic Committee" and walked away.

The next day I went to Theron during breakfast. He listened to me for a change, but he said that I must work at the Quarry. When I came out the warder asked what Theron had said. I lied blatantly, "I have to work in your *span*". The warder, who was a bit silly, just took me along. He was in charge of the *siektespan*.

There was no alternative but to get on. A PAC guy once put it very well. He said that when you hear the wake up bell, it is like a chain-saw cutting right through you. "Will I get a hammer today, a pick . . . Will I loose meals?" It was permanent daily torture. You against them in a badly unequal battle. And you were alone.

There was not that much talking together between us comrades because we were not yet conditioned. It was only after about two months, when we were moved from A1 into B1 that we began to find our bearings. They had moved us after Billy complained about the conditions. Everyone was shoved into different cells and broken up.

We were all so traumatised that we never spoke much. Each of us thinking his own things. We had been selfish and separate during detention, then one after being charged, one again through Leeukop, but now we split up again. The oneness disappeared and no one seemed to know how to find it again. It would take us two years to really find our bearings. By that stage I was in C3 with Curnick. This meant a lot to me. It was only then when we had acclimatised that we could adjust to the long sentences.

When we landed we did not think we could survive more than a day or so. The beatings were horrific. Your senses became atomised, nearly into nothingness.

When we arrived there were only eleven ANC chaps on the Island. We brought the number to fifty one. Within six months of our arrival there would have been well over eight hundred of us ANC.

Right from the beginning we had what was called a Disciplinary Committee. Until the ANC leadership arrived, the DC was the top ANC body on the Island. They were appointed by a senior ANC comrade. In the early days there were five on the DC. Curnick, Billy, Phillip Mathews, Masondo and Jeremiah Francis. Always one non-African.

The DC would meet regularly and discuss various things amongst themselves. Like the conditions, the attitude of the PAC towards us and, say, food. And, very importantly, if something happened in one of the cells, like if two chaps fought, it would go the DC. The DC would resolve the issue and reprimand the fellows. Times were hard and people would easily loose their tempers: often over the most small, inconsequential matters. But it did not seem like that at the time.

Somewhere in '65 or '66 these structures expanded. Then we had a Public Relations Officer below the DC and group leaders in each cell dormitory wing. Within the lock up you would group together in fours. At the beginning I was with Jeremiah Francis, Gloria Mdingi and Masondo.

This was to keep discipline amongst us and to ensure that order and unity was kept throughout. And it always had to be done in small groups. This because if the warders found you meeting in big groups, which was very difficult anyway during those early years, the warders would accuse you of having a political meeting. Then you loose three meals.

And in the cells it was easy to arrange. The PAC all lay and slept on one side and us on the other. The night bell only goes for lights out at eight so you just lay close together and talked quietly.

But during those first months I was scared and alone. Maybe I still felt stigmatised. I tried to go off alone.

I worked in the *siektespan* for about a month and a half. It was easy work.

The hospital was in *zinktronk*. It had two medical orderlies, named Nel and Van der Berg. Nel was a sergeant and a real Boer who never wanted to speak English with us. His task was to stop politicos from seeing the doctor. No matter how ill one was, hospitalisation in 1963 and 1964 was out of the question. In winter when we went to see the doctor, we were told to go and have a shower before seeing the doctor. Just imagine the cold wind freezing your body and on top of that to go and have a cold shower. It was terrible! Every prisoner, before the cells were opened had already had a cold water shower. This second shower was to deter people from seeing the doctor. Even if you had the second shower, you still have to stand naked in the cold wind brought in by the Benguela current. This inhuman treatment was carried out by Nel in winter.

In the absence of Nel, Van der Berg did not put us through this inhuman act of persecution. Under the prison conditions of the early sixties, Van der Berg was what we would call in ordinary terms a darling.

Two criminals also worked there. Lucas Dry was a Coloured convict from Durban and Tezzar an African convict from Johannesburg. They thought that they were Boers.

Lucas Dry was really the worst chap. When comrades went to the hospital to have our blisters attended to he used to say, "Aye *Poqo*, just piss on your palms and continue pushing the *kruiwa*". If we objected he would beat us up. Being a sodomist, he took vitamin oil from the hospital and kept drinking it to maintain his virility. I also saw him taking other stuff too. We were shocked one day to see him kiss his *wyfie* in front of Nel. Nel liked Lucas. Lucas was his *voetagterryer*.

In 1980, Lucas Draai was shot dead in Wills Road, Durban. I saw him that day, in Prince Edward Street. I just looked at him and said "You bastard!". He just looked down. Later that day he shot a taxi driver and within two hours the other taxi drivers had got him.

Tezzar was Van der Berg's pet. In many ways Tezzar was better than Lucas Dry. Though arrogant, at least he treated us with some respect.

Soon I was sent to the dock workers team. I was not that happy. As we go out Theron sees me and laughs "Daardie Koelie will vrek vandag".[12] I took no notice of him and went along with the group of Paarl politicos who made up most of the *span*.

On reaching the wharf we took off our jackets and got into the hold of the waiting ship. It was full of cement bags. Two of us would carry the bag and place it in the cargo net. The crane would then load it to shore. It was a back breaking job. By mid-morning my clothes and hair were full of cement and I looked like a clown, what with the cement and my Buck Jones hat which I had got by bartering some tobacco. Luckily 'Oom Robbie' Robertson, the warder in charge told me to stand on the wharf and unhook the net when it comes by. I felt relieved to get away from the cement bags.

---

[12] Afrikaans for "Today that Indian will die".

But the next day I did not go back there. The reason was that I was an Indian and Indians were not allowed to work at the docks.

So the next day I was again in the *losspan*. Once we were taken near the sea where new sewerage pipes were being laid. When that ended we went to broaden the road in the town. Criminals would load stones into our barrows and we would carry the stones along and dump them at the side of the road. Convicts would level the things out then a heavy roller was pulled across to push the road flat. It was okay work because the stones were not boulders.

It was here that I learnt how to measure time. We would work out that it took us about ten minutes to carry the stones from the pile across the road to the hole. One would just keep count of how many times you crossed the road and so you could work out when lunch and other breaks were.

I also managed to get into the group of *losspan* who would have to go every Monday to the GI Store and collect the wheelbarrows. On Friday afternoon we would knock off early so that we could hand them back. These were good times to waste time.

At the store I managed to contact some Coloured chaps who kept me supplied with tobacco and sometimes slipped me newspapers. My best contact there was Achmat, a Cape Malay. We got along very well. I would circulate the newspapers amongst the comrades in the evenings. They were always pleased.

Some of the criminals at GI Stores added fat to our mealie rice and made thick *puzamandla* with sugar and shared it with us at lunch break. It was delicious.

These criminals told me a lot about their life. They had their own law of the jungle. All the men were in gangs and each gang had their own law courts, with a magistrate, prosecutor and defence lawyers. Witnesses are called. Only members of the particular gang could be witnesses. Everything is an internal matter in these courts. When the magistrate pronounces judgment and sentence there is no appeal procedure. Sentences range from one blow to the head with a mug filled with sand to death but as far as I know no one ever received the ultimate penalty.

Once guilty you have to take your punishment like a man. A doctor will examine you, declare you fit and he gives it to you himself! The doctor in the Desperados trial was Brancas. A nice chap, always laughing. When he was drafted he cried, "I am a *Poqo*, I am a *Poqo*!"

When two gangs fought, it was done in the course of duty and no one was punished for this.

Magistrates would spend a lot of their time hearing cases where people wanted to swap *laaities*. Sometimes one party was aggrieved and things could get quite complex. But even if both parties agreed to the swap you still had to get it confirmed by the magistrate.

When a man wanted a *laaitie* who belonged to another gang then it was time for a fight. The winner takes the prize and the new member becomes part of the household. This was how Poonas was killed. He wanted to rape a 'Springbok'. They fought and Poonas was no more! The youngster put thirty two holes into Poonas' body.

The head of the household has to buy or barter for bread to satisfy the wants of the household. Lucas Draai, who worked in the hospital, would often help families out by arranging for the medics to put criminals on special diet. Lucas' survival depended on him doing favours for the households.

After working some weeks here I saw Karnakemp at our *span*. He saw me working with my wheelbarrow, stops, and tells a convict to overload my barrow. He started to threaten me when I refused to push the damn thing. When he insisted I told him to take me to the chief warder. When he refused I insisted on being taken to the hospital. He refused again, so I just tipped my wheelbarrow over and took a walk. He came after me, but saw Theron walking by and so backed off. This was the end of June 1964. I was sent back to the quarry.

The Quarry

So back to those bastards the Kleynhans brothers. It was the same stuff, us carting sand and rubble to build the dyke.

One day Jan Kleynhans thought of a new idea. He took Siva Pillay and a PAC youngster from East London and handcuffed them to a pole in a standing position with their arms above their heads in the blistering heat. They were kept like this till our lunch break.

Jan Kleynhans and his brother Piet enjoyed this type of torture. Piet and Jan had as aides such sadists as Du Preez, Fourie or 'Gigeleza' as we knew him, Mouton and Karnakemp. To top it all the Big Fives were four square behind them in seeing us get beaten.

It took us some months to build the dyke. During this time the old quarry was closed. With the closing of this quarry lots more *bandiete* arrived. And lots of criminals came too. And Sergeant Delport, 'Oom Dellie', who had a blasting ticket came over from the old quarry to take charge of us from Sergeant Jordaan. When he came over to us to check things out he would be on horseback. The whole place just swarmed with us like ants.

We had the feeling that 'Oom Jorrie' had been sent over to us to watch over the Kleynhans two. During his time with us things cooled down a lot for us politicians. Oom Jorrie was a nice guy, but because he could speak Xhosa, he left us to go to the censor's office.

In the quarry we had a number of different *spans*. The *kruiwaspan* had to load rubble and dump it on the dyke site. The *grawespan* would fill the dyke with the rubble. Both these *spans* had to load crushed stones to the heap, and to bring blue stones to the *knaplyn* to be crushed for concrete mixture.

The *sifspan* sifted the crushed stones on a big sieve and the residue was brought back to be crushed smaller.

The *knaplyn* was the biggest *span* in the quarry. They crushed blue stones for concrete mixture. One had to crush them to the size of sugar beans. Each had to crush a wheel barrow and a half a day. There would often be many comrades failing. If you failed to meet the quota you lost three meals the following day. But usually this punishment was carried out on weekends when there was meat for supper. Rumour was that the quarry warders planned it this way quietly with the GI Store so that they could take the meat away themselves and hold *braaivleis*.[13] This could be a lot of meat.

The *boorspan* would drill holes in the blue stone with a pneumatic drill worked by a compressor. Then prisoners, working with fourteen pound hammers, would insert a chisel and bits into the hole and start hammering it till the wall cracked. It could take days. Always working in unity, they grunted together. 'Hosh . . .! Hosh . . .! Hosh . . .!' Then they would use the *gala*, a six foot steel crowbar, to prize the rock away from the wall. This was hard work and only the fittest were taken in this *span*.

This was where the *toutrekspan* of Gabes and Sitho came in. They had to hook a thick twisted steel cable around the rock and drag the thing away. Then the drill would punch more holes into the rock so that it could be broken into smaller pieces. The *toutrekspan* would then drag these to the stone dressers.

They would have to make them into wall stones or corner stones, depending upon the thickness of the stone. In the early period a stone dresser worked as an apprentice to Anthony Souza, a PAC guy, for about six months or so. Souza, as with many PAC chaps, had been there from '63. He had picked the job up quickly and he was easy to work with as he was not a *hardegat* PAC. Then a fellow would be recommended by 'Oom Dellie' for a gratuity. Most of the stone dressers started with a gratuity of fifty cents a month and would end up earning R1.50 after three or four years, depending upon Oom Dellie's recommendation.

The *baksteenmakerspan* made bricks. They made a couple of thousand bricks a day. They also fell under the gratuity class.

---

[13] Afrikaans for barbecue.

The *lorriespan* was about twenty five prisoners who would go to the shore and pick sea sand up and load it into the lorry which Oom Dellie drove. This was then sifted by the *sifspan* and used for making cement.

There was also the *koekepanspan*. The *koekepan*[14] was the tipper which used to run on railway lines. The Desperados used to drive it, bringing the stones from the quarry to the *knaplyn*. Two fellows would stand on the back plate and, as the thing went downhill, they would just kick out at any of the Big Fives who happened to be near. In three years time this *span* was stopped altogether. I think they found the Desperados were playing more fool than working.

The terrace *span* came into being in '65 or '66. It consisted mainly of the Coloured and Indian political prisoners. We had to build terraces at the quarry and elsewhere and plant proteas and wild flowers to beautify what was in reality a hell hole. These *boere* think in different ways. They thought us Indians, being sugar farmers and gardeners, were all the same! In charge was Sergeant 'Hotdorsh'.

There was one time there; we were just fooling around, doing nothing. Hotdorsh just looked at us and held his arm out, looking at his watch. A long time later he calls us: George Naicker, me and some eight or nine others.

"Look you *Poqos*! For the last twenty minutes you have been doing just fuck all. Give me you cards."

He takes us to Theron. It was a Wednesday, a shooting day when we were supposed to knock off at midday. Theron asks us why we are not working. We give some silly fool reply and so he tells Hotdorsh to take us out for the afternoon to work at the main gate. That was okay for us because that was where you could score tobacco. At the quarry there was no chance. That is why we always tried to get to the main gate.

From June 1964 for the next two years I was in the *knaplyn* trying to fill my daily quota. Then I became an apprentice wall dresser. Somewhere around 1967 I started getting a gratuity. In 1969 I was on R1.50 a month.

In the midst of all this there was also the trench. Because Mandela and the other leaders were in the old jail, awaiting the completion of the single cells, we could not walk past the old jail on our way to the quarry. The warders changed our route to the quarry. Then one day the Colonel we called 'Staalbaard' because of his thick wiry beard arrives and tells Oom Dellie that we have to dig a six foot deep trench from the jail gate to the quarry. We started digging the trench

---

[14] At Coedmore we used to call this the *Gollovan*.

having no idea whatsoever why. When we were halfway through with the trench, Oom Dellie could not keep it a secret anymore and told his *agterryers* what the trench was going to be used for: for us to walk in. From the *agterryers* it came to the ears of the *bandiete* and from there it came to us.

Once the secret was out the work slowed down. The *bandiete* didn't like walking in a trench and so they slowed down the progress of the trench too. Most of us who were using spades and wheelbarrows also had a sinking feeling that the trench was going to be a replica of Nazi trenches of Auschwitz and Bergen Belsen. One day the *boere* would just mow us down. Comrade 'Zed' said "This is it boys! Nazi Germany repeating itself." *Bandiete* looked for a slight excuse to break into a gang war and we were very depressed. The mood prevailed for some time.

Then one day Oom Dellie told us to cover the trench up. We were all so happy. We covered it in a week.

Later we heard that some officials from Pretoria had seen the trench and got very angry. "What are we going to say to the International Red Cross when they come down here?" They totally rejected the plan and ordered that a barbed wire fence of the same width be erected with barbed wire covering on top. They also fenced the whole quarry area.

Now we were in a caged prison within a prison. We did not like it at the beginning but as time went on we got used to the idea. There was one advantage. The warders walked outside the fence and could not hit us even if their hand itched. The fence created a barrier between the beasts outside and the human beings inside.

Trouble Shooters and Slim Mense

When we first arrived political prisoners were not allowed to buy anything. We needed toilet things like soap. We queried this but nothing happened. If you spoke up you were a *slim mens*. What we would call a trouble shooter. But soon we heard that a new Colonel, who was the new commanding officer, was coming round on inspection. We in Cell B1 decided to raise this matter and the beatings with him.

So that Sunday at inspection Billy raises the matter. Colonel Wessels listened attentively and ordered Theron to issue order papers to every cell and told Billy that he would go into the matter of beatings.

The same day we were issued with the requisition paper to order soap, toothpaste, razors and blades. This was a great victory to us.

But the following morning Theron comes with the yard warder, Van der Berg and separates the Indian comrades to different cells. While weeding us out he says "Jy, Koelie, is 'n slim mens".[15] From that day on trouble shooters became *slim mense*.

I think the main problem was that warders just couldn't understand Indians joining Africans in the struggle. This made it hard for us, and Coloured comrades. We were always beaten and pushed around by the warders.

There was one incident which I remember well. After eating we used to line up in four rows. Each row was counted and sent to its respective cell. While in the line this sadist used to go up and down with his baton in his hand and approach an Indian comrade and say "Koelie, jou ma se moer".[16] He would say this every time he passed an Indian comrade. After some time the Indian comrades from Durban, who did not understand Afrikaans, came to know what it meant and they retaliated by saying in vernacular "Tari Ben-ni bosadi".[17]

Resistance could come in many guises. Ebbie for instance would often report sick, go to the hospital and get given light duty work.

Soon after we arrived the more militant of APDUSA, the *Yu Chi Chan* guys arrived on Robben Island to serve various sentences: Neville Alexander, Lesley van Heerden, Don Davies, Fikile Bham, Lionel Davies, Marcus Solomon and Gordon Hendricks. They were to suffer badly at the quarry but they put up a strong resistance to the Kleynhans group.

They seemed to have managed this in an interesting way. A lot of Coloured prisoners had been brought to Robben Island from Bellville Prison. There was some respect amongst these blokes to the *Yu Chi Chan* comrades who managed to change the attitudes of the members of the Desperados and the '28s' towards the political prisoners. After this the attitude of the Desparados changed completely and they became very friendly and often protected us from the Big Fives. Kleynhans' allies were watching their step.

However their hardness soon attracted the wrath of the warders. They were trouble shooters. So they had to take frequent trips to the single cells in the isolation section.

There was a day when Piet Kleynhans started handling George Naicker. This infuriated Don Davies who goes up to Kleynhans and tells him to stop it and rather handle him instead. So Kleynhans takes him to reception to be charged. Nothing came of it.

---

[15] Afrikaans for "You Coolie, you are a *slim mens*".
[16] Afrikaans for "Coolie, your mother's cunt".
[17] *Gujarati* for "Your sister's cunt".

The first of our group to get isolation was Billy. A frequent visitor to the isolation cells was Indris Naidoo. For some reason 'Cofimvaba' hated his guts.

Saamwerk

The term 'saamwerk' is old as the racial settler colonial rule. In English it probably means 'co-operation' or 'let's work together'. The Afrikaners got a narrow, twisted and sinister interpretation. To them 'saamwerk' means inform or pimp on your friends. For that you get treated a bit better and may even end up sleeping on a bed at the prison hospital. The Big Fives, other gangster criminals, and even some politicos without commitment became pimps and had cozy work.

We would hear the words 'julle moet saamwerk'[18] till it stank. We knew what it meant and shied away from such overtures.

They would never use the term 'saampraat'. To discuss our problems with them was out of the question. Although they did listen to the Rivonia group, whenever we got official visits from Pretoria Headquarters, it was an eyewash manoeuvre. All they wanted was to hear their pimps and not hear of our complaints. Brigadier Aucamp from Prison Services was really bad. He was definitely Vorster's man, getting promoted very quickly and loving to see politicos being beaten.

Robben Island's most notorious pimp was a 'sky pilot', a priest and a so-called political prisoner from Grahamstown. The day he put his foot on Robben Island, he became a pimp. He had the easiest life with his pimping. Every warder was his 'Baas'. This man had no scruples but had a stomach that loved the special privileges offered to a number one pimp. In the beginning he worked at reception but quickly he moved to the hospital and was sleeping there.

Once he was scheduled to go to Cape Town for a chest X-ray. However as the boat taking the 'sky pilot' and the usual lot of prison warders' wives and so on to Cape Town was supposed to leave, he gets called to commanding officer Willemse's office. An official from Pretoria wished to see him. The boat was instructed to wait for him. We never knew of the boat being made to wait for other people.

By the time the little coward was working at the study office, which processed all our correspondence with schools and universities, he started stopping all UNISA and State Library books. By hook or by crook he also managed to enrol with an American university

---

[18] Afrikaans for "You must co-operate".

and got his doctorate. It was only on receiving his doctorate certificate that the study officer came to know the trick that had been played on him.

Soon he got so big for his boots that eventually he started pimping the warders and became the centre of hatred, from the prisoners and warders alike. He was moved from the study centre and he went back to the hospital to work till he was drafted. He changed working places but never his hospital bed.

One day a PAC prisoner named Mboswana, who was sleeping in his ward, tried to choke him with his hands but the other prisoners stopped him. We heard the following day that the pimp was shivering like a leaf and was unable to speak for a lengthy period of time. The whole thing was reported to Prins at reception. Prins calls Mboswana in, but none of the warders wanted to do Prins' bidding and beat him up. Everyone just left him alone.

After a few months we got a report that the cook at the hospital had beaten him up. The blue-eyed boy got real black-eyes! It's ironical isn't it?

There were other *saamwerkers*. PAC leaders, like John Pokela, who was very friendly with comrade James Kati and was vociferous in condemning smuggling, were wanting some sort of working unity with the ANC. PAC guys; Leballo's boys resented this and pimped their leadership into isolation cells.

Us politicos felt that smuggling was bad. For when you smuggled, or as others would have it, stole from the kitchen, you were taking food away from your comrades.

Smuggling of things like *dalav* was a big issue. One of Johnson Malambo's eyes was dug out with a spoon by one of his PAC call mates because Johnson opposed that kind of smuggling.

Robben Island Prison

What is an institution? Is Robben Island an institution? Yes it is in the sense that the Boers used it as their chosen battlefield. They wanted to wage war against us, so they dreamt up all the rules and the punishments and tried to kick us into them.

But then you see things get messy. If they want us to breathe terror and suffering, this same air will get to their lungs as well. This was a crucial thing to learn. At the time we often spoke about how some American black civil rights activist had said that to keep a black man down someone would have to hold him down there all the time. Everyone on Robben Island could become a degenerate. But most of us *Poqos* resisted. But look at how the common law prisoners turned into wives, sodomists, pimps and smugglers? And how the warders would encourage this. In so doing, as the warders made people into the scum of the prison, so some of them became the scums of the earth.

At first many officials and warders did not know how to handle political prisoners. For the first time they were coming into touch with political prisoners. They were supposed to demoralise us and the best way they thought that they could do it was by beating us and harassing us.

Chief warder Theron got caught up in this mess. He had to show that he is not soft on us and at the same time he tried and succeeded in being a tyrant. He was unable to stop the atrocities of the Kleynhans group. If he did so he would become a scapegoat of the informers of the higher ups. The difficult task was to find an equilibrium between these two tendencies. And in this regard he was an incapable man.

Comrades Indris Naidoo and Moses Dlamini portray Theron as a tyrant with his owl like eyes and stance, but I think he was a victim of circumstances and his rebelling attitude to higher ups made him a rebel with no cause. To somehow make himself popular he did stupid things which now made him unpopular with the politicos.

A Cape Town comrade once approached Theron and asked him for tobacco. Theron laughed and said that he should make his own plans for tobacco as he was not in the position to supply any.

Theron also knew that the politicos were not thieves, and he used to say, "The *Poqos* won't steal a cent if they worked in town, but they will definitely smuggle papers". He knew this, therefore he tried to send politicos to work in town.

He did not want an attorney to visit us. When charged and we asked for a letter to our attorney, he would persuade the warders to drop the charges. As far as he was concerned, an attorney meant messages going out about atrocities.

I remember Theron when John Vorster came visiting. It was Saturday and Vorster arrived just after we had taken lunch and were locked up. Through the windows we saw Vorster with the Colonel and Theron standing near the kitchen. Theron kept looking at his watch and, it being his lunch time, he left the Colonel and Vorster and walked towards the reception with his bandy legs. He hated superiors and never liked authority.

One day when we were lined up to go to the quarry, Colonel 'Staalbaard' Prinsloo came with Theron and stood looking at the *spans* going out. Sergeant 'Dup' Du Plessis pulled two politicos out of the quarry line and brought them to Theron.

"Gehoor jy die twee *Poqos* praat in die lyn."

"Wat het jy gehoor?"
"Ek't gehoor die twee *Poqos* praat!"
"Ek hoor jou, maar ek vra wat het jy gehoor?"
"Ek weet nie!"
"Fuck off!'[19]

Theron just looked at 'Staalbaard' and smiled.

On our way to the quarry, one of the criminals told us Theron was bombed out of Bellville Prison by 'Dup' in cohorts with Staalbaard and that is why Theron acted like that. He was trying to convey to Staalbaard, "See what I do to your pimp!". As long as Theron was on the Island he had instructed Oom Dellie to keep 'Dup' in the Hell Hole.

Theron was sent to Tulbagh, a farm prison. A convict new to the Island told us that there Theron had again caused trouble. A farmer brought his convicts back to the prison late one day. Amongst the prisoners was one carrying this basket of fruit which the farmer offers to Theron. Theron had kicked the basket over saying that he would buy his own fruit and that his prisoners should be in by four thirty.

I suppose in essence, Theron was an ignorant, self-conscious introvert who became a victim of his own system and came to be known as a tyrant.

At this time we had a Captain Visser on the Island. He was educated and reasonable. It was he who opened study facilities and allowed us to buy stationery and books. He was helped by warder Terreblanche. He was also good. But good people don't last on Robben Island. Visser was transferred to Pretoria and rose rapidly to the rank of a Brigadier.

There was prejudice among the Boers against the English. It was very rife and easily noticeable. A Sergeant Sutherland, an Englishman, worked or was made to work on a quarry post till he left. This was naked prejudice. He was a Sergeant and could have taken any small *span* out, but they preferred to give it to any ordinary Afrikaner warder.

There were only about five or six Englishmen on the Island. One was Whitfield or Wakefield, who was in charge of the GI Stores. Then there was Captain Mann, his son chief warder Mann, dock chief Southeby and about two working at the Docks.

Chief warder Southeby was working at the dock. Barring Indians and Coloureds, Africans used to work at the docks. While working

---

[19] Afrikaans for "Did you hear these two *poqos* talking in the line?"; "What did you hear?", "I heard these two *Poqos* talking!", "I hear you, but I am asking what did you hear?", "I do not know!", "Fuck off!"

there Southeby used to call one of the youngsters and tell him to go through the *Cape Times* and tell all his comrades about the news. He stood guard at the door and said that if he coughed, the youngster should know that a Boer is approaching and he should quickly put the newspaper away and pretend to clean the office. This was his way of helping us. He was kept on on the Island because he was there for the last twenty five years and knew all about the boats.

In 1969 or 1970 he rose in rank and became a Captain and would regularly take weekend inspections. When it was his turn he was accompanied for inspection by an Afrikaner chief warder and 'Masiki', a nice old *Boer*. And he knew the pimps.

In he comes carrying his heavy bulk, red-faced and aged. If anyone complained he would explode.

> "You terrorists! Moscow Satellites! You complain! If you complain in Russia, you would be shot! Russians send their prisoners to icy Siberia! Siberia! You hear!"

Then he walks out and stands in the passage like a tired hound. We heard this lecture whenever he came.

But before coming for inspection he used to leave the Sunday papers at reception where, by this time, all the cleaners were politicos. By the time he returned all the papers were gone. The cleaners had cleaned up. If they weren't, he would shout again.

> "Why is this place not clean. Take those papers away immediately!"
> "Captain, I did not have a chance! Sergeant Augard was here!"
> "OK but be quick and take it away!"

This aged old red-faced Southeby married a young girl from Cape Town. He bought her new furniture, a TV set and a kitchen unit. But one morning old Southeby was found dead in his bed. He had died of a heart attack. The wife left Robben Island after the funeral with all the furniture and never came back. Rumours had it that she inherited everything in the will and that amounted to a huge sum.

Cofimvaba

After Theron, Naude alias 'Cofimvaba' alias 'Haal hom toe'[20] became the jailer. He often pronounced that he was "haal hom toe van Cofimvaba af!".[21] In no time he was promoted to a Lieutenant. Before he left, he was a Captain. He was the most whimsical person I ever met. He looked like the cartoon character from Beetle Bailey who gives Bailey a rough time.

He was never a tyrant but a whimsical and impulsive character who did much harm to the politicos in different ways. He spent

---

[20] Afrikaans for "Hand him in". *Bandiet-taal* for "Lock him up".
[21] Cofimvaba is a place in the Transkei, apparently where Naude came from.

about four years as an official and during that time he removed the criminals from amongst us and cut our supply of newspapers.

When he took charge of studies he also ran amok. Once he drove comrade Stanley Maghoba and me to headquarters to write exams. Within half an hour he was back. "Maghoba! Take your articles! You are being drafted."

Stanley tried to protest but Cofimvaba just went and snatched his paper away and left no alternative for Maghoba. I was so shaken up by the crude behaviour that I stopped writing and handed my paper in to the invigilator.

It was he who raided the quarry and destroyed all the shelters and started the court case. That day he made sure that chief warder Davies remained outside the quarry fence. Some of the warders with their rubber baton or 'donkey *piele*' were on the verge of attacking us but he saw it and shouted, "Stadig mense, stadig!"[22] This stopped them and an outbreak of violence was averted. It was then that Lungile Dwaba and Steven Tshwete and others were taken away by two vans and locked in a special cell vacated in D Section. They were about eighteen in all. The situation at the quarry was very tense that day.

One day he gets hold of a letter which some PAC comrades in our group had written to their isolated leaders in D Section about unity in action with the ANC. The following morning when we were going for our breakfast he stood against the wall swinging his key ring on his finger and created a rhythm and sang,

"ANC and PAC want to come together,
ANC and PAC want to come together,
But that will be the day!
But that will be the day!
ANC and PAC want to come together,
But that will be the day!"

After this charming recital he laughed and marched away.

He had the habit of picking up empty bottles: beer bottles, cold drink bottles and brandy bottles from all over town. One day while he was on this spree he saw a *span* warder looking over a hedge while the prisoners were pulling weeds. He drove over there and looked over the hedge and saw warder Spencer's sister-in-law having a suntan with only a bikini covering her private parts and her breast nipples pointed towards the sky.

He took off with the warder and told him to move his *span* somewhere else. Then he went through the gate and told the girl to get dressed and take her things as she was leaving the Island.

---

[22] Afrikaans for "Carefully men, carefully!".

Spencer's wife tried to intervene but he shouted her down. The girl dressed and came out with a bag. Cofimvaba told her to get into the back of the van and drove her to the docks and told her never to come back to the Island.

Robben Island has a small town with homes for married warders, a primary school, a hall, sickbay, single quarters for single warders, a sports ground, tennis courts, mess room for single warders plus a guest house for visiting officials.

Warders choose servants from amongst the common law prisoners to do domestic work in their houses. Criminals also clean the single quarters and cook and serve in the warders' mess rooms.

With the warders working long hours, the wives get lonely and when the husband returns he is unable to converse intelligently. The only conversation she hears is that, "Vanaand, het ek die kaffirtjie lekker geslaan,"[23] and so on. He, in his crude behaviour never could reach out to her understanding of things. She sulks and her sexual urge wanes. They feel lonely and lost. The following day she feels lonely and seeks some solace from the house monitor.

The *bandiete* are great conversationalists and their conversation draws the women closer and the sexual urge rises again. The *bandiet* is always ready.

With Wednesdays being shooting practice days, half the quarry *span* would go out for half a day's work while the rest were locked up. In the afternoon the others went out to work. One such afternoon we are locked up in B4 with one of these house monitors. He was tall, about six foot, dark and a damn good story teller. He was sitting next to old man Jack, a *bandiet*, chatting away in *bandiet-taal*. Jack sympathised with him and let him talk. Jack listened and interpreted for us.

There was a warder who we named 'Umhlanyo' after the green medicinal herb to fix coughs and grew on the Island. Why I don't know. His wife was a pretty woman. They had this *bandiet* as their house monitor. The pretty woman fell for his talks and started having sex with him.

However a warder we called 'Lampies' was after her and one day unexpectedly he came to visit her. He walked in through the back and entered the house. Thinking she was in the bedroom he opened the door which was shut but not latched and saw the *bandiet* on top of her. He being wise, reported the matter to her husband and the husband, being a fool, reported the matter to Lieutenant Bosch, who was our jailer.

---

[23] Afrikaans for "This evening I really beat the little kaffir up good and proper".

The *bandiet* was taken off and told to work in the yard. He worked in the yard for some time, but always looking for an opportunity to go out and see her.

He told Jack that he loved the woman and she was deeply in love with him. He said that as soon as he reached the house he would prepare breakfast and coffee for both of them and take it to her in the bedroom. They then ate breakfast together and sipped their coffee in bed and all the while his hands moved up and down her thighs. He would then mount her for one and a half hours with her legs around his waist. He said that the woman was so good that she moved with each thrust of his and her lips never left his. He said that after that she would get up and go have a bath. He would prepare lunch and clean the house while she was bathing. After lunch they would get into the bed and start all over again. He said that if he was in a mainland prison he would escape with her. He even said that one day he would get even with Lampies.

One day the *bandiet* did manage to break out of his *span* and sneak off. He was found out and that was the end of this. But we heard that eventually the woman started prostituting herself for three Rands or more for a round.

As all the *bandiete* were scattered amongst us politicos we would hear their stories whenever we liked. One of the Desperado *bandiete* knew something about hypnotism. He was a capable chap who could put a person to sleep with his head and back on one chair and his legs on the other and then ask two people to stand on his stomach. He taught his tricks to a warder who used it on other warders.

What this warder did not know was that this chap would also visit his wife during lunch breaks for sex. He told us that the Boer woman like Black men because of their ability to satisfy. The warder found out soon enough and got his transfer.

Nelletjie's wife was big and used to beat her servants up. The *bandiete* never understood her and would ask for a transfer. One of the replacements was also beaten up and got transferred. But she complained to Nelletjie and back he went. Soon she has him on the ground again, straddled her legs, sat on him and started tickling him. The monitor sees that she has no panties on, so he toppled her over and mounted her with his lips on her. She gripped his back and started muttering, "You son of a bitch, this is what you were running away from, eh! Now give it to me, its all yours honey!"

This monitor related the story to the other monitors and they were sorry for running away from her place of work.

There was also the warder who tried to fight with a *bandiet* called Billy. Billy floored him easily and it was only when the other warders came by and held him that he got badly beaten. This poor young warder met and married this Cape Town woman who must have been in her mid-thirties. Soon after she arrived on the Island she started a lucrative business of prostitution with the other warders.

The Malawian convict who always supplied us with newspapers and tobacco found out what was going on and threatened to tell her husband. She compromised with him and went to bed with him on and off. One day the warder comes home, finds his wife with another warder and shoots but misses as the warder flies through the window. The warder was transferred. We came to know of this from the Malawian *bandiet*.

There was however an occasion when a *bandiet* having sex with a warder's wife was found out by another warder's wife. She called her husband, 'Jigeleza', who got a group of warders together and shot the *bandiet* dead. To cover up the murder, the authorities said that the *bandiet* was shot while escaping from being caught for theft.

A Colonel was also having an affair with a young warder's wife. He promised that he would give her husband promotion up to Sergeant when the next Merit Board sits. He blackmailed her into having sex by making false promises as he never gave the promotion. Eventually the Colonel moved off looking for new pastures.

One day she forgot all about her dignity and reported him. The receptionist at headquarters had to help calm her, for by then she had completely broken down and was crying her heart out. She and her husband soon moved away to another prison.

There was also a yard warder who was found to be having sodomy with a *bandiet* and the case of a Lieutenant having an affair with a bald-headed young warder. This warder was one of the guys who tried to swim across to Blouberg Strand with Sergeant Kaminga. He never made it and was picked up by a boat just in time. To hush up the whole thing the bald-headed guy was transferred to another prison.

These crude immoral affairs came to our ears through the *bandiete* grapevine or from friendly warders. The affairs gave us something to talk about, laugh and while away our incarceration days, thinking the scum had no morality because they came from a degenerate breed.

This was the main reason why Captain Naude never allowed Indian and Coloured politicos to work in town or near the place. Not that he ever distrusted us but he never trusted his breed of women folk.

Strip Search

Strip searching was a common occurrence. Mostly done at night, it was a harrowing experience making life more miserable than it was.

One day in B1 a criminal named Ralph put a note into one of the PAC inmate's blankets. The note was linked with Robert Sobukwe and the inmates. He then informed head warder Van der Berg. A search was made and the note found. There was chaos after this. Some eight to nine people were taken to single cells. Among them were ANC members.

When Theron came around, our cleaner called 'Viskop', (just because his face looked all scaley like a fish's head, and he was ugly anyway), went straight to the chief and explained everything. The men were brought back from the single cells. This type of thuggery was called 'a bomb' in prison language. The 'bomb' backfired and Ralph himself landed in single cells.

In the second raid I remember, the warders came running, opened all the cells and the windows. "Staan teen die muur en trek julle klere uit."[24] We stood naked and freezing with up-stretched hands on the wall. We stood shivering and if we looked sideways the baton strap would sting our buttocks.

They threw the blankets and our clothes here and there and kept on taunting us, "Kyk die koelietjie se klein pieltjie!".[25] and so forth. This went on for an hour and in the end, at random, they took about twenty prison tickets.

After they left we found that all our blankets and bedding had been 'skommelled op'.[26] Luckily we had already marked our things and we settled down soon. From all the B Section cells they collected about eighty prison tickets and these comrades were charged for illegal possession of reading material.

We appeared in front of Captain Kellerman, 'Fat Mobs'. The prosecutor was the chief who conducted the raid. Amongst our group were George Mbele, Joshua Zulu, Matthews Meyiwa, Siva Pillay, two PAC chaps, Makana and George Rafuza, some others and me.

George Mbele and Makana pleaded that the search was improperly conducted and the prosecution could not show which article was found where. There was an adjournment and after some time we were called in. He said that the prosecution was withdrawing charges and we could go.

---

[24] Afrikaans for "Stand against the wall and remove your clothes".
[25] Afrikaans for "Look at that little Coolie's small penis!".
[26] Afrikaans for "messed up".

But the Big Fives kept on making bombs against us and pimping on the prisoners working in the GI Store. First a rumour was spread that the politicos were going to attack the warders while working at the quarry. Panic stations arrived and we were kept locked up, only coming out to eat and to exercise, which we had to do with our hands above our heads. The Kleynhans brothers were keen for us but the whole thing fizzled out when they found it was a bomb.

Sometime after this another bomb came. The Big Fives reported that some criminals sympathetic to us had hidden an escape boat for us in the bush. There may have been such a boat, but we never really found out. However what did happen just after this was the removal of a huge draft of 'A' and 'B' group criminals from the Island. We were sorry to see them leave as we then had to make new contacts for our newspapers and things.

In 1968 the warders raided C section. They had been given some information by an *impimpi*. They walked straight to Siddiq Isaacs' drawer, lifted some books in the corner and found a hand-made master key. It was said by the warders that this key could open any prison door in South Africa. All the prison locks were made by *Josiah Parkes and Co* of London. Siddiq was taken to reception, charged and off to single cells. The following day they raided everywhere, including the quarry.

On another occasion, Lieutenant Fourie, the bastard, raided the single cells one night. With a howling wind outside the sons of the land were fast asleep. "Trek jou klere uit en staan teen die muur!" Govan Mbeki was not well and could not take this. He collapsed in a heap and Fikile Bham got angry. He moved towards 'Oom Gov' but Lesley van Heerden stopped him. He had to lie there until the search was over.

Fourie was a degenerate sadist and, being the blue-eyed boy of Brigadier Aucamp, lusted after power. With his security network he planted about six small radios at the quarry and the *landbou-span's* work place. He then raided and caused all kinds of trouble. We were angry when we heard about it, but because no one was charged we cooled it. But some of the warders did not like what he was doing and they told us about Fourie's *laaitie*. This is how we came to know about his evil acts with 'baldie'.

'Spy 13'

When we arrived on the Island we found a well-dressed gentleman with a carnation in his buttonhole and always a felt hat. We had not a clue about him until some other comrades said that he was 'Spy 13', a security prison official. He would drive around the Island all day in a bakkie with binoculars on the seat next to him. He looked like a guy that comes out of a James Bond thriller.

The story went that his brother was Victor Verster, a big shot in the Prison Department and so the prison was named after him. He was a very diplomatic person and had the mannerisms of an Englishman. Now and then he used to call us for an interrogation. The first thing he would say, "Gentlemen, I am getting you all a holiday and away from the Kleynhans brothers. Isn't that nice?"

At the end of 1965 he called about twenty five of us to the *zinktronk*. That day I was with comrade George Naicker. He called George and asked him to be seated and started a monologue which went something like this:

"You Indians are Aryans who came from the North through the Himalaya Passes many millions of years ago. Your ancestors settled in the plains of the Indus River and slowly advanced to the southern tip of India where the Natives were Dravidians. Your ancestors conquered them and they assimilated with your people. Now you people are called Indians—a very civilised race.

The Aryans were a very clever race. They brought with them knowledge and skills and taught them to the Natives—the Dravidians. The Dravidians were a backward people and lived in primitive conditions. The Aryans changed all that.

The Vedas are your people's classical literatures. Lord Krishna and Lord Rama paved the way to prosperity and a culture you can be proud of.

Your civilisation is thousands of years old, even older than the European civilisation, but what I do not understand is how these monkeys managed to get you people involved into their politics!"

Comrade George replied with his usual cynical smile.

"Mr Verster you are under the wrong impression if you think I am an Aryan. I am not! I am a native of India called Dravidians. We Dravidians accepted the Aryans without any wars; and in the same way the Africans whom you call monkeys accepted us without any wars. They even tried to accept your people with open arms but your White Tribe had ulterior motives. You did not want to share with them, but wanted all that they had—and it was land! Precious land on which they survived. You took it away from their welcoming hands by the wars of dispossession. I am a Native of India, born in South Africa and now a fully fledged African of South Africa!"

"Mr Naicker, nice talking to you! You see, I have learnt some history of which I was ignorant!"

The interrogation which was really a palaver, ended. But he was an intelligent bugger. A *boer* would not know the things he did. I was called. The topic changed.

"I do not like what is happening at the quarry, but I am in no position to do anything about it. Have you seen how the Kleynhans group bend the tops of their caps upwards like the Nazis? They are the same breed as the Jew killers. Don't worry, they will not be here for long. Right! Next gentleman!"

This was his way of talking. He did not harm us in anyway and usually kept himself aloof from trouble spots. He was later transferred.

Influx Starts

It was clear the outside world was having a tough time. The drafts just flowed in. Loads of them being shunted around the country and reaching their final destination with us. Soon C section was opened and filled, mainly by people who had study rights. Most of the drafts from the Eastern Cape and Border regions went into D section. By the end of 1965 the cells were full with inmates sleeping sixty five or seventy to a cell right up to the bathrooms. Even to get us all in there they took some of our criminals to *zinktronk*.

Of course work at the quarry continued. There we were banging away with our hammers filling our quotas. Because of the pace of work we had to keep the four hills of crushed stones high. I was there sitting on my rock place, *knapping* away. It was hard and boring work, with no shelter and the wind howling around. At least the *spans* working the *kruiwas* could move around. And since they had broken down the little shelter we had constructed there was no place to hide or rest.

As with us, the newcomers found the ropes quickly. As with us, they learnt when to try for the wheelbarrows and when to go for the four pound hammers. During winter the wheelbarrows were the favourites because at least you could try and keep warm by moving.

The politicos who worked with the pneumatic drill and the fourteen pounders were the toughest of us. And they were Oom Dellie's favourites. And they were allowed to knock off early so they could wash all the dust off themselves properly.

The wall around the dyke had been finished. About sixteen feet high and nicely built out of flat stones. The new quarry was taking on its own real shape. There was the fence around it with two large gates at one end and then the fence right up to the prison yard.

All this happened but one thing remained constant. Meal stops. On each Friday enough tickets were taken from the *knaplyn* to fill a cell.

Piet and Jan Kleynhans were transferred sometime before the end of 1965. Of their group of bad bastards, Du Preez was later moved to stores while Fourie went to train as a male nurse and then returned to the Island. It was at around the same time that we heard through the grapevine that the now Captain Killian had told Karnakemp to cool it with the politicos.

Kleynhans' group was hated by Sergeant Jaapie Smith's *bougroepspan*. Jaapie was a good soul. So much so that at weekends they would take clubs and staffs into the warders' pub and beat shit out of the Kleynhans' group. Someone from the group would come around on Mondays with a black eye or a hand in plaster. It got out of hand so people were stopped from going to the pub with clubs.

When the *bougroepspan* was on duty over weekends, Sergeants Joubert and Opperman would raid the kitchen for *dalav* for the politicos. However we had a strict rule not to take things from warders so they would always have to throw it away.

The *bougroepspan* did help us in fighting tyranny and smuggling but when the prison complex was finished they left the Island.

It was at around the time that a whole bunch of criminals were taken off the Island to make room for more of us that we began to complain. Maybe it was easier then. Tools were in short supply and the old wheelbarrow wheels were all buckled and they were hard to push in the sea sand. We complained.

Lieutenant Bosch

He was a new guy to the Island, coming to replace Cofimvaba. He was a humble person who did not know the ropes well. So Cofimvaba sees the gap and offers to show him around. He was all so full of himself because he was now promoted to Captain and in charge of security and studies.

"So you have not yet visited the single cells. You must visit them every day. Let me take you there and introduce you to President Mandela and his Cabinet."

He thought he was very funny.

As I was then studying for a Chartered Institute of Secretaries diploma, I would always get invitations from the Cape Town branch of the CIS to attend meetings. One day I took the invitation to Cofimvaba:

"Why of course you can attend. Why not? Just as long as you have the money to pay for the warders accompanying you."

He laughed and walked off.

It was at around this time that the warders started looking for politicos to become house monitors. Oom Dellie wanted James Marsh but he declined. Joseph Dlamini agreed, but jokingly says to Dellie that he would work but not wash Dellie's wife's panties. Oom Dellie replies:

"No you will not do that. If she gives it to you to wash then I will kick her puss."

Sergeant van Wyk of the bamboo *span* wanted Edward Mkhize.

We in the ANC got worried and discussed the matter at length. It was an attractive option but against this was the fact that 'Umhlanyo's' wife and her friends were part-time operatives running their own 'blue light' district. They would have party evenings playing Johnny Mathis and other blues songs. Arguments were strongly put that these women would lure politicos into bed. We decided to reject the idea.

'Umhlanyo' had a tough time. One of the criminals had messed with his wife. 'Umhlanyo' suspected the right criminal. So one day when we come back from the quarry we all have to strip as usual. The *bandiet* hands his clothes to a warder, gives a click of the tongue and jumps real high, legs very wide. When 'Umhlanyo' sees the size of the *bandiet's* penis he closed his eyes and held his head. We all laughed.

Anyway nothing came of it because we heard that Cofimvaba turned the idea down flat.

Us politicos had a high reputation in the town. Whenever we worked there some of the women would send their monitors along to us with a jug of coffee and some bread and things. One day Oom Dellie's wife did this and one of us went up to her and asked for some dripping. She got very cross and when he came back and told us what he had done we asked him not to belong to a town *span* again.

During the Captain's time there were two chief warders, Davies and Van Tonder. Davies was very violent but reasonable, whereas Van Tonder was a lay preacher so he never swore or anything but he was a real sadist. In his behaviour he was the devil itself. He would love to take away a criminal's bread if he saw any coat buttons undone. When they saw him coming at meal times the common law blokes would hook their bread on the barbed wire and gulp down their coffee and then get stuck into the bread. When you did this you had to watch for the seagulls as they were always swooping about and stealing. They were a nuisance but one day one shitted on Van Tonder. We all could not help but laugh.

Van Tonder could make you very cross. On one occasion Ronnie, one of the Desperados, threw a hot plate of porridge at him. Right into his face. From then onwards Van Tonder became 'Sopapa'.[27] Ronnie went straight to the isolation ward for a beating up.

Bosch was reasonable. His sense of diplomacy helped him to take us lot. Everyday Ephraim Mbele from Umlazi would stand in the queue for complaints. Bosch asks him why he stands in this queue

---

[27] From the Afrikaans 'pap', meaning porridge.

everyday. Bosch gets told that there was so much wrong with the place that he, Mbele, could come up with a new complaint every five minutes. Bosch just takes Mbele into his office and sorts the thing out easily.

Hunger-strike

The last Friday but one in March 1966 turned out to be a scorcher. But we were all hard at work *knapping* our barrow and a half of stones. No one wanted to loose any meal tickets and miss the Saturday meat ration. In fact a lot of us had already filled a barrow full so we were taking it easy and allowing our stomachs to rumble along. It was nearly lunch time anyway.

This did not last long. One of the *agterryers* comes along and tells us that we would only be getting a half ration at lunch. The reason seemed obscure. The tension rose quickly and Comrades Dip, Steve Tshwetè, Majaja and Simon Brander took over. Word passed around that no one was to take lunch. The Indian and Coloured comrades had to be warned as they were the first to get their plates of food.

The *phaka* bell rang and we fell into a line. As usual we stood in the front of the line, waiting for our 'D' diet, specially for Indians and Coloureds: mealie rice and cow peas at lunch time. There was only half a plate, so we just walked past with anger and defiance; quite sadly and cross. This was an idea whose time had come. You feel it in your bones and it carries you forward. That is what power is all about. The rest did the same. All the other politico *spans* from other work places did the same.

We all sat down and in a few minutes the ANC, PAC and NEUM representatives met and came to a unanimous decision. We were on hunger-strike until our demands were met. We wanted better quality of food, soaked properly with a reasonable amount of fat, better clothing, harassment by the warders must stop and recreational facilities should be provided by the Prison Department. The list went on. Our delegates told us to discuss the matters in our cells and come up with constructive ideas.

The warders were of course badly taken aback. They tried to push us around but to no avail. Back to work we went and then, when we started lining up to troop back after knock off time they waited, lining the way. We put some of our militant men in the front so that the hunger-strike could not be sabotaged.

After being searched in the prison yard, the hunger-strikers just walked straight past the food counter. We were counted and locked up.

That evening our cell, by this time C3, we decided to recommend that we should only break the strike if the authorities agreed to see a delegation. Decisions passed through the cells via the telephone.

The next day there, enticing us, was a breakfast offer of pure white mealie meal. No one touched it. We fell in for our half day Saturday work.

At the quarry there was much discussion and in fact some conflict within the PAC fellows. Most of the PAC comrades from the Transvaal and the Cape were supporters of Leballo. There was however a group led by Hamilton Keke from East London who followed Sobukwe. This little group gathered and listened as Popo, an old man from East London, told the group that they should not follow the communists in the hunger-strike. That lunch time these East Londoners did in fact take the meal. We felt this was a stab in the back.

We were all locked up after lunch, but soon the grilles clanged open and the warders took all the sell-outs who had eaten out and away to D block. They were taken out so that they could not be beaten up, and as far as I was concerned, I knew Popo had approached the authorities to take them out of the cell where the hunger-strikers were.

In our cell nine were taken out, including Popo. Their fears were genuine, because the young Leballo group would have definitely beaten them up. This was a common practice in prison. There was some difference between these two groups. Robert Sobukwe's followers, who were a minority, were regularly getting beaten up by Leballo's youths headed by their general, 'Hunchback'.

We had forsaken four meals and were still going strong. Our determination grew stronger after the sell-outs were taken out. The stigma of being sell-outs stayed with these guys for a long time.

Late that afternoon the supper came early and was brought to our cells. Of course we strolled past and obviously there was some variety. The meat was cooked well with slices of tomatoes. The soup was nice and thick and the porridge had some fat on it. It was probably the best food any of us had seen in years. As the criminals brought it into each cell the warders informed us that the other cells and blocks were eating well and everything was settled. But we left it. "Why are you being so silly, it is all settled", the warders said.

Our communications were far too good for this ruse. In fact we had even heard that by Friday evening the single cell politicos had heard of the strike and come out on a sympathy strike. And some of the criminals had done likewise. I remember one of these chaps was a good guy called Mandla. They got it badly though. They went into isolation, lost their gratuities and 'A' group privileges.

On Sunday we heard that the hospital patients had also come out.

We quickly met and resolved that the patients should not jeopardise their health and should take food.

That day young Qwentshe, the son of the man I met in East London all those years ago, had three epileptic fits. He refused our pleas for him to get into the hospital quick. However after the next bout we pointed out to him that he was not selling anyone out. Full of remorse he gave in and the warders took him away.

On our seventh meal, the Sunday lunch, Sergeant Loubscher praised the food, tasting some, telling us that he himself had helped prepare it and so forth. A Captain just stood by as we filed past the food trays in the cell passage and went back to our cells.

After not eating supper we all started singing freedom songs, being led by Jacob Zuma. We ended with *Nkosi sikelele i Afrika* and went off to sleep feeling better than for a long time.

But the nightmare began the next morning. It was a Monday, which meant back to the quarry and trouble. We had already noticed how Lieutenant Bosch had avoided us during the past few days.

We entered the barbed wire covered hole and started to walk to the quarry. Although the warders shouted and screamed at us to walk faster we took it very slowly. It must have taken us all of half an hour to reach hell hole. The comrades at the back had it really rough. The dogs were let loose and a couple, like comrade January, got nasty bites. We told Oom Dellie that we wanted to lay charges against the dog handlers but he ignored us.

We carried on working at a very slackened pace. After all, what could they do? Withdraw our prison cards? But it felt like a helluva time till lunch. But for us lunch meant not just no food but also that only half the day had gone. When the bell rang some stood up reluctantly and others just sat where they were.

After lunch break the work slowed down more and more. The wheelbarrows stopped moving, the spade *span* leaned on their spades, the *toutrekspan* sat in a circle, the fourteen pound hammer *span* sat next to their hammers, the stone dressers leaned against the wall. Occasionally one could hear the *knaplyn* hammer. Even the breeze stood still and the day dragged on.

When the bell went for *shayile* we slowly stood up, dumped our tools in the shed and fell into a line. We had one thing in mind and that was to hit the hay as soon as we were in the cell.

We were counted and we started our tortuous journey to the prison. Now however Oom Dellie asked the dog handlers to walk outside the fence. They were getting worried.

In the cells and with no food, most just rolled out their mats and crashed. Some played bridge or draughts.

I think it was the first time that the three toilet-pans had a rest. And they must have enjoyed the rest, because they often became the victim of sixty to sixty five buttocks of all sizes spewing mess on their clean water and shining circular mouth. On the morning of the fifth day I peeped into the toilet-pan and I think it smiled at me. Was I becoming crazy? How can a toilet-pan smile! Must be hallucinations!

Walking even more slowly to the quarry began to irritate some of us. It was all dragging on and our nerves began to fray. Everyone was on edge and a small thing could spark an argument. My niece was to have visited me the coming Sunday, but it looked like all visits were cancelled. I got depressed not knowing when it would be possible for her to come again. And there is George Naicker walking with me and Molefe and Alfred Duma. George was needling them with remarks on capitalism and socialism. This comrade had a tiny structure but enormous courage but he seemed to have little sense of time and place. "Natoo, are you with us?" This broke my revere. "Comrade, I was drifting on a high plain!" I replied. He let it go at that.

At our work places the *toutrekspan* tried to sing freedom songs but their voices cracked up and fell silent. Sometime that morning a comrade from East London fainted. Some comrades carried him to the shed and sprinkled water on his face and told him to lie down. Before noon another two had joined him in the shed. After lunch the *kruiwaspan* just lay in the barrows, despite Oom Dellie's orders to keep moving.

I think this is when Oom Dellie had enough. He went to his office and phoned. Bosch arrived in a bakkie. He told Oom Dellie that he wanted to see a delegation of the hunger-strikers. Our leaders went forward to hear him say he was willing to hear our complaints and try to solve it as best as he could. He told the delegation to climb into the van so that he could meet them in his office and sort out our problems.

Our demand was met, so, quickly, we decided to notify everyone that the hunger-strike was now off, and that we should take our supper.

We walked back quickly. Some pimps who had been eating started to call for the boycott to continue. They were over-ruled. When we reached the yard the warders did not even count us. The kitchen gate was wide open and the food waiting on the food counter. We went to the kitchen and took our food. At last the hunger-strike was called off. Much later the delegation came out and we saw them taking food. We had won.

On Wednesday during lunch break our leaders told us that

promises had been made. And indeed they were kept. The food did improve and we did get better clothing along with shoes and socks. And the greatest victory was that we were not stripped naked anymore for search after work. The *tausa* had met its end and we had got stronger.

The *tausa*, done in all prisons, was very humiliating. At the end of a day's work you would form up and strip in the prison yard. Clothes in one hand and the hoes and socks in the other. Warders like the Kleynhans group would wait till all the prisoners had stripped and only then would they search and throw our clothes in all directions. This made it hard for us to find our clothes but easy for the Big Fives to pinch.

In winter this ritual was very grim. After suffering the day in the chilling Benguela Current wind to stand shivering and be searched! We hated it!

This was where the *tausa* came in. The warder would search your clothes while you had to jump in the air with open wide legs, at the same time clicking your tongue and bending down to show your anus. The criminals seemed to have made this into their own form of dance. And when they landed on the ground again, bent over and legs wide, they would shout 'King!'. Still, even doing this, the criminals would be able to hide the most amazing kinds of contraband. I do not know how they do it. All politicos always refused to jump. Instead, we just undressed, raised our arms, turned around and walked away. In 1967 that stopped as well. No undressing, nothing! They would just pat your clothes. It was a big victory!

Nearly all the criminals had deep lash marks on their buttocks and walked with a limp. This came from cutting the ankle tendons so you could earn a long rest at the hospital.

As time went on, we got a spare coat, spare trousers, spare shoes and socks, spare shirt and a set of jerseys: one polo neck and one 'V' neck.

In September, 1967 we were given permission to order tobacco, *Rizla* and matches. Before this, smoking was an offence and if caught one gets three meals off or land in isolation cells.

Recreational facilities were promised by Lieutenant Bosch, but they again only came in 1967.

Man is a human being with emotions, intelligence and certain beliefs and as such the environment around him affects his lifestyle, his manners, his way of thinking and his outlook of the world. Our hunger-strike had a terrific impact on the bachelor warders and it galvanised them into action within three months.

The bachelor warders in all the *spans* got about four slices of brown bread with a miserable splash of gooseberry or raspberry jam and a bottle of coffee for lunch. This was delivered to them at their work place. One day Meintjies, Smith and company threw down their rations of food as soon as they received it and told the van driver that they were going on hunger-strike. Meintjies said:

"Die *Poqos* is reg! Hulle ken wat julle moet doen. Ons moet *vuga*! Ons wil nie die vuilkos eet nie!"[28]

Within the hour the van came back with food: rice, soup and meat. This was a great victory for the bachelor warders. Right through the years they had been eating that greased gooseberry jam, bread and coffee. Meintjies and Smith walked high with a big smile on their faces. This victory was due to our struggle. They realised it and somehow their behaviour towards us also changed. Where there was harshness, they now sometimes showed respect.

It was around then that we began to acclimatise to our predicament. Our structures had expanded and so people knew the line. As more and more SACTU people came to the Island they would go straight into the 'DC' structures. They knew about organisation and discipline. The SACTU comrades from the Eastern Cape were particularly strong.

With Mandela and the top leadership with us, the structures could sometimes work hard. He and the single cell chaps had their own structures. They would send stuff down for us to discuss. It would come to the DC and they would notify the dormitory 'PRO', who would then inform the group leaders. From there it would come to us in our groups of four. Matters would be discussed; our small decisions then taken back to the group leaders and then higher upwards.

There was the possibility of democracy in all of these structures. But there is also the chance for top down telephones. Sometimes we would talk back to the leadership and tell them they are talking nonsense. Or it could work the other way around. Like when George Matanzima came unannounced to visit Mandela. Nelson did not know. He met with George and took off with him. "How could you want to just come and see me, what about Walter. . .?" We heard about it and decided that Nelson should never see George again.

But later George says he wants to come back and bring Sabata Dalindyebo along. By now Nelson had learnt his stuff and we discussed the whole thing. We said that he should only see Sabata

---

[28] Afrikaans for "The *Poqos* are right! They know what they are doing. We must strike! We will not eat filthy food!"

alone. That was in the late '60s. But Nelson decided not to see anybody. Oh well!

The messages would come through the channels written on small pieces of paper. But we kept nothing. Not even a document from Nelson. It was read then destroyed. Everything was written in cryptic code. Two people in our cell block were responsible for the code: Curnick and Ebbie. The code came from the single cells where Joe Gqabi was the whizz. Nelson would hand something over to Joe who would then encode it and send it over to whoever was on the DC in the single cells. From then it came to us.

This was a tough job, this encoding and decoding. Nelson would write long documents!

We could also then sit and think about our sentences and think about the past. Sometimes that was tough. It was curious because if you thought too hard about the past then you might find too many weaknesses and say that it was all for nothing. And then you have to look forward and all you find are years and years stretching ahead. For nothing? This could screw your head around and around.

But we would look back and see where things went wrong. Somehow we needed to. It was particularly tough when Stephen Dlamini would say "You chaps were becoming terrorists!" Maybe we were but that was a big load to carry. But I do remember Curnick and I often saying that we should be relieved that we were picked up when we were. Some of the operations that may have been planned for us seemed dangerous. Lives could have gone and we could have swung. Small reliefs!

And then there were the funny things. Like wanting to rob Phyllis' sister for money. In India I had begged and here I was turning into a fucking bank robber! And Ronnie. We would often laugh about him. He was a driven hooligan! Man, he was good at it! And the guys who wanted to screw around at Atlas Chambers. That was a bit much. We all had little stories and memories that we made up or just scattered around anyhow.

With the hunger-strike we were back conducting political struggle so I suppose it was fine that we could look back.

July 1966

I was working in the quarry when Sergeant Du Plessis tells me to get ready to leave. I knew what this could be about. We had read in the newspapers that Rowley and MD had been detained. I went across to where Joe Gqabi, Stephen Dlamini and Ebbie were working and told them that something is in the air. They told me not to worry and that they had full confidence in me.

At reception I was told to get all my things together. I was off to Pretoria.

On the boat with my leg-irons and handcuffs on, Magalies kept on trying to rattle me, saying that I was going to hang.

"Die koolie is slim. Hy gaan hangpaal toe!"[29]

And a Lieutenant asked if I was the 'dynamite coolie' who had fainted at Leeukop. Magalies took great glee in saying that I was the one.

At Pollsmoor I met up with 'Perdekop' whose head really did look like a horse's, hence his name and he was Theron's stooge, and Champagne, one of the NLF guys and six stroppy criminals who were part of his group. They were all hardened criminals, each with two or three blue *baadjies*, which meant that they were in for between ten and fifteen years. They were being taken to Barberton Prison after having tried to escape from Pollsmoor.

At Colesberg that evening some of the criminals started looking for *wyfies* as we settled down for sleep but an old NLF guy told me not to worry and I made my bed next to his. I felt safe but started to think of Rowley and MD.

It was probably the sour herb soup, for on the way to Leeukop all our stomachs started to go rotten. Soon the bucket was full and the toilet paper had run out. When we arrived we were all stinking of shit.

During that first night at Leeukop something must have happened because in the morning Champagne and another criminal, Tony, had a boxing fight according to the gang code. Champagne won and things cooled down.

That day I was taken to the better accommodation in the hospital section. I had barely been locked there for forty five minutes or so, when a warder comes and tells me to get all my books and things. Brigadier Aucamp was booking me out and taking me to New Look Prison. There I was given cold porridge and coffee and put into a single cell. My thoughts were running riot. Greenwood Park, Point, 'Maritzburg, Durban Central. What of tomorrow. Luckily I had some tobacco and my *slatch*, so I lit up and relaxed.

I found out that there were guys in the cell next to me.

"What are you doing here?"
"I was brought here for interrogation. And you?"
"We were got for slogan painting."
"Just keep mum and do not answer any questions."
"Thanks for the encouragement. How long are you doing?"

---

[29] Afrikaans for "This Coolie is a *slim mens*. He's going to the gallows!"

"Sixteen years."

"'Hey! That's a helluva long time."

"Yes it is. I know."

I sounded brave but inside I was scared.

After my conviction in 1964, the SBs had come to Robben Island and interrogated all eighteen of us 'Maritizburg politicos. Now I was alone to face the music. They left me there for four days before anything happened.

On the Tuesday I was taken out, given a set of new khaki pants and safari-type jacket. Aucamp was there with Captain Steenkamp, who had been in charge of our trial.

On the way to COMPOL buildings in Pretoria, Aucamp turned his bulldog face around to me sitting alone in the back of the car and tells me that I must use this opportunity to cooperate with the Security Branch. In the office I was introduced to a Lieutenant Stadler who offered me a Lexington, his favourite brand. I hesitated.

"Take it easy and smoke slowly. How do you feel?"

"I should be alright."

"I felt very sorry for you when Lieutenant Prins was bashing you about. But it is over now."

"Yes it is over now."

"Natoo, we have two statements made by Dan and Iqbal. They say that M. D. Naidoo addressed some activists at your place. You must please think it over and let me know. I shall be back soon."

I felt irritated and trapped. Now they were coming with the soft touch and using my first name as well.

I then asked Stadler about the cricket. He spoke freely until Steenkamp came back. Back to business.

"They are lying if they say that 'MD' addressed a meeting at my place."

"Dan says he introduced 'MD' at that meeting."

"How could he have? I was the organising secretary. As far as I know 'MD' never attended any meeting at my place."

"What about Rowley Arenstein. Did he not give you leaflets to distribute?"

"I told you guys in 1963 that that parcel of leaflets came from Jo'burg with a stamp mark on it. I wouldn't distribute that crap about sabotage being an adventurous act."

"No, Natoo. You are shielding these people. How long are you serving?"

They knew anyway. Why reply? Steenkamp said that I should think things through and that they would see me in the morning.

I was taken back to New Look, where I had a hot bath and then supper. Some *puzamandla* and mealie rice. I smoked one of the four cigarettes I had stolen from Stadler. I lay down and was angry with Dan and Iqbal. They had falsely implicated MD. Rowley's matter was another thing.

The next day Steenkamp was busy writing out 'my' statement. I refused.

> "Natoo, I have given you a chance to come clean. I even promised you that you will get out of prison. Now you are throwing that chance away. When you are on Robben Island and you find things hard do not blame us."

The next morning I was in one of the New Look work teams. This on Aucamp's insistence. The warder did not want a politico in his *span*. It was hard work, pushing wheelbarrow loads of rubble up a hilly incline. One day I just stopped, telling the warder that I had an attack of vertigo. I was soon alright and then they put me in the *span* preparing a rugby field. The work was not that bad and I liked it. I worked there for about three weeks after which I was flown back to Robben Island on a military plane. Kathy Kathrada, Govan Mbeki, Walter Sisulu and others were also in that plane. Kathy and I chatted in *Gujarati* about my interrogation. He seemed to feel very pleased with the way things had gone and was relieved to hear that they had not beaten me up.

At reception I was given a new prison card. My new number was 295/66. Previously it had been 68/64. Then I was taken to a single cell. I was furious. Chief warder Fourie just ignored me. 'Oom Gov' was there and he tried to console me by telling me that it was not too bad in single cells.

I was cross and demanded to see Brigadier Aucamp. 'Cofimvaba' also said that I belonged in the main section. He was going to take me there, with all my books and things. The Sergeant at reception asked why I wanted to see Aucamp and I said that it did not matter any more. Fourie still wanted me in the single cells but Cofimvaba had his way.

After supper, which I had been sharing with Curnick for the past two years, I related the whole thing to Curnick. He was happy that I had refused to give evidence.

Curnick was the live wire of our cell. He would relate stories of preachers preaching away in a way that would make us all crack up with laughter. On Saturdays when we would all wait for our letters; if there was no letter for him, he would just sing "No letter today! No letter today!" It was a sad song and he put a lot of emotion and feeling into it.

When he came back to the cells after Saturday soccer I would ask him how it had gone. "The buggers play for themselves! They never pass and we lose."

But you could always see, just by looking at his face if his team had won. Then we were treated to an action replay of all the best shots. But he would get very serious when we discussed politics.

Campaign Against Tyranny

Then we started to defy the quota system. Cofimvaba came to the quarry and took eighteen politicos away to the lock up as ring leaders. They were charged and we decided to get legal counsel to defend them. We won the case. Apparently there was nothing in the Prisons Act which stipulated quotas. It was a great legal victory.

After some time many politicos were brought back from Paarl and we received more *knaplyn* hammers, wheelbarrows with rubber wheels and spades. Now the quarry was really overcrowded.

Oom Dellie found a way to cope with the overcrowded place. When he found any politico not working hard enough he made them line up on the dyke facing the sea. It was bitterly cold with the sea and wind slashing your face. They had to stand there for hours shuffling their feet to keep warm. One comrade, Douglas Tyutyu, was seriously affected. He was later moved to a mental hospital in Cape Town.

Soon the politicos started building shelters with stone walls to protect them from the cold. One day Cofimvaba just tore them down. Revolt was soon in coming. Comrades just refused to sit against the dyke wall, even when he came along with a squad of warders with FN rifles and dogs. Indris, Lungile Dwaba and Steve Tshwete played a big role in this.

A few months after this Colonel van Aarde sent Sergeant Van den Berg to take charge of the quarry. Working conditions improved immediately and he was always satisfied with what we did, which was more or less very little. We were just sitting around. Instead of a wheelbarrow and a half a day, sometimes we could just manage a very, very small pile.

Some of us Indian comrades made a vegetable garden at the back of the quarry shed. George Naicker, who we nicknamed 'slave master' because he was so zealous about his garden, was in charge. We grew cauliflower, beetroot, pumpkin, spinach and carrots.

Zed, Hector Ntshanyana and myself were in charge of supervising the making of the targets for the shooting range. 'Dip' and others started putting traps down for the rabbits and partridges. Harry Gwala and Mashaya were in charge of the mess hall.

The warders also set traps and could sometimes catch three or four partridges a day. Comrade Ernest Malgas would cook their's for them. Comrade Reggie Vandeyar would cook ours.

One day Dip's trap bagged a peacock. All trapper's activities were suspended for a while. But soon the thing was forgotten and the trappers moved in again. But our main problem were the wild cats, which would often get to the traps before the trappers. Then there would only be bones left.

Things in the quarry were looking very bright. During lunch time a group would be listening to the *Mpukane*. Others would form bridge foursomes and play on a knock out basis. Norman Metshane, alias Captain Devil, Peter Magano, January and myself were together. So were Mike Maimane, Anthony Souza, Molefe and Ebbie. And there was Reggie, Indris, Shirish and Sunny. Others would lie about playing draughts or dominoes.

This went on until the master-key episode. Warders raided the quarry but found nothing.

Oom Dellie was now doing his first year BA and needed someone to help him. Slowly Oom Dellie started accepting the changed conditions in the quarry, realising that we were gaining the upper hand. So Ernest Moseneke agreed to help Oom Dellie.

Since Oom Dellie's head was turning the *toutrekspan* began singing songs as they heaved away. Gabes or Sitho would lead:

> "Mpakmiseni uMunt' o Fileyo
> nase kuseni madoda asinaluvalo"

And the others would come in:

> "Uyakhala' ujuju
> Uyakhala' ujuju Yho! Asinaluvalo
> Uyakhala' ujuju tina Asinaluvalo!"[30]

Another favourite was of course:

> "Shosholoza . . . shosholoza
> Shosholoza . . . shosholoza
> Kwezontaba istimela sishona e-Wankie
> Shosholoza . . . shosholoza
> Wen 'uyabaleka . . . wen 'uyubaleka
> Wen 'uyabaleka . . . wen 'uyubaleka
> Kwezontaba istimela sishona e-Wankie
> Shosholoza . . . shosholoza
> Wen 'uyabaleka . . . wen 'uyubaleka
> Wen 'uyabaleka . . . wen 'uyubaleka
> Shosholoza . . . shosholoza"[31]

Some of these songs were hummed. It is obvious why. Listen with the lead and the chorus following line after line.

---

[30] We used to sing it, but I never saw it; it's Zulu for
'Raise the dead martyr
Even in the morning comrades we are not scared'
Juju is crying
Juju is crying. Oh! we are not scared
Juju is crying. We are not scared!'
[31] The gist being Zulu 'Forward coming through Wankie on a train . . .'

"Mukhulu mukhulu lomsebenzi"
"Umsebenzi . . . umsebenzi . . . umsebenzi"
"Umsebenzi wenkululeko"
"Umsebenzi . . . umsebenzi . . . umsebenzi"
"u Tambo ufuna amajoni
u Mandela ufuna amajoni"
"amajoni . . . amajoni . . . amajoni"
"amajoni enkululeko"
"amajoni . . . amajoni . . . amajoni"[32]

One day Oom Dellie called comrade 'Lavai', Lombard Mbata, to his office.

"Lombard jy is 'n vuil . . . vuil kaffir."
"Delport jy is 'n vuil . . . vuil Boer en 'n hond."[33]

With this preliminary courtesy over Delport invited him to sit, which Lavai did. Oom Dellie opened up. His parents had died when he was very young. His very poor grandparents brought him up. They had no electricity or tap water so Dellie did all the house chores, fetched river water and chopped wood. He never managed to get beyond Standard Eight until he joined the Prisons. He became a brute with a criminal mentality. But now working with us lot had changed his mentality. He could see that we were disciplined politicos fighting for what we believed was correct. He even said he hoped we succeeded.

"From now on I do not want to do anything wrong."

And he did not from then until the day he left us.

The day after this he followed Billy Malgas around the quarry wanting to apologise for having hit him. Billy told him not to worry him and to stop traipsing around.

"Oom Dellie you have hit many people, made many suffer, taken hundreds of people's meal tickets away and lined your stomach. Why do you want to apologise to me. Go and apologise to everyone you have tortured."

Dejectedly Oom Dellie went to his office and sat down with his head in his hands. This was it. One more neutralised.

Education and Culture Struggles Begin

If you do not watch out prison can put your brain to death. So right from the very beginning, during the Christmas period, we would stage plays. It allowed our minds to be preoccupied.

---

[32] 'The task is heavy
The taste of freedom
Tambo and Mandela need soldiers
soldiers for freedom fighting'
[33] Afrikaans for "Lombard you are a dirty, dirty kaffir".
"Delport you are a dirty, dirty Boer and a dog."

Shiresh Nanabhai and Kisten were in charge of the stage. I was the make-up artist. Other interested comrades helped in various departments.

Our first play was *Auntie Selina* which we staged that first Christmas, 1964. Comrade Mike Ngubeni was the director. Its about a witchdoctor, Selina, who dishes out all kinds of potions; for love, sexual potency, removing the *tokolosh*. All the things needed by weak minded people of both sexes. But somebody dies after taking her potion. Auntie Selina is brought to court and tried.

Jacob Zuma played Selina, Judson Khuzwayo was the prosecutor, Gordon Hendricks the magistrate and I was the defending lawyer. It was a great success. This is what prompted me to write my *Sophia* and comrade Mike to script *Ides of March*. Long before Christmas in 1965 we were both hard at work preparing for the performances.

Ides of March is about the workers' struggle. All the dialogue was in workers' language with some very stinging, razor-edged retorts. Comrades Zuma, Khuzwayo, 'Doktela', Billy Malgas, Mayekiso, Xolisile Roxo, Liso Sithotho, Alfred Khonza and others all took part. Between them they chose the stage manager who was also the director.

As usual the stage was made of coir mats. The screen was jail blankets.

There was an eye-catching scene. The workers are in a bus going home to New Brighton. Doktela was the bus driver, clutching the broomstick steering wheel, swinging to and fro as if taking bends at terrifying speed and now and then hooting with his mouth. The workers sat in two rows behind him swerving with him and bubbling away enthusiastically about an impending strike. In the aisle was Billy Malgas with a pile of 'newspapers'; *'New Age*! . . . *amadoda* . . . *New Age*! . . . Read all about the strike!'[34] The workers buy *New Age* and then the bus comes to a halt. There on the roadside sits comrade Dip with bananas; *'Tenga banana baba! Tenga banana*! . . . *Diblish ukala*! And the workers buy his bananas because they like the *fanagalo* of this Indian.[35]

The play was very successful and had to be performed in two different cell blocks on consecutive nights.

Sophia was staged in B1. It is about a slave uprising in a small Greek enclave ruled by a King. But the real dominant force is actually Sophia, the sister of the King. Xolisile Roxo was Sophia; Richard Quentela the King; and Mike Ngubeni, Babana, the leading

---

[34] Zulu for *"New Age! . . . men . . . New Age! . . ."*
[35] *Fanagalo* for 'Buy bananas, old man! It will only cost you one penny!'

black slave. Nelson Diale was the gladiator with Mayekiso, Billy Malgas, Doktela, Alfred Khonza and Patrick Bopela as senators.

The slaves are in jail. However, led by Babana they refuse to fight the gladiators. An uprising takes place, supported by Sophia and they are set free with the help of the gladiators and slaves from outside.

Ides of March and *Sophia* were so popular that we had to repeat them the following year: with a bit more sophistication. Prison conditions allowing of course. That year Xolisile looked stunning as Sophia. I had used water colours to get his lips crimson red and eyebrows slanting with a touch of mascara. Comrade Phillips made us laugh that year when he made liberal use of the water colours to look white.

In 1967, Lwamek Loabile came up with a trade union play. All the dialogue had to be impromptu. So the key was to select the actors and explain the characters and plot: leaders being charged for holding an illegal strike. Ebbie played the magistrate, I was the prosecutor, Henry Makhoti defence, with Isaac Tlale as the court orderly and Patrick Bopela, Nelson Diale and Molefe as the union leaders.

In '68 *Ides of March* played again. Then came a clampdown. No more plays. This lasted for two years.

In '70 comrade Mike staged *Echoes of Congo* which was very successful. He also wrote *Ché Guevera*, but after it played once the clampdown came back again.

While we were staging these plays our PAC counterparts put on *Animal Farm*, which was very successful and also *From the Backyard*. Or something like that. It was about the evils of the *lobola* system. But they never seemed to be as interested in these things as we were.

Of course all the plays had a political message. For days after the showings comrades would discuss the merits and weaknesses of the productions and their meanings.

During December some of the Desperados, with comrade Monde Nqunqwana and a PAC jazz artist, used to move from one cell to another singing songs. Johnny Mathis was Monde's favourite speciality. The Desperados sang, "There would be peace in my valley" and they sang it very well. If one hears them sing this song then one would forget that they were common law prisoners. Being Coloureds and from around District Six they knew how to harmonise and they were the best.

During these times the criminals were playing soccer and had indoor games. Why not us? One day I asked Colonel 'Staalbaard'. He just bit his teeth, "As long as I am standing on my two feet, you *Poqos* will never have any recreational things whatsoever."

'Perdekop', one of the very lowest was standing there, "Jy is reg, my groot baas."[36]

So we relied on our own ingenuity and made our own games. Shirish and I both made scrabble boards out of thin card and there was a chess set with pieces fashioned out of bottle corks. Things were on the move but of course the warders could not help being boorish. The games would go in the night raids and we would have to remake them. But eventually I had managed to make a scrabble board with eight squares for quadruple scores and two hundred and twenty pieces.

At the end of game, comrade Tonjeni was always fooling around by not counting the 'Q' in his hand. He would hide it or slip it into the bag when we collected new pieces. This was his way of making the game less serious. One look at his face and we used to know that he has picked up a Q or a Z and all eyes would be on him to see what he was going to do.

It was fun having comrade Tonjeni around. 'Dip' always played with Tonjeni's huge paunch, tickling him. Tonjeni would laugh. All eyes would look at his paunch going up and down. He never got angry with Dip's antics.

Incarcerated for a very long time one has to think seriously of the future. And to achieve things which could not be done on the racist mainland. On the Island, 'peoples' education' finally became a possibility and it brought new enthusiasm into one's life. Literacy was the main problem. Many, like Ernest Malgas and Samson Fadana could speak English but they could not read and write. Teachers and tutors were selected in each cell and lessons began almost immediately. I was involved in teaching English to beginners. In our cell comrades Jacob Zuma, Doktela, Isaac Tlale, Lombard Mbatha, Shumi Tutu, Nene, Masuku and others joined the beginner's class.

Proudly we could say that we brought the literacy rate to 99.9%. There was only one PAC member, Poyi, left out. A big guy, he worked long hours in the kitchen and did not seem to find the time. As more politicos came to the Island, he learnt from others. Everyone on the Island could read and write. We got to 100%.

I also held Arithmetic and Bookkeeping classes. Comrades like Harry Gwala, Griffiths Mxenge, Gloria Mdingi, Henry Makhoti and Zola Nqini taught the matric parts. The whole idea of 'people's education' was also taught.

---

[36] Afrikaans for "You are correct, my great master!".

In the early days our main problem was stationery. We would use cement bags. Once the study office was opened up by Captain Visser in 1965, we were able to buy stationery and books. Comrades who had money bought reams of newsprint paper, pencils and things and shared it with other comrades who had no money. The will to learn conquered all obstacles.

Culture Takes Off

1967 brought in a new era to all political prisoners. Recreation was allowed.

Soccer! What a wait for so many of us! Teams formed immediately. However it was a pity that they formed along organisational lines. The PAC and ANC both had four teams. In strength order I would rank the PAC teams as first *Manong* then *Gunners*, *Mphatalazana* and lastly *Ikhwezi*. Likewise I would rank the best ANC team as *Bucks* then *Rangers*, *Hotspurs* and bringing up the rear, *Dynamos*.

The most unlucky team was my team, *Dynamos*. George Naicker suggested the name. One Wednesday we had come back from the quarry at midday. We decided to form the team, so, firstly, we elected an executive committee. The president was comrade George Naicker, our secretary Gordon Hendricks, I was treasurer and Marcus Solomon was also on the committee. Our team captain was Douglas Pithi with Benson Fihla as vice-captain. None of us had played soccer before. After two years *Dynamos* and *Hotspurs* merged, with the remaining players forming up as our 'b' team, the *Naughty Boys*.

However in the beginning there was deadlock because we did not have a football association to arrange fixtures. Indris tried and tried to arrange matters with Judas, a *Gunners* player with PAC leanings. Judas would, for some reason or another always run away and only arrange things if he felt like it.

Through the energies of Anthony Souza of *Manong* and Ernest Moseneke of *Mphatalazana* we eventually formed the *Makana Football Association* with a sound constitution. President was Moseneke, Indris was secretary and there were five other executive members. From then onwards fixtures were properly arranged and teams would battle it out every Saturday and Sunday. However after the good Colonel Van Aarde left, Sundays became the Sabbath. All games were banned.

In the very first games *Dynamos* played, there was never any positional play. We would just tear around after the ball. In the first game Benson Fihla tried to head the ball, headed it well and he promptly landed straight on his arse. We cracked up. We had to get

Dimake Malepe, a real pro from *Manong*, to give us some idea. We soon picked our game up.

Once, a veterans game was arranged. It was great to see old guys like 'General', Caleb Motsabi and Joe Moroelong playing havoc with their dribbling tactics. However this proved a short-lived treat. Someone swiped Harry Gwala off his feet and he landed up in hospital with a fractured wrist.

In 1968 rugby games started. This made the Eastern Cape comrades very happy. They had two formidable sides which regularly battled it out against each other. As far as us Natalians and Transvaalers were concerned rugby was very rough. Indres and Dip tried to play, but gave up after one or two games.

But the game was always played in good spirit and no fights ever took place. But when there was a scrum or a load of players piled on top of each other and a scream came out, we always knew that someone's balls were being squeezed by Steve Tshwete.

The warders also had their own teams and warders like Munro would come and watch our guys. There were also rumours that the womenfolk in town wanted to see these two teams clash, but permission had been refused.

Chief Fourie introduced boxing in around 1967. He got about six pairs of gloves, some gum guards, skipping ropes and constructed a ring. As usual we formed clubs on organisational lines. The PAC club was *Vala a Mehlo*,[37] while Michael Ngubeni, a skilled boxer himself, trained our comrades. Comrades Stetho Phillips and Lombard Mbatha were good, but the best was surely George Moffat of *Vala a Mehlo*.

Bouts would only last three rounds. No one had the stamina to go further than that and Fourie would always stop the contest when he saw someone tiring badly.

The clubs only lasted about three months. It was one thing to train and learn to box, but another thing when opponents from two different organisations came together with the intention of bashing each other up.

Inside the cells, bridge was a big hit. Nearly all the Indian comrades knew the game well. We formed a bridge club with Reggie Vandeyar as chair, Gali Tembani as secretary and me as treasurer. Lungile Dwaba and Cansibe Nxigki were on the committee as well. To promote this seemingly strange game we would go from cell to cell teaching comrades and soon, in just over three months, we had over a hundred members.

---

[37] *Fanagalo* for 'Close the eyes'.

Competitions, based on a knock out system, were held each year and pairs were picked from a hat. Reggie Vandeyar, Indres, Shirish, Dip, Anthony Souze, Magano, Tembani, Nxigki, Metshane, Mapukata, Moonsamy and Moses were all good players.

Draughts was also popular, as were dominoes; particularly with the Eastern Cape comrades. Champion players were Joshua Manqunqu, Souze and Magalies. Whenever Magalies played Manqunqu he would always shout, 'I am going to show you pieces of ice . . . You hear, pieces of ice!' But he never won.[38]

In chess the indisputable champion was always Reggie Vandeyar. When Indres got a caramboard and cue from home this prompted great excitement. The game had to circulate amongst the cells. Then Anthony Souza made a board and I three cues out of broomsticks with leather tips. Eventually more appeared out of nowhere. While we were at work, yard warder Crous and another youngster used to practice with our boards. They challenged us one day, beating Ephraim Mbele and me and then also Mbele and Souza in doubles. But in singles I could easily thrash Crous.

Once a couple of table tennis tables were set aside for us, we formed a table tennis committee and the whole game took off. The star was Brian Mzo who was full of acrobatic manoeuvres. He was too much; even for Benson Fihla. Much, much later, four tennis courts were prepared and the game got going. In the annual competitions a lot of the youngsters from 1976 dominated.

Douglas Sparks and George Rafuza took an interest in ballroom dancing and they were very good at it. They started to teach whoever was interested. In a few months they had about fifty pairs dancing. Jacob Zuma became a keen enthusiast and soon could dance with grace.

I used to call Zuma 'Machine gun Zuma' because of the rattling way he laughed. He had a lot of hidden talent which came to the fore when the opportunity arose. This rural boy was so good in whatever he laid his hands on that he won the ballroom championship with his graceful steps. He also took interest in high jumping and here again he excelled and won an annual event.

His interest in politics took him to great heights. In the time he spent on the Island, he was able to analyse a given situation dialectically and come up with a brilliant synthesis. Credit for this goes to Mtu Madala and Stephen Dlamini.

In time it was inevitable that we would have to form a recreation committee to coordinate all these activities. During the Christmas

---

[38] *Bandiete-taal* for "I'll make you cold—defeat you!".

recess the committee arranged all kinds of events. It was a tough and complex task but us politicos already had a commitment in life and were already very sound in our beliefs. This, though the racist minority government kept on telling the world that we were being kept for rehabilitation. It's ironical isn't it?

As recreation and 'people's education' progressed so did our cultural development. Japtha Masemola was the first to make a statue. It was of an African with a bow and arrow. Mark Shinners, Nick Kekane and I started being artists while Kisten Moonsamy and Siddiq Isaacs were good sign writers. We would also hold writing competitions; under the umbrella of the Robben Island Academy of Fine Arts and the Robben Island Institute of Education. In 1973 Mark Shinners took the painting award while in 1974 I received first prize in the short story competition.

We also had some good choir groups. One was led by Arthur Bongani from Port Elizabeth with others by Judson Khuzwayo, Selborne Maponya and Bernard Nkosi with his *Zulu Choir*. Bongani had a style of his own. While conducting he moved around as a ballet dancer and swayed the audience with his moves. His *metier* was freedom songs. When singing about unity through Congress he would move towards an Indian or Coloured comrade, touch the comrade's head, spread his own hands upwards, look up and then with a smooth movement bring his hands down. His choir was more inspirational and cultural than classical.

In competitions the winners were often the PAC young gospel choir. They were all from the Transvaal, the mecca of music in the fifties.

We also had two groups of traditional dancers. Zakhele Mdlalose led the Zulu dancers which included Jacob Zuma, Masuku, Isaac Tlale, or 'Budda Ike' as we knew him, Lombard Mbatha and Bernard Nkosi. Marcus Solomon later joined then and became quite a star. Comrade Kakhaza led the Xhosa group. Later this dancing was banned because the authorities felt that we were sending some sort of war signal. What war signal?

We had our own gumboot dancers, led by David Pitje and George Moffat. They were very good, particularly some Mamelodi boys.

Our Own Comedian

Simanca Simancanda known to all of us as 'Blues'. From the Paarl politicos who came to the Island in 1963, he was a comedian of the first order. Short, stocky, always walking swankily he often suffered from severe bouts of asthma. But when he was not coughing he kept rattling on in a mixture of English, Afrikaans and Xhosa. Even when he spoke this *gamtaal* and people laughed, this did not deter him. His determination to speak this 'taal' made him a comedian, loved by all sectors of the political spectrum, including the foe.

His dialogue with fellow prisoners went something like this:

"How are you today Blue?"

"You not good. Fuckin' khoslo-khoslo pla you." (I am not well. Fucking cough is worrying me).

"Why don't you take medicine for your cough?"

"You soek pomp! Daai khoslo—khoslo medisyne no good for you." (I want asthma-pump! That cough medicine is not good for me).

"I see. But you go every morning for medicine."

"You is pelile. You drink pyn medisyne, asthma medisyne, kitten medisyne, but you like malt baie. Give you amandla." (I am finished. I drink pain medicine, asthma medicine, kidney medicine, but I like malt a lot. It gives me strength).

"Why don't' you ask for malt?"

"Ayi khona. Daai Boere no give you. Suster is lekker. I gives malt." (No. Those Boers would not give me. Sister is nice. She gives malt).

"You mean Sister Saayman?"

"Ja! Ja! I ken hom! Suster Soiman!"

(Yes! Yes! You know her! Sister Saayman!)

"Why you like malt?"

"Thixo! Thixo! I mampara. Malt give you lot amandla. You play mooi volley-ball. Why I no play volleyball?" (Oh God! God! You are a fool. Malt gives me a lot of strength. I play very good volleyball. Why don't you play volleyball?)

"I am old."

"No Old! I still chicken." (Not old! You are still young).

"I get very tired!"

"Must be I heart fucked up. I engine no good. I buy new engine." (It must be that your heart is fucked up. Your engine is not good. You must buy new engine).

"Where can I buy new engine?"

"Buy from dood mense! Hospitals khona baie dood mense. Chris Barnard maak I reg." (Buy from the dead people! Hospitals got a lot of dead bodies. Chris Barnard will fix you up).

Conversation like this always brought laughter. Anthony Xaba was Blue's teacher, trying to get his pronouns right. He failed.

Blues would always tell stories. Like the one about his friends on Friday afternoons in Cape townships. A pretty woman ran a dice game in the street while workers were going home with their pay packets. Wearing a wrap around skirt she sits on her haunches as the workers play her game. She rattles the dice in one hand, shouts "So Vula", and with the other hand flicks open her skirt. As the skirt opened they would peep and so they would loose their money on her loaded dice.

Flea Invasion

In the latter part of the sixties the Island was invaded by a swarm of fleas. There they were, massive black clouds of them jumping around. In the morning you would be full of little red marks and scratches. We washed our blankets with carbolic soap, rubbed our bodies with 'winter green' but nothing seemed to help.

Only when they became fattened could you catch them and squeeze them dead. In our cell Mayekiso used to pile their bodies in a clam shell to show to the yard Sergeant. He could fill half a shell a night without really trying. If we work it out arithmetically, leaving out those that got away, we have fifty five to sixty to a cell, multiplied by half a shell we get half a litre of dead pests. Now multiply that by the cells in A, B, C and D Section; sixteen cells in all, and we get eight litres of the invading pest and about the same quantity that got away. What a total!

And that leaving out the hospital, single cells, kitchen and the Robben Island town itself, which could easily bring another twelve litres of black, shrivelled, deadly dead pests.

Twenty litres containing 20 000 bodies in each litre brings the grand total of 400 000 pests. Add to it approximately another 600 000 pests and we find one million tiny nincompoops every day, trying to bring into submission about 2 500 inhabitants of the Island!

Don't laugh when I get into a hypothetically mathematical progression. If one pest sucked one tenth of a drop of blood, that means they drank 100 000 drops of blood a day. Hey, isn't that a lot?

The whole Island was infected. So everywhere was sprayed but that did not help. Colonel Van Aarde said that they had asked the government laboratories to prepare something stronger and that worked. The first night after this spraying we slept in peace and two days later we were told that we could now wash our blankets. At last Van Aarde, the humble soul had conquered the pests. It was a relief not to scratch our buttocks and backs again.

This invasion lasted two weeks. I'll leave the figures up to you.

Mary

The Mary we knew on Robben Island was not the Mary from the Holy Bible. It was a triangle stand with straps to hold a prisoner's hands and feet. On this Mary the strapped prisoner was given cuts with a cane on his bare buttocks.

Offences were hardly that at all. Often it could all just start through the sadistic whim of a warder. At the trial which preceded a whipping the officer would most often just uphold the warder's words. If you are not defended by an attorney then you hear

remarks from the presiding officer like "Die baas praat die waar-
heid" or "Jy lieg kaffirtjie!".[39] Then come three or six cuts with a
light or heavy cane.

The sight of Mary is ominous. When one is being strapped on the
tension increases. The doctor merely passes you fit and stands there
for an emergency. When the cuts are given a heart piercing scream
is heard. Usually 'M..a..a..ama! M. . .a. . .a. . .ama! Sometimes the
belly empties mess through the anus. It's a pathetic sight to watch!

Indris Naidoo, Johnson Mlambo and Tshweni were victims of the
Mary. They were working at the quarry, removing stones to a heap.
Near the working place was a pool of stagnant water full of algae
and insects. The warder in charge ordered comrade Indris, Mlambo
and Tshweni to get into the pool and remove stones lying there.

The three refused. Their prison cards were taken and in the
afternoon at *shayile* time they were marched to reception and
charged. Indris asked for a letter to his attorney and he was given
one. The other two did not want to be represented and so their case
came up earlier. They were each to receive three cuts with a light
cane.

When Indris' lawyer wrote asking for details and date of trial and
authorities replied that the case was a very minor one and if found
guilty, he may get three meal stops. The attorney on receiving this
letter did not come. Indris was tried, found guilty and was
sentenced to three cuts with the light cane.

They all took the cuts bravely, but when we saw their buttocks we
shivered. The cuts take about two to three weeks to heal completely
but the scar is a life long companion.

Siddiq Isaacs, Achmat Cassim and James Marsh also received cuts
for attempting to escape from Pollsmoor but they received their cuts
off the Island.

Spare-diet

Spare-diet was another form of punishment. Gali Thembani from
Port Elizabeth was caught with some news items. He was charged,
found guilty and sentenced to twenty one days spare-diet.

You get taken to the isolation cells. There you get plain mealie rice
and water for the first two days and then on the third day a half
ration of mealies. Twenty one days go like this. On the twenty
second day he was brought out to have his normal meals.

When I left the Island in 1979 the system had changed. Spare-diet
was now a half ration daily.

---

[39] Afrikaans for "The master speaks the truth" or "Little kaffir, you lie!"

Air Manoeuvres

After our victory over the quota system of work, we were sitting around at lunch time at the quarry. Someone asked me how I could draw so well. My whole family was good in some or other form of art. This prompted a discussion which was to last three days, on whether art was a hereditary or an environmental effect on the person. Comrades quoted Marx and Engels and several other authorities. The conclusion we came to was that the home and school environment of a particular person affects one's tendency.

After lunch we heard loud sounds in the sea and saw warplanes flying over our heads. We stood up and watched five South African Air Force planes trying to sink an old ship by air bombardment. The planes flew low and dropped bombs and rose skywards. They all missed. We laughed at this with derision. We were seeing the shattered image of the force everyone told us was so powerful. One little unarmed dead ship and they cannot sink it!

A trained *Umkhonto we Sizwe* soldier next to me laughs 'S. . .pl. . .a. . .a. . .S.H! Ha. . .Ha. . .a. . .H. . .A!' 'Oh! No!' S. . .pl. . .a. . .a. . .S.H!' Ha. . .H. . .a. . .a. . .H. . .A! H. . .o. . .o. . .o!' His eyes watered with glee.

All of a sudden the *shayile* bell rang. Early! Clearly they did not want us to see this disaster. On the way back all the comrades boasted about how we would have been able to do a far better job. The next morning the ship was gone.

News

News was the food and inspiration of our comrades. When I came to the Island I was constantly amazed by comrades' ability to get hold of newspapers and disseminate news reports. It was a very difficult and dangerous task, made possible only by the common law prisoners who through sympathy with us or because of their bartering activities would filter papers to us.

One thing was of primary importance to us. The security network of the prison authorities and our own security network had to work in harmony but also very differently. If the warders' tightened up, then our security structures had to find alternative means of sustaining us. This would obviously mean taking a few chances for the benefit of the rest.

Things were of course a bit difficult in the early days. But in 1965 one of our comrades made contact with a common law short term prisoner. He would supply daily papers, especially *Die Burger* and the weekend editions and pass them on every Tuesday and Thursday. He would leave them at an arranged spot. A comrade working in town would collect and hand them to another comrade who would take them to a specifically designated cell.

Here only three comrades would deal with the news. There would be two who could read Afrikaans and translate into English. As far as we were concerned the leader pages were the king pin. The third comrade would make a copy of this. The copies were distributed to cells with the original going to the Rivonia cells. When our SWAPO comrades started arriving, the second copy of our news reports would be sent to them. At times when the security situation became difficult news was given orally. Gradually the news would spread through the hospital, *zinktronk* and everywhere.

Cofimvaba hated Indris and would always just look for a feeble excuse to lock him away in singles. One time Indris sat for three weeks. The weird part of this punishment was that Indris was brought from the single cell to eat and work with us at the quarry. This made it easier for us to send news and give him gossipy tit bits. He wasn't supposed to be with us, but, well! . . . Cofimvaba was a weird comical character.

The News Committee had only three members. They had to decide where the news should go. We had to be vigilant at all times so the News Committee would constantly move from cell to cell. The translators were known only to their cell mates. The cells where the translators worked had to be failsafe with no pimps. Sometimes newspapers were brought in by warders, so one had to be doubly aware of the security risks and keep everything tight.

The people who read, translated and copied the newspapers were all students who had to sacrifice their study time for this important work. Only one of the News Committee would be exposed to the comrades at any given time. He would have to memorise all the important news items and brief us in the mess hall or at the quarry during lunch break. Before the strip-search was done away with it was a tough task but still done. How? No more revelations!

It became easier once strip-search was done away. But throughout, the security was extremely good. None of the news disseminators were ever caught. All credit goes to the comrades who worked hard in making it possible for comrades to get news. They worked in difficult conditions. Particularly the people given the task of collecting the papers and bringing them in. Some were called smugglers, a term of criticism and denigration because the line between smugglers and *impimpi's* was often too thin. They would be told not to go to certain places but were instructed to weather the storm and not worry about being called names. Comrades who read this should now know that those who at times were called smugglers were not smugglers in its true meaning but were elite members of an elite underground network.

This elite network only had about ten members. The elite members who brought it in were only known to the elite operative inside the prison yard. No one had the right to query where and how the newspapers came in. This secrecy had to be observed at all costs.

From around '66 to '71, Gali Thembani and myself were in charge of newspapers. He could read Afrikaans and then I would transcribe. One copy for the single cells, one for Namibians, one for the kitchen and one to take to the quarry to read out at lunch time. It was okay to do that because by then there were no warders around during lunch break. They were having their lunch. But sometimes if the security was bad I would not take the paper with me. I would memorise and speak.

There were also political education lessons during lunch time at the quarry. These were led by Harry Gwala, Stephen Dlamini and Joe Gqabi. There were always about twenty or thirty fellows attending. I could never attend because I was busy reading news. And I think these were Party classes.

In the cells we would also discuss ANC history and current news issues. In our cell Ebbie would give news analysis every month or so. He was beautiful. A very good speaker.

The News Committee of the ANC and the PAC's group would work together. The cell receiving the newspapers had the most difficult task. If the ANC got the newspaper then they would go through it first, translate it and pass it on to the PAC group. If they got a newspaper the same procedure is followed.

It is alright when you get one newspaper but very difficult when there are more than one. Our News Committee would pass the other onto the PAC, they would work at it and pass it back late at night.

To destroy the papers was crucial. One of the News Committee would leave the paper to soak for about half an hour in a bucket of water and then tear the newspaper into shreds and rub it with his palms till it became like pulp. Then he would throw a handful in each toilet pan so that they do not get clogged and flush it away. He would then clean the bucket and soap his hands, making sure that all the blackness has gone. One cannot be haphazard in this work. A blackened palm will give the game away.

One day George Naicker went to the kitchen to fetch hot water. The kitchen warder refused, but George tried to push his way through. The warder pushed him and so felt something in George's shirt pocket. Radio batteries! George went straight to reception. They really wanted to know where George had got them from. "What batteries you people are talking about?", George asks blankly. They took him to the single cell lock up and put him in a strait-jacket and left him. "Die Koelie is baie slim maar more jy sal vrek."[40]

We had heard about this and were worried. We were relieved to hear that the next morning they had taken the strait-jacket off.

George was released on Monday morning. That day we found the quarry walls tampered with and the shed was in a shambles. One of our security said the warders had found two radios at the quarry and one at the lime quarry where the single cell comrades toiled.

Only one comrade was ever caught red handed with a newspaper. He got twenty one days spare-diet. It was not carelessness. Just an unlucky day.

One winter Wednesday it was just passed *shayile* time at the quarry. It was cold and we were irritable. As we queued, Mannie Abrahams was in front of me and Andrew Masondo just behind me. Smith was searching and Mannie had not left his quarry pants behind. Smith asked him to stand on one side. This made Andrew angry and he started arguing for Mannie. Smith tells him to stand aside. Then my turn. I had my eye-protection netting wire glasses in my pocket. I joined them.

We were taken to B2 and told to strip. I spoke up.

"Look here, Meneer, I really forgot to leave this thing behind. We were all in a hurry. I could have thrown them on the road, but I did not do it. If I threw it I wouldn't be standing in front of you. Can't you overlook this honest mistake?"

This convinced Smith. "Fuck off from here all of you!" We left hurriedly. And then I took off with them.

"Andrew, Mannie, I don't want you two to stand in my queue. Don't you people know that my both shoes are loaded with news cuttings! Why argue over a small matter. He would have left you people! Remember! Don't stand in my queue!"

That was that! I regretted my behaviour but it had to be done. It could have landed me in deep trouble, possibly a twenty one day spare-diet or three lashes with a light cane.

In the late seventies we started getting news through speakers in every cell. The evening news broadcasts were taped, censored and then played to us in the evenings from the room upstairs near the reception. It was all bullshit. But if we caused trouble they would often threaten to cut the thing off.

[40] Afrikaans for "This Coolie is too clever but tomorrow he will die".

Hospital

In the early years, the visiting district surgeon was Van der Bergen. To this day I wonder if he ever was really a doctor! More people died while Dr Van der Bergen was visiting the Island than other district surgeons. In 1964 five people died on the Island: a PAC youth, an ANC comrade whom we called Sipho and three criminals. Even when politicos were seriously ill, his diagnosis was N.A.D.: Nothing Abnormal Discerned. We felt very upset.

When Lwamek Loabile went to him complaining about his throat all he gave was aspirin. Later when Doctor Gosling arrived he diagnosed throat cancer. Poor Loabile died of the disease in a Cape Town hospital and was buried in Johannesburg with full ANC honours.

Another doctor who was bad and hated the political prisoners was Dr Poliansky. He went with the South African rugby team to Britain as a spectator. In the anti-apartheid demonstrations he was beaten up and when he came back he changed his name to Dr Pallet.

While he was with us the new wing of the hospital was opened, adjoining the reception. It was later extended with another hospital section. It was here that a SWAPO comrade died of cancer. Another SWAPO, Rudolf Kadikwa, contacted tuberculosis but Dr Pallet did not seem worried. It was Sergeant 'Quarry' van den Berg who insisted that he be transferred to Victoria Hospital in Cape Town. Van den Berg also arranged for one of our comrades to go to a specialist and for X-ray.

At this time prisoners who had piles, nose problems and tonsillitis and so forth were operated on in the Island's Sick Bay. Matthews Magalima went for a nose operation at the sick bay but Pallet did not mention that he was suffering from hypertension. The operation was a near disaster. The specialist transferred him to Cape Town. Magalima was the last person to undergo an operation in the Sick Bay.

Another district surgeon was Dr Rom. He died in a mysterious way. We heard that he committed suicide by jumping from his balcony. We could not believe this because he was very good to his patients. We believed the rumour that the system threw him off. Dr Gosling, who retired in the late 1970s was also good as was Dr Siroky, a Czechoslovakian refugee from '68. He resigned and joined another state department.

But Drs Biesot, Edelstein and Kaplan were like all other district surgeons: they worry more about their pay than their patients. The same with Doctor Gordon, who was fond of using cheap psychology on patients. Alfred Khonza was suffering from a brain injury and went to see him. Dr Gordon looked into his ears, praised him for keeping them clean and discharged him. He was sent to Cape Town by the medical orderlies where he died. If this is not negligence on the part of the doctor, then what is it?

To protect the patients from these animals was Sister Saayman. She was a nurse in the truest sense of the word. She would always wait on the other side of the iron door in the dispensary and after the doctor had gone, come in and care for us. And she would give instructions to the hospital cleaners or the night warder to call her if anything happened. She was a real sister.

In 1974 the Kiwi 'flu hit the Island and the situation became critical. Two cells were quarantined with politicos with high temperatures. The hospital beds were full and victims slept on the corridor. The Sister and her staff worked very hard throughout the epidemic. It was a credit to them and the cooperation they received from the political prisoners which avoided any loss of lives. The team was good.

Nelson Mandela was taken to a Cape Town hospital for a minor operation on his lower part of the leg. He was operated on and in bed when comrades Moumbaris, Jenkins and Lee escaped from the Pretoria Central Prison. The prison authorities just bundled comrade Mandela in his pyjamas and brought him to Robben Island. They wanted to put him in the isolation section of the hospital.

Mandela argued that if he is not allowed to share the ward with other political prisoners then he might as well go to his own isolation cell and converse with his other comrades there. He won.

Suicides

Incarceration and harsh treatment for a long period of time badly affects the minds of those incarcerated. Politicos in the main sections were a lot better off. They had a comrade or a son of the soil sleeping next to them and could talk in whispers about whatever they wanted to talk about. This was not so in the two single cell sections. For them it was thirteen, sometimes fourteen hours complete silence. Locked up at four or five in the afternoon and only let out at five in the morning. Their books, if studying, became their silent partners, companions and comfort. If they felt like expressing their thoughts, they couldn't. Being bottled up they suffered psychological effects. If one could go through some mind-reading machine of these politicos' minds, it would be a heart rending and very disconcerting experience.

Political leaders stay in this way for years on end. You have to fight otherwise you will be cast in stone. Through physical and psychological tortures our men of steel bore the brunt of this two-pronged attack on their minds and bodies.

The warders working on the watch posts for six hours a night were also isolated. They were fresh from College to crush our morale. They had been indoctrinated with false utterances. Political prisoners were terrorists who wanted to kill all the whites by poisoning the drinking water and driving the remaining whites into the sea. Many could hardly understand things when they met us. Having no zest for life they took a way out: suicide.

The first white warder to shoot himself was working on the post in the middle of the *zinktronk*. The second shot himself in the passage of C Section, near cell C1. Inmates heard the shots and heard a voice say "Ma! Ma!" and then nothing. The third shot himself dead near the hospital cells.

It's pathetic to see the young die in this way.

A fat youth named Basson, nicknamed 'Mumbele' from the Xhosa for a fat cow, worked in the *knaplyne* and used to call our working place 'the sabotage zone' and never allowed other warders or prisoners to come near us. He often chatted with us and came to know why we were really there. One day out of the blue he said:

"Julle kan al die land in Suid Afrika vat, maar jy moet net nie Stellenbosch vat nie!"[41]

Surely he could not stay like that forever? Did he commit suicide?

There was another youngster also working in the *knaplyn*. After the 1968 court ruling against the quotas, he came and apologised to us.

"Look gentlemen, I am married and my wife is expecting a baby. To make ends meet I work in the prison department, and at the same time I am studying for my matriculation examination. Please do not kill me when the war starts. I haven't done anything bad—I haven't ill-treated any prisoner. Please remember my face and do not kill me and my family!"

These utterances rocked us. We felt very sorry for his ignorance. Shadrack Mapumulo was good to him. He explained why we were in prison. And that we did not want to kill them but neutralise and win over.

We had a bad Colonel around 1975 or 1976. His name was Roelofse. One day he walked into the censorship room and picked up a five line letter which was already censored and insisted the youth censor it again. The youth became angry and resigned.

We had a policy to be civil to the youngsters who were not troublesome and we tried to get into some political discussion with them without touching religious issues. If one could get hold of all

---

[41] Afrikaans for "You can take all the land in South Africa, but not Stellenbosch!".

CAST IN STONE IN A HELL HOLE   185

the resignations from the Prison Services, one would appreciate the
soundness of our policy.

Our Second Hunger-strike

In the early seventies the situation got tense. Lieutenant Fourie,
the security officer, was running amok trying to turn the clock back
on all our hard fought victories. In the absence of Colonel Van
Aarde, he sought an argument with young Ernest Moseneke and
locked him up in the isolation cell.

We did not take this lying down. We met and decided to go on
hunger-strike. It steam-rolled for three days. And we had the
support of the quarry warders! Maybe they were becoming politicised, but they were certainly sick and tired of Fourie's ways.

Colonel van Aarde heard about it when he was in Cape Town. He
came back, drove his combi down to the quarry and wanted to
know why we were not working. For by this time we had decided
to stop work as well. Dip, humorous as ever fired back:

> "Colonel, how can we work when we have no strength to work. The food
> is rubbish. You know Colonel, if I cut myself no blood will come out but
> instead you will see just *pap!*"

This outburst broke the tension and the Colonel laughed.
Moseneke was out that afternoon and the hunger-strike was called
off. The Colonel wanted volunteers to help the kitchen improve the
food. A new lot of people went to work in the kitchen. Amongst
them was a cook called Don Mata, a very good friend of Reverend
Hermanus, the 'good pimp'.

Record Club

As time went on conditions started improving on Robben Island
Prison. We were allowed to write to our families to send us records
of our choice. These started coming in; including some Indian
records and, as the numbers of records increased it became necessary to form a record club. Kisten Moonsamy, Indris, Hector
Ntshanyana and a few others administered the club with the
permission of the officials.

The club's task was to draw up a programme for the whole week.
Once a cell gets the programme it knows exactly what record is
played on a certain day. Requests from each cell were taken into
consideration. As time went on we asked, through the officials, for
the people in single cells to also set a weekly programme once a
month. This was done. Democracy prevailed and people's education thrived theoretically and practically.

back to George. Sunny refuses and tells the warder George was to
see his lawyer about this nonsense. Eventually, after letting the
warder fry for a while, Sonny relents but tells the warder to stay
away from George. It was all a huge ruse. George had no lawyer
coming to him. It was just a tactic to keep the warders in line.

One day at the *knaplyn* 'Lavai' sits down humming '*Uncha rahe
janda hamara, Janda na niche jukana*'.[42] Indris and the others joined in.
I could not stop laughing. Lavai had known Dadoo well during the
Alexandra Bus Boycott and he must have picked up this favourite
Transvaal Indian Congress song from them.

'Blou' Makelani was a Transkeian from Cape Town who had been
caught up in the Paarl riots. On the Island he worked with me and
Lavai as a stone-dresser. One day Blou starts singing the home
coming song of the youths returning from circumcision schools in
the hills. Now they are no longer *Kwedini*.[43] Blou was singing the
girls' part of the song, a refrain that went something like this, '*Thina
sithanda lento yakho*'.[44] George and other Indian comrades had no
idea what he was singing about and did not know about the
circumcision rituals. George asked him and he just laughed and
shouted, '*Aye!, kwedini* get away from here!' After this whenever I
saw Blou I would always sing '*thina sithanda lento yakho*' to him and
he would chase me around the quarry. This kind of jovial atmosphere kept us going.

'Captain Devil' was Norman Metshane, one of our bridge players.
He had gone outside for military training and when he returned had
been captured and badly tortured.

One day coming through the wire from the quarry one of the PAC
guys jokingly gripped Captain Devil from the back. This PAC chap
worked with the big hammers and was tough and well built. But
this did not stop Captain Devil from throwing him to the ground. It
was hard to persuade Captain Devil that the guy had been joking.

The next day comrades went and spoke to Captain Devil but he
just sat on his stone on the *knaplyn* fuming. Eventually he did
apologise. But at least it made the warders treat him carefully.

Captain Devil's draft had included Patrick Bopela, who later gave
evidence in Braam Fischer's trial. He left the Island after a couple of
years and thus became the first political prisoner to leave the Island
before his sentence had expired.

---

[42] Marathi for 'Keep the flag flying, don't let the flag down, don't let the flag down'.
[43] Xhosa for circumcised male adults.
[44] Basically Xhosa for 'We like your thing'.

'Jam Loot' was a warder who used to love barking orders at us in the quarry. And he gossiped in secretive undertones about the women in the town. On weekends he worked in the kitchen. He loved it. He ate all his meals with enough fat to grease his belly. Then afterwards, with his cotton hat in one hand, he would come and ask the prisoners for contributions. Mostly people gave him the smallest pieces, but George Moffat was fond of needling him so he would give him a little more, saying 'My scavenger, the lost son of the white laager'.

George Naicker, Steve Dlamini, Joe Gqabi and Joe Moroelong always worked together in the *sifspan*. They were our 'Four Musketeers'. They would use a spade as if it were a gun with a bayonet, thrusting and parrying and then use the butt to crash onto someone's skull. And they would have lengthy discussions on Marxism-Leninism. They were good theoreticians.

One of the discussions we had in the changed circumstances at the quarry concerned tigers and leopards. In South Africa there are no tigers, but leopards are plentiful. The question arose: 'Were the chiefs wearing a mantle of leopard or tiger skin?' Many joined in. Blues argued it was tiger skin. Many supported him. Anthony Aba declared it was leopard skin. Some tried to argue that *Ingwe* was a word used for 'tiger' because there was no other word for 'tiger'. Others argued that there was a word for 'leopard': *Ihlosi*. After two weeks most of the quarry was debating this fine point of language and politics. I felt that people were wasting their time, but to them it was food for thought. No compromise was reached. I think the people responsible for drawing up the dictionary were responsible for this debate. The *Ingwe* died a natural death when people stopped discussing it.

In 1965 when us students were separated from our comrades, I was moved to C3. There I met 'Bra Jeff', by profession a teacher and a committed PAC guy who had been on the Island before I arrived.

I got along well with him. Whenever I ran short of tobacco I would go to him and ask for say, two *zols* worth. He would tell me to take whatever he gave because then other PAC guys could approach me. He was against smuggling.

He was doing his BA and we got closer together when he asked me to explain certain lines in *A Passage To India* for him. He was also a regular member of our scrabble games. Bra Jeff worked in the quarry as a blacksmith, sharpening our chisels and punches for us.

In around 1966 Bra Jeff was slowly isolated by his PAC mates. At this time I had organised a common law prisoner to get the newspapers. A comrade who worked in town was told where to pick it up. After Gali Tembani, who could speak Afrikaans, had translated and copied it I took it to our PAC comrades. They returned it, but before I had the chance to destroy it Bra Jeff asks me if he could read it. His news team were not giving him anything. This seems to be because he followed Sobukwe while his hometown Mamelodi boys supported Leballo.

Bra Jeff was keen to escape, but the second time he tried, his PAC guys felt that he was endangering their position. They sent their 'PRO' to ours, Lungile Dwaba, who went to Bra Jeff and explained the feelings. But he never stopped trying. It was actually he who made the master key. He gave it to Siddiq Isaacs.

One evening we heard a huge rumble coming from the quarry. In a few seconds the walls shook and before we could collect our thoughts another rumble shook us. We all ran around helter skelter not knowing what to do. Dip was reading a novel and the book just started to wobble around. Soon one word passed around: "Nigima!".[45]

Soon Colonel van Aarde came around and said that it seemed as if everything was alright. However if it got worse he would let all of us out of the building. It was apparently really bad at Tulbagh.

The rain was lashing the Island and tidal waves were creeping up towards us. At times it rained so heavy that the mood of the sea changed and a hurricane wind lashed everything. After two days it subsided and Captain Claasen went around putting pegs in the ground showing the flood water marks. The leadership raised the question of our safety but they were assured that although the storm was bad, we were quite safe.

Hospital Cleaner

In October 1971, I was admitted to the Island hospital for suspected tonsillitis. Doctor Pallet refused my request to see the ENT specialist, saying that I was a 'slim koelie'. But Sergeant van den Berg looked after me in the sickbay and after my tonsils were removed he kept me on as a cleaner. I worked there for the next eight years.

I had to keep the ward allotted to me clean and help Sergeant Pienaar in the medical bulk stores. In the beginning he did not like me but after a while recognised my abilities and became friendly. I created a good impression.

It was because of this that I was able to converse with the Rivonia comrades. When Mandela came in for heat treatments to his knee I used to rub his knees and thighs. He was curious as to where I learnt

---

[45] Zulu for 'Run!'.

about physiotherapy. I had learnt it from the orderlies and was only allowed to assist if told to by an orderly.

The Rivonia comrades used to stand around in the garden waiting for their turn for treatment. I had planted a big chilli tree in the garden. They would walk round it and look at the hospital windows, but they never took a single chilli unless I said it was okay to take as many as they wanted. I also had tomato bushes there. It all started through some seeds I got from the warders. In a good season I could get up to six hundred tomatoes.

Somehow, as cleaners, we managed to establish links between the single cells and the main section. 'Mac' Maharaj was the courier. Anything which came from the single cells was passed through us to the contact in the main section. None of us ever opened the parcels to see what was written down. We were responsible cadres. Many of the messages came in match boxes with small pieces of paper with very small writing on them carefully slipped into the boxes.

One of my tasks was to weigh anyone who reported to the hospital. As they took their clothes off they would hand the box to me. Then I would wait for the cook, an ANC member, who would bring us food, give him the box and pass the message, saying "give to Curnick." I collected match boxes up until around 1975.

Mac would also come in for heat treatment. While I was rubbing his neck one day he told me that he had married MD's sister. I asked him if he was the guy who used to come visiting at MD's to chat with Vasie, Phyllis' sister. It was him.

One day a friendly young medical orderly asked who I would like to see that weekend. I said Mac. He brought Mac along and left us chatting to our hearts' content. But the Colonel appeared and so the orderly told Mac to hide in the TB section yard. As the Colonel walked around he let Mac out. A ticklish situation was averted.

One day comrade Mbeki, 'Zizi' to us, came in for treatment. He wanted our cook to add some salt to his soup. We refused, despite his pleadings because he was on a saltless diet. He was just trying us out and using his mild manner! I said "No comrade! We still need you!"

When Xolisile, with his paralysed half-body, was with us in hospital, Mbeki asked to see the dying man but permission was refused. He was actually the fourth person whose eyes I closed. The first was comrade Mkumbuzi and the second Petrus Nailenge and the third a BCM youth. It was our task to bathe the body, place cotton wool in the ears and anus and a tag with their number and name on their toes. When Xolisile was dying Sergeant Schoeman did all he could. We all cried when he passed away.

Comrade Johannes Shiponeni, a SWAPO comrade, had his leg amputated and spent his recuperation time in our hospital. He started to correspond with my daughter, Veena. These SWAPO people were very close to me. Shiponeni knew Eleanor Anderson from his days in Dar. They would see her on the beaches. We would chat about her, politics and all kinds of other things.

While I was at the hospital I finished my Chartered Institute of Secretaries course. I came out first in southern Africa and in my Company Law exams, the highest in the British Commonwealth.

On the evening of the 21st of September 1974 I collapsed in the kitchen. I had a heart attack. Lawrence Phokanoka carried me to my bed and in no time Sister Saayman and Sergeant Pienaar had the oxygen machine working. I was sent to Cape Town and spent about three weeks in hospital there. As soon as I returned to the Island hospital I found a note in *Gujarati*, "Get well comrade!". That was good but I had lost all hope. I decided to make a will.

I suppose what concentrated my mind so was that whilst I was in hospital recuperating I received a letter from India giving me power of attorney over insurance money that had been lodged in my name twenty five years previously. I asked George Naicker, our great financial whiz what to do. I did not want funds coming into the country. George said I should send the money to sister Shanti but I did not have her address.

I then decided to give my power of attorney to Prime Minister Indira Gandhi for her to do what she saw fit. I wrote the letter sending it to her, care of the Delhi Secretariat, New Delhi. The authorities wanted to know if this person was the Indian Prime Minister, but I just said she was a colleague of mine from the old days. They believed me. Ha! You buggers! You think you are clever!

After some time I was called to reception and shown a letter. It said 'The Prime Minister's Relief Fund'.

In 1976 I had another heart attack and went back to Woodstock Hospital.

SWAPO

In around 1968 we heard rumours that new people were to join us. They were the SWAPO cadres from PLAN. They were kept separate from us. A fence was put up and they were removed to D section, which had been the old B section. As time went on they were taken out to chop trees. It was only when I was in the hospital that I could talk to these comrades easily.

They told me about the training they had received in various countries and how the Nyerere government had given the ANC,

SWAPO and FRELIMO vast tracts of land in Tanzania. Each organisation's camp was a short distance from the others. It was here that the guerrillas trained, discussed strategies and tactics and became conversant with Marxism-Leninism.

At around the same time another new group of prisoners came. They too were sent to the Namibian section. They were APDUSA members. Later they were sent to single cells.

For a while tensions crept in. These people were Trotskyites. They had still not forgotten about world revolution and anti-Soviet propaganda started to float around with pro-Chinese idealism becoming the order of the day.

Comrade Johnny Shiponeni and I would talk often about it. He was worried but understood these guys. He maintained that their propaganda was full of flaws. They said that the Soviet Union was sending us old AK 47s, while the Chinese manufactured AK assault rifle was of much better quality. When they went to single cells, they again formed an unholy alliance against us, but our single cell comrades knew what was happening.

The unholy alliance was between APDUSA, the PAC and the SASO group. Against them were the ANC, SWAPO and the lone ranger, Eddie Daniels, the Liberal Party member of ARM. As SASO started disintegrating, more vociferous utterances were made against us.

In one of our discussions Jerry Ekandjo and Ben Uulenga pointed out the futility of arguing with people who think that Marxism-Leninism is dogma. Once you arrive at this premise then a theory loses its value. Comrade Jerry pointed out that most of the SWAPO members were peasants and that they were interested in one thing only and that was to get independence free of any sort of exploitation.

At the hospital I met comrade Lawrence Phokanoka, a trained MK cadre and a political commissar. On the Island he became a cleaner. His knowledge of Marxism-Leninism was of exceptional value to us and the SWAPO section comrades. He would see to it that the SWAPO chaps regularly got his lecture materials. This got him into hot water on many an occasion, but because he was a likable chap the medical orderlies overlooked these small violations. His analytical mind worked like a machine so he was able to counter any polemics that came from the APDUSA chaps. I got him interested in Russian novelists. His favourites were Popov's *The Steel and the Slag*, Pavlenko's *Happiness*, Boris Borgatov's *Tara's Family* and Nina Fedorova's *The Children*.

If we were not discussing books then we spoke about politics. He related stories about his life in MK camps, his capture during the Wankie campaign and the torture he had endured. Or we spoke about our families and their sufferings. While he was on the Island his mother passed away. He told me about his Esther and asked me to send John Paul Satre's *Germinal* to her as a birthday gift from him once I was out. This I did.

Bad Guys

The early seventies saw a bunch of bad guys come to our Island. Among them were chief warder Van der Westhuizen, chief warder Nortje, Lieutenant Prins and security officer Lieutenant Fourie. They got lots of pimps working again and began to make life miserable for the politicos. And Brigadier Aucamp became a regular visitor to the Island. Some of these bad guys were transferred while others stayed.

Around that time Colonel Willemse came to the Island. He got Sister Saayman there. Things simmered down a little. It was then that I got permission to work in the bulk medicine stores.

After he left Colonel Roelofse came. He was a tyrant. He terrorised the warders and started interfering in the hospital.

I had a lot of problems with him. One day he decided to do inspection on Sunday and came and started searching my pockets. He found nothing. The next time he came I was in the garden pulling weeds. He shouted at me and when I told him that I was pulling weeds he told a warder to lock us up. Then one day he found me watering my tomatoes. He chased me and told the warders to stop us getting outside. He also got very cross when he found me packing medical supplies.

By this time I had already had two heart attacks. So I wrote a letter to the Colonel. A week later the Colonel sent for me. Chief Du Plessis was with him. 'Dup' did not like the Colonel. The Colonel asked me it I had written the letter. I said yes.

"You know I can take away your gratuity?"

"Colonel that is your privilege! It does not bother me."

"I can also demote you to a lower group."

"That is your privilege. You can do whatever you please. But one thing I want to tell you is that you hate Indians because of their involvement with the ANC."

"No! I do not hate you! But I want to know why you wrote that if anything happens to you, you will hold me responsible for your death?"

"Colonel, since you saw me in the hospital, you have always tried to intimidate me! Isn't it true because you wanted me out of the hospital?"

"You are arrogant! You can go now."

Soon he was transferred to a small jail in De Aar. That is what the grapevine told us.

Still Lieutenant Prins was still there! He banned me from leaving the hospital. I was prohibited from going to see films or sports. This did not demoralise me as I could spend more time with Jonas Shimwefeleni. He was on the dialysis machine.

TV Generation

The 1976 Soweto revolt and the student uprising brought new problems. Youths arrived with various political thoughts and some with no political understanding of the struggle.

There was a whole generation gap between the youths and their elder leadership. The youth's own experiences had led them to think racially. Student movements formed, fumbled and tried to find a Black Consciousness which was in truth no solution at all. What it did was to boggle their minds and made them forget about the national democratic struggle and that they were the working class of tomorrow.

They forgot this and instead, started to throw abuses at the generation that came before them. This, to a generation that lived through many trials and tribulations. Nasty incidents became the order of the day and there were people who were eager to exploit the situation. Lieutenant Prins was not up to this, but Captain Harding was much more diplomatic. Some were taken to what had been known as C and D Sections. Now B Section became E Section. Single cells were also divided up.

This changed the whole character of the jail. The *zinktronk* was broken down and a new prison built for common laws. *Zinktronk* became our sports field with four new tennis courts.

One guy in the new E section said one day that he belonged to the National Party. M'tu Madala just laughed. Someone said that at least we have one Nat amongst us. In a very short time this guy was released.

The ones who really tried to turn the clock back were the guys who had no political roots. They had no inkling of the struggles we had launched, the hunger strikes and the quota system, which by the time they arrived, had all gone. Work was now just an outing to get some fresh air. The quarry had in fact closed down.

We tried to explain to them that they should behave like politicians. Some took note of this.

I call them the 'TV generation' because they were born when television came to South Africa. They had seen too much American trash, liked it and had become Americanised. They were not of the calibre of the older generation.

Farewell! Comrades! Release!

In the last week in February 1980 I was told to get ready for the draft. I went to say farewell. When I went to Jonas Shimwefeeni, he pulled my hands and kissed them. I knew he was crying with his head covered.

I went to reception to get my stuff: my identity document and some books of mine which had been confiscated. I put these into my canvas bag. I signed for it, ducked back out and went and passed the books through the grille to the comrades. I was leaving these for them. In no time I was back.

Our draft landed at Cape Town docks where Vusani and I, both cardiac cases, were told to get into a car. The others went into a big pickup. They were handcuffed. Vusani and I were not.

After the night at Pollsmoor we left for Leeukop, stopping at a farm to pick up some grapes for Brigadier Aucamp. At Bloemfontein the medical orderly who was accompanying us bought me a packet of *Texan* plains and a box of matches. That was the first time a warder ever bought cigarettes for me.

It was there that I also drank my first *Coca Cola* in sixteen years. The medical orderly also bought this for us. After I drank it I just passed wind non-stop for a long time. The same with Vusani. Our tummies just could not believe what we were giving them!

We reached Leeukop later than scheduled because the fan belt of the car broke, but along the way we had an interesting discussion with Lieutenant Miller about Botha's reforms and whether the Afrikaners would be willing to let him do too little too late.

On the 26th of February 1980 I left Leeukop for Durban, accompanied by the same medical orderly and a Captain.

At Durban Central Prison the Captain called me aside and told me that my exit visa had been approved by the Minister of Police. He said that I should approach the security police for further information. I was taken to an isolation cell but I insisted that a warder bring me a mattress and some bedding. They did and I was in for my last night.

My mind wandered. My daughter and son! I had left my daughter when she was nine years of age. I had only seen her once since then and that was in 1973 when we had to talk through a telephone with thick glass between us. For most of that time my baby and I cried. Visits depressed me. Now she was a Sister at R K Khan Hospital in Durban. I knew my daughter would come to fetch me.

The next day I was taken to the District Surgeon who filled out some forms saying I was fine, my photograph was taken and then I was rushed to get some clothes. This I insisted on. I got a shirt, a pair of trousers and shoes and pair of socks. No coat! They said they didn't have. The shoes were very good and that was that.

As I was finger-printed for arrest, so too with my release. Pat

Moodley and two other SBs waited for me. They led me through the back entrance and whisked me away. My daughter and family waited in the front entrance.

Somehow Omar Badsha and a youth rushed to the back entrance and an argument developed between them and the SBs. I intervened. Pat Moodley said that as they had taken me from my home, they were taking me back there. This they did, dropping me off and telling me that I lived in number three.

I carried my cardboard box and went in. A strange girl was there. She was puzzled because I looked strange in my oversized clothes. I told her I was Babenia. She embraced in an embarrassed way. Then I heard footsteps. It was Pravina. I was out! I was free! And here was my cute little grand-daughter Anisha.

Soon a lot of friends and political leaders came to see me. Of course, Indians! I felt I was in another atmosphere. I felt like crying. Where was Doktela, Jonas, Dlamini, Solly, *Mputi*? *Umkhonto we Sizwe* had made me an African. A little while later that day Poomoney Moodley and A K M Docrat came round. I was very happy.

Just before I was released 'Veena, my daughter had got me a flat. I installed myself and tried to get used to the outside world. It is not easy to get used to the outside world after sixteen years of incarceration. I observed that no one really understood why we had been to jail. This was worst amongst the Indian community. Maybe the leadership of the NIC was not up to the calibre of it's past leaders? All the while the African comrades in the townships were fighting, the Indian moderates were intellectualising. It was a pathetic sight.

After a few days rest I started treading the streets of the Grey Street area looking for work. I was a marked man. A saboteur does not get a job easily. A chance meeting put me in touch with Chimanlal Patel. Sixteen years ago he had been a student of mine when I taught him the vernacular. At first I could not recognise him. Chiman promised to get a couple of students for me to teach English subjects to. Some of these children, including Chiman's nephew, I took right up to when they went to university.

In 1983 I also managed to fix a half-day job at a drapery store. When I would come home early in the afternoon to teach, there would always be the phone call. From a white woman; 'I am sorry wrong number'. Besides this, the SBs would often pop around to ask me how I was.

One day they made me furious because they said I had done more than my fair share of time and that I should get on their payroll.

Afterall, they said, Tambo and Slovo were driving around in Mercedes Benz's. This riled me but they kept on watching me.

I asked my daughter to fix an exit visa for me, but she said that when she was in London, Dadoo had told her that at all costs I was not to leave the country. That was that.

I had two heart attacks after being released. The drug 'Pexid' had been prescribed for me, but it was taken off the market after some five years. Its side effects had adverse affects on my health. I could not walk fifty yards without my calves giving me excruciating pain. My lower limbs were becoming useless and I decided that 'this is it!'

As an MK cadre I have attended several funerals of fallen comrades. This was the least I could do. The first funeral was that for David Mkhize in Greytown. Dip and Shadrack Mapumulo have also passed away. The rest of us are still living. I still believe in the principles of our vanguard organisation and the struggle that it is shouldering. But as a victim of harsh conditions and failing heart conditions, I stayed conscious of the world revolving and things happening, always hopeful and never despondent. Knowing 'Just is Might' I could never become a pessimist. In a struggle like ours, pessimism is a belief of a coward.

In 1980 I came out of incarceration and on the 5th of January 1987, I was detained under Section 29. I was released on the 21st of March 1987 from Wentworth Hospital. My heart condition had deteriorated to such an extent that the doctors consulted the surgeons and, with fifty percent chance of being saved, Dr Shama, a Venezuelan doctor at Wentworth opened me up and did a triple coronary by-pass operation. It was successful.

I live, I breathe and I walk. The post operation period was hell. Pain and depression became my companions for a long time but I live with the hope of seeing victory for the oppressed masses; not in a distant future, but in the near future.

A man is a social being and he has commitment to his family, and the family being a component of society, and society being a tiny structure of the nation; man has commitment to the nation.

I have learnt to love my daughter, who has been a tower of strength to me. She took care of me and nursed me to what I am today. She is Pravina my beloved child, now a grown woman.

Whenever she was hurt, I was hurt. When she cried, I cried. The understanding between us is not of a father and daughter, but one of oneness. She is a symbol to me, as our ANC flag is a symbol to us. I dedicate this book to Pravina and millions of my children who in this country have been hounded by police, the SADF, vigilantes,

Askaris, the Inkatha and the puppets of a racist minority settler colonialists.

These children of mine sleep in the bushes, defend themselves with stones and carry arms to eliminate the peoples' enemy. These children of mine die and in the process fertilise the mother earth with their precious red blood, so that it could produce more qualitative children to ease the pain of the nation and bring love, warmth and peace to this country and to this nation in a way that soon we can bask in the glory of a free society.

GLOSSARY

Language is a crucial form of power. South Africa has eleven officially recognised languages, all of which are spoken, written and have standardised grammars and vocabularies. There are, in addition, other languages and also a large variety of colloquial *lingua franca*, terms and expressions: for example *bandiet-taal*, *fanagalo*, *gamtaal* and political terms created during 'The Struggle'. The differences between languages and their relationship to other rejected or otherwise unrecognised terms and words is often inherently conflictual and deliberate. Further, words and terms can have different, conflicting and sometimes sanitised meanings, in different contexts or when spoken, written, listened to or read.

Many of the terms which were either made by or had to be part of political prisoners' lives will probably not become part of any official language. The age of the Robben Island political prisoner has now ended. Other words and terms do remain. The complex historical origins and very gendered meanings of many terms used by Babenia have not yet been fully analysed. The meanings as given here must thus be tentative.

Agterryer—Afrikaans from Dutch, originally associated with male hunting or armed commando expeditions, used to describe an obsequious mounted male attendant, with *voet*, Afrikaans for feet, simply meaning a lackey of even further diminished status. In prison, a dismissive term for a man in charge of a labour gang; as in the English boss boy. Used by both superiors and other prisoners, but rarely by the actual man in question, who could use terms like *spanleier*, as in the English foreman. For other prisoners, the term can be synonymous with both bully and *impimpi*. For other prisoners, but not politicos, it can also be associated with loyalty and male bonding. Often associated with gang leaders or their deputies.

Anavil Brahmin—Gujarati, the highest landlord caste in India.

Ashram—Gujarati, a Hindu communal religious retreat offering accommodation to the destitute.

Baa(i)djie—Afrikaans from the Malay for a naval-type jacket. Colloquials have various spellings. In prison it refers to both the white-ish coloured canvas jacket issued to all male prisoners and the military style woolen hip jackets issued to male 'A' and 'B' group prisoners.

Baas—Afrikaans from Dutch, the male owner, master or he who gives orders, the term is still recognised in standard Afrikaans dictionaries as the term used by 'Coloureds' and 'Bantus' when addressing a white man.

Bande Mataram—Derived from *Sanskrit*, 'Motherland We Bow To Thee' was the anthem of India, including the Princely States and the All India Congress in the period before and immediately after independence.

200   MEMOIRS OF A SABOTEUR

Subsequently the anthem became *'Jana Gana, Adhinayak Bharat Bhagya Vudhata! Jaja Jaihao, Jaiho!'*

Bandiet—Afrikaans from the Dutch word for convict and possibly also robber or brigand and now accepted standardised and colloquial Afrikaans word for convict. However, it is very different from the Afrikaans word *gevangene* meaning prisoner. *Gevangene* is part of the discursive language of the state. *Bandiet* is a pejorative term used by warders as a generic for all male prisoners and a word of self-identification used by jailed men. To both warder and prisoner the word implies outsider and untamed status; for the former implying the need to discipline and for the latter conveying heroic qualities. The term is sometimes used by both to refer, partly respectfully, to long-term male prisoners. *Bandiete* also used other terms for themselves, these often being essentially part of prison gang social networks. The word is not used by drafted released prisoners. The term was not accepted by *politicos* for themselves.

Bhagwa Janda—Gujarati, the flag of the King of Gaekwad.

Bhajia—Hindi, a dish made from spinach leaves and pea flour.

Blou Baaidjie—A prison term for a male habitual criminal or a long-term prisoner who has escaped and then been recaptured or has been drafted and then convicted of another or other offences carrying long prison terms. Although having no clothing which separates him from other prisoners, he is known and spoken of as different. Warders will speak of him as such; to his face and to others, and he himself will announce himself as such and thereby claim authority. However ordinary prisoners will rarely use the term when speaking directly to him.

Bidi—Gujarati, hand made leaf cigarettes.

Boer—From Dutch; Afrikaans for white male farmer, settler or freedom fighter, within white Afrikaans-speaking society the word has huge nationalist political connotations. With the rise of Afrikaner Nationalism the word becomes a pivotal derisory word in the lexicon of black anti-Apartheid politics.

Boesman—Afrikaans from Dutch, a derogatory term for a Coloured man.

Coolie—From Hindi and Urdu *kuli* or 'porter', British imperialists used the term as a generic derogatory for oriental male manual labourers, including Indian and Chinese. Historical origins in South Africa are obscure, initially possibly referring to Indian male indentured labour, but probably much earlier, it is accepted as being a racist generic term of abuse for South African Indian men; with the feminine often being *'Coolie* Mary'.

Charro—From *char*, probably from the Anglo-Indian *charwallah*: a British official's Indian male servant serving tea and the Afrikaans *ou* as in 'fellow'. South African Indians can use the term in a jocular way, but in South Africa it can be a very derogatory term for any Indian man.

Chotra—Gujarati, a meeting place.

Dacoit—*Gujarati* name for a bandit or brigand.

Dalav—*Bandiet-taal* for the cake made from fat, sugar, *puzamandla* and the porridge crust from the bottom of the cooking pan.

Deepavali—From Sanskrit, one of the most important Hindu religious festivals, 'The Festival of Lights' is held each year in October or November.

Dhal—Gujarati for dry yellow split lentils.

Donkeypiel—Colloquial spoken Afrikaans and *bandiet-taal* for a police baton; with heavy masculine sexual insult towards the wielder: 'donkey' inferring loyal stupidity; this may be via both Nguni and English; where in the latter 'donkey' displaced 'ass' and its associated 'arse', and with *piel* being Afrikaans for 'penis' or more colloquially and properly denigratory, 'cock' or 'prick'.

Drafted—In prison language, when one is moved from one prison to another or finally released.

Dynamite *coolie*—Term of abuse used by policemen and male prison warders to describe and thereby insult South African Indian cadres of *Umkhonto we Sizwe*.

Fahfee—An illicit Chinese numbers gambling game, with thirty six named numbers, usually associated with mine compound and African and South African Indian proletarian life.

Fanagalo—Literally 'Do it like this!', a bastardised, simplified and basically verbal *lingua franca* comprised of short essentially commandist phrases made up from various southern African languages; mainly Afrikaans, English and Zulu. Used on mines, but not originating there, historically it is also the simplified trading language between Africans, Indians and whites. Not used in prisons.

Gala—Originally Xhosa, a mining term to describe the iron bar, pointed at both ends, which is used to dislodge pieces of rock. Those who use the *gala* are respected for their strength.

Gamtaal—A spoken and very fluid, very fast moving *lingua franca*, mainly within male gangs, comprising of a mixture of Afrikaans, English and Xhosa; from *Gamat*: derogatory Afrikaans for Coloureds.

Gandhiji—Gujarati, an affectionate term for Gandhi.

Ghee—Gujarati, clarified dairy fat.

Hardegat—Colloquial Afrikaans, a mainly masculine term, directly associated with the anus and implying powerful rejection of existing or threatened established authority, with the direct English equivalent being 'hard-arsed' or, as conventionally but imperfectly translated, 'truculent'. In prison, as elsewhere, the mere use of the word by an authority figure implies imminent punishment whilst, as self-identification, it conveys notions of both refusal and dangerous isolation. Can be corrupted to simply meaning cheeky, or also *slim mens*.

Harijans—Gujarati for God's People, Gandhi's term for untouchables.

Impimpi—Possibly derived from the English pimp; modern Nguni, collo-quial South African and a mainly spoken political slogan for male or female sell-out, informer and often more generalised to any male or female quisling of the Apartheid State. The term is at its most powerful and often very deadly when conveyed verbally and by the grapevine.

Isolomuzi—Nguni, the term the ANC gave to its civic structures which operated during the very late 1950s and in the 1960s. The term's origins date back to Christian Eastern Cape communities in the later nine-teenth century. The term's modern political meaning would be 'Eye of the Township', having the notions of all-seeing vigilante and, although often underground, also having the legitimacy of being leaders of the homestead: *muzi*, Nguni for homestead. These community structures were not necessarily the same as 'M' Plan networks.

Jayanti—Gujarati, for the celebration of the anniversary of birth.

Kaffir—Arabic for unbeliever or non-Muslim, many historic South African usages, it became but is now a mainly archaic term of very deliberate insult used by racist South Africans for any African; *kaffirtjie* being the Afrikaans diminutive. In Afrikaans the diminutive can often be affec-tionate: in this case it is a further implicitly paternalistic insult.

Kaia—From the Nguni, *khaye*, for 'house' but then *Fanagalo* for the live-in single quarters for black men and women employed as domestic servants by whites.

Kakaji—A Gujarati word conveying the respect and affection for one's father.

Kanna—Tamil for darling boy.

Khosan—After the Nguni *Nkosana*; a politically correct term amongst Indian South Africans, within the Congress Alliance movement during the later 1950s and early 1960s for an Indian male sell-out. It translated Zulu masculinity, patronage and respect into urban Indian 'Struggle' politics: not *impimpi* and not 'boss boy'; it was a derogatory term conveying respect for the paternal, autocratic and effective power of the Indian opponent.

Knap—Afrikaans, a noun for the short snapping sound of something cracking.

Knaplyn—The rows of prisoners and the place where they broke stones at the Robben Island quarry.

Kwedini—Xhosa, a boy, with implicit and often very explicit reference to his obviously uncircumcised status. When used in reference to a male adult, the term is highly insulting.

Laaitie—Afrikaans, carpentry term referring to a moveable object with handles that slides in and out of a piece of furniture. Modern meanings have very personal, masculine and sexual inferences. Possibly origi-nally urban African, it is also colloquial gangland-speak and was also a white urban term for a brave, free male street adolescent or youth. In prison it refers to the desired for or subservient partner in a

There were a few politicos in the main sections who liked the same records as the cadres in the single cells. They were however in the minority. I can see a clear difference between the tastes of our leadership and us. We were not that keen on the classical stuff.

When comrades Indris, Shirish and Reggie went out in late 1973, they sent us dozens of records. All those individuals who got records from outside had to leave them behind and they automatically became record club property.

Amongst us the most popular records were Beethoven's 6th and 9th symphonies, Miriam Makeba and Harry Belafonte; although these were soon banned, as were *The Cossacks*. We also enjoyed Aretha Franklin, Nat King Cole, Diana Ross, Johnny Mathis, *The Beatles*, Cliff Richard, Satchmo, Frank Sinatra and Bing Crosby. Our Indian favourites were Ravi Shankar, Pankaj Mullick, C H Atma, Pradeep and Hathi Mera Sathi.

The record club also took charge of the film shows; which were shown on Saturdays. Makana knew how to operate the projector and in this way became very valuable to us.

I think the very first film we saw was *Heidi*. This was the very first time that our cells were opened up in the evening. As we waited to go into the mess hall, we stood around watching the stars. It was a very wonderful feeling. Like being free.

Quickly we were told to march to the hall. We sat on benches and saw the film. It was definitely good and we expected to see many more like that. Brigadier Aucamp had different ideas. He started bringing in propaganda films from the Information Bureau on the prosperity of the homelands. We saw the first one and then stopped going to the film shows.

Film shows were then suspended for some time. Eventually we won on the campaign and better films were shown. Even a time came when one could hire a film to be shown to the inmates. Our main problem was that all films were censored.

Tit Bits

In around 1969 or 1970, conditions at the quarry improved considerably. The days of harassment under the Kleynhans' had gone and we suffered no more verbal taunts and physical abuse.

One day George and Sunny were pushing a wheelbarrow. A new warder stops them and asks George for his card. George asks why and is told that he has been talking. George hands the tickets over and says, out aloud, to Sunny that he is going to fix the warder.

The warder follows the two of them around for a while and then goes up to Sunny, gives him George's card and asks him to give it homosexual sexual conquest. In prison, it is rarely a term of self-identification. For prisoners outside of the encounter, the word can be either derisory and/or have the sympathetic connotations as in 'victim'. For prison warders the term can be a generic abuse.

Lobola—Nguni for bride wealth.

Mamie—Gujarati for maternal auntie.

Meleko—Colloquial African urban term for the large three ton police pick up vans. They acquired various colloquial names, the most popular being either *Meleko* or *Kwela* vans. *Meleko* simply derives from milk as the vans looked similar to dairy delivery trucks, while *kwela* is the basic *Fanagalo* command for 'jump!', a verbal command usually given by police to those having to climb into the trucks. Although having earlier origins, the term is mostly associated with state enforcement of the pass laws during the 1950s.

Meneer—Afrikaans from Dutch, a form of respectful address to an adult man by a man or woman of lower status. It can often be subverted by the lowly into a term of insult and mocking.

Mahila Mandal—Gujarati; the women's organisation within the All India National Congress.

Mhlungu—Nguni, possibly originally referring to flotsam and jetsam deposited on the sea shore, the word is now commonly used as a politicised generic term of insult for white people.

Moer—Afrikaans, from Dutch, and now recognised and colloquial Afrikaans. As recognised and also in certain colloquials, an expression of abuse which can be used by both men and women towards peers of either sex and mostly towards younger persons as '*Jou ma se moer!*' ('Your mother's mother!'). Colloquially it can often be so sanitised. However, in Afrikaans, *moer* can mean not simply mother, but also refers to an animal mother and the flat metal object with a hole in the middle through which to pass a screwdriver in order to screw in a 'female' screw in a male-female bolting where the two bolts turn in opposite directions and tighten against each other. Thus, despite attempts to cleanse the word, it is very much more often part of male language with the sexual insult emphasised and womanhood demonised: for example as in '*Loop na jou moer!*' ('Go to the Devil!'), with the words matrix and womb being linked and inferring extremely diabolical characteristics. Here the word deliberately uses the very denigratory use of the word 'cunt', with '*Jou ma se moer!*' meaning for example either 'Fuck your mother!' or 'Your mother's cunt!'.

Motabhai—Gujarati for big brother.

Mpukane—Xhosa for a fly, in prison the term refers to news from a smuggled newspaper and is synonomous with the term grapevine.

Nkosana—A *Fanagalo* term conveying the patronage meaning of father.

Oke—From Afrikaans, a male street term of respect.

Phaka—*Fanagalo* for food.

Pap—Afrikaans for mealie meal porridge.

Platteland—Afrikaans for the southern African highveld region, encapsulating the notion of white Afrikaans-speaking rural identity.

Politico—Insisted on and used by political prisoners as a term of self-identification against terms like *Poqo* and *bandiet* as used by prison warders and common law prisoners. Both the South African and South West African authorities refused to accept the notion of political prisoners, so the term became an absolutely fundamental means whereby political prisoners would attempt to both challenge the State and distinguish themselves from simply being seen as criminals lacking any political fibre or political organisational legitimacy and capacity. It was a crucial term essentially deriving its modern meaning from Robben Island: a *politico* is an imprisoned cadre. A *politico* is not a volunteer. It was only during the post-1990 negotiations over amnesty releases that the concept of political offences became legally recognised, albeit in a jurisprudentially confusing and politically contested fashion.

Poqo—Xhosa for 'alone' or 'pure', the term has Eastern Cape Christian separatist church origins and was later the name of the PAC inspired insurrectionist Poqo movement (often as in 'We go it alone'). During the political crisis of the early 1960s, most of the first political prisoners to be incarcerated on Robben Island were PAC cadres. The word quickly became used by prison warders as a generic term of identification and abuse for all male political prisoners.

Praja Mandal—Gujarati for 'People's Organisation'.

Puzamandla—Fanagalo, meaning strong drink, this is a cold, sour tasting drink made from maize meal.

Red Square—Officially Nicol Square, the large open space between Grey, Commercial, Field and Pine streets in Durban, it was one of the main venues for mass, mainly black political meetings. It acquired its popular name during the late 1920s as a result of the many Communist Party of South Africa meetings held there.

Saampraat—Afrikaans; literally 'let's talk together and understand each other', but very often far more ominous, really meaning 'you must listen and cooperate with me'.

Satyagraha—First coined by M K Gandhi whilst in Durban, derived from Sanskrit *satya* or 'true and honest' and *agraha* or 'firmness' or 'obstinacy'. The word really means 'soul force' but does incorporate a more popular and wider political notion of non-violent anti-colonial struggle.

SB—A South African Police Security Branch policeman.

Shayile—Nguni, but also *Fanagalo* for the end of a working day or 'time up!'.

Slatch—A very small piece off the ignitable side of a match-box cover.

Slim mens—Literally clever person but Afrikaans colloquial and prison warders' abusive term for a man too clever for his own good and deliberately or otherwise subverting prevailing white authority.

GLOSSARY   205

Span—Afrikaans for team. Also as in 'baksteenmakerspan' (brick making
    team); 'bombelaspan' (quarry team); 'dokspan' (harbour team);
    'grawespan' (digging team); 'houtspan' (timber team); 'kalkspan'
    (limestone team); 'koekepanspan' (quarry railway team); 'landbou-
    span' (farming team); 'lorriespan' (lorry team); 'losspan' (general
    team); 'siektespan' (sick parade); 'sifspan' (sieving team); 'steenmaker-
    span' (masonry team) and 'toutrekspan' (rope pulling team).

Stompie—Afrikaans colloquial for the dead butt end of a cigarette and,
    partly through prison *taal*, also the small burning smokable remaining
    part of the cigarette.

Stuk—Afrikaans for a broken off piece of a larger inanimate object, in
    colloquial Afrikaans and in prison it can refer to anything, either
    human or otherwise, having an unendurable but cherished and possi-
    bly also secretive or illicitly hidden quality.

Taluka—Gujarati for an administrative sub-district.

Tausa—Prison and *bandiet-taal*. A commandist verb and noun describing the
    ritual dance, focusing on the anus, which black male prisoners had to
    do after labouring shifts, ostensibly to show they had not stolen or
    concealed anything. The act is one of public self-denigration and was
    one of the main rituals used daily by the state to humiliate captured
    men. Common law prisoners turned the ritual into their own cer-
    emony, which, through their ability to still conceal objects and its
    legend, became a dance of defiance. *Politicos* hated the ritual and
    largely refused to fully participate.

Tokolosh—Bantu term for an evil spirit or a devil.

Tshombe—From the Congolese crisis of the early 1960s, within South African
    'Struggle' politics it became politically correct and trendy to use Moise
    Tshombe's name as a specific and relevant synonym for an *impimpi*.

Vinnig Loop!—An Afrikaans military and penal term: 'Run fast!', it is the
    commandist part of a normal Afrikaans sentence.

Volk—Utilised by Afrikaner Nationalist politicians in their rise to power,
    their meaning defined all white Afrikaans speakers as belonging to the
    volk. Within the black political lexicon, the term is denigratory and links
    the *volk* with the Apartheid State.

Wyfie—An Afrikaans colloquial and prison word for a male subservient
    lover in a homosexual relationship, the word has meanings which
    range from sexual chattel to emotional loyalty. Derives from both the
    Afrikaans word *wyf*: mean woman, vixen, shrewish or effeminate and
    wyfie: female animal. Can be used in derisory ways by warders,
    heterosexual prisoners and other male homosexual prisoners.

Zinktronk—Afrikaans, the corrugated iron cell block on Robben Island.

Zol—A hand-made cigarette, rolled in newsprint and containing either
    tobacco or marijuana.